HOUSEKEEPING BY DESIGN

Hotels and Labor

DAVID BRODY

The University of Chicago Press CHICAGO AND LONDON

DAVID BRODY is associate professor of design studies
at Parsons School of Design, the New School.

The University of Chicago Press, Chicago 60637
The University of Chicago Press, Ltd., London
© 2016 by The University of Chicago
All rights reserved. Published 2016.
Printed in the United States of America

25 24 23 22 21 20 19 18 17 16   1 2 3 4 5

ISBN-13: 978-0-226-38909-7 (cloth)
ISBN-13: 978-0-226-38912-7 (paper)
ISBN-13: 978-0-226-38926-4 (e-book)
DOI: 10.7208/chicago/9780226389264.001.0001

Library of Congress Cataloging-in-Publication Data

Names: Brody, David, 1968– author.
Title: Housekeeping by design : hotels and labor / David Brody.
Description: Chicago ; London : The University of Chicago Press, 2016. |
Includes bibliographical references and index.
Identifiers: LCCN 2016007243| ISBN 9780226389097 (cloth : alk. paper) |
ISBN 9780226389127 (pbk. : alk. paper) | ISBN 9780226389264 (e-book)
Subjects: LCSH: Hotel housekeeping—United States. | Hotels—
United States—Employees. | Hotels—United States—Design and
construction. | Sustainable buildings—United States—Design and
construction.
Classification: LCC TX928 .B764 2016 | DDC 647.94068—dc23
LC record available at http://lccn.loc.gov/2016007243

♾ This paper meets the requirements of ANSI/NISO Z39.48-1992
(Permanence of Paper).

CONTENTS

INTRODUCTION

It was September 3, 1984. I was sixteen and my brother Jonathan was thirteen. Since the new school year was beginning the next day, my parents decided that we should go out for an end-of-summer celebration. We took two separate cars to Tony Roma's, a fairly casual chain restaurant famous for its ribs. The drive from our house in Potomac, Maryland, to Bethesda was uneventful, and I do not really remember the meal, but what I do remember vividly was the drive home with my brother. About five minutes into the twenty-minute trip we left my parents' car behind at a traffic light. I sped ahead quickly and continued driving along a series of one- and two-lane roads until I got just outside our tract housing development. Approaching Trotters Trail Road from Bells Mill Road, we noticed a fire truck. This was not a common occurrence in our suburban neighborhood, so Jonathan shouted, "Follow it!"

I did not have to be encouraged. I sped up and made the left into our neighborhood, following on the tail of the giant red truck. Outside of accelerating, which is never an issue for a sixteen-year-old boy, I did not have to deviate from my planned route. The truck appeared to be going along the same path that I would have taken home. It was after making the left onto Crossing Creek Road, and driving about a hundred feet down that street's steep hill, that I realized something was amiss. The truck decelerated, as it followed the bend in the road to the right and made—much to my jaw-dropping amazement—the right turn into our cul-de-sac driveway.

In front of our house were two other fire trucks. My parents arrived a few moments later and did exactly what you are not supposed to do in these situations: they ran into the house. The firemen urged us not to follow. My brother and I did not need this encouragement. We sat silently as smoke billowed out of open windows and the roof. I did not see flames, but the dark plumes made it obvious that something had gone wrong. My parents emerged minutes later carrying, of all things, our bar mitzvah photo albums. The fire marshal arrived about thirty minutes later and explained that there was extensive smoke damage throughout the house and that we would not be able to live there for some time. Lightning, we were told, had hit the television antenna (remember, this was 1984) and had traveled down the antenna wire and into the VCR box, triggering an electrical fire. The marshal told us to stay with friends or to get a hotel room.

While the events that followed, including the outrageous attempts at dry cleaning all of the clothes that were in the house and the enormous effort it took to clean the house's ventilation ducts, took a toll on my parents' patience and goodwill, it is the hotel story that developed out of this fire that continues to intrigue me. The fire and my three-month hotel stay at the Bethesda Marriott inspired this book.

The Bethesda Marriott is a fairly large hotel located in Bethesda, Maryland, about fifteen minutes outside Washington D.C. The hotel has about four hundred rooms, and while its Brutalist-influenced facade does not foster a bucolic sensibility, the grounds surrounding the parking area are well manicured and verdant. The rooms have always been rather corporate: think staid colonial revival furniture accompanied by banal browns and tans for paint, along with industrial carpeting created to evoke a faux sense of hominess. This is neither a funky boutique hotel nor a luxury property. Most guests stay here because of its convenient location near tourist attractions and corporate parks.

What I remember most about the hotel was the food. The restaurant on the ground floor was American-bistro-meets-suburbia: fantasyland for a teenage boy. Hamburgers, french fries, onion soup, and cheesecake filled the menu's pages. Thanks to a generous insurance policy, I had my own room (my brother had decamped down the hall to get away from my parents and me) and loads of unhealthy food during our prolonged stay.

What I remember least about the hotel was housekeeping. Nonetheless, the daily housekeeping at the hotel must have been on my mind. Being at the hotel, with someone there to make my bed and pick up after me, meant that the ritual upkeep of my room at home was no longer paramount. And, like any other teenager, I had things I wanted hidden from view, so I must have been keenly aware of when housekeeping came and what parts of the room they cleaned and which spaces they left alone. However, even though the food is still clear in my mind, the women who came to my room each day to tidy up my messy space, change the sheets, and disinfect the bathroom are barely even a distant memory, obscured by almost thirty years.

As I have discovered while writing this book, the invisible nature of housekeeping at the Bethesda Marriott, and the fact that guests take this labor for granted, is intentional. The hotel industry does everything in its power to make certain that guests do not have to think about the hard work involved in cleaning guest rooms. As each chapter of *Housekeeping by Design* explores, hotels turn to housekeeping as a way to maintain the guest rooms' design integrity, while making certain that guests feel they are staying in a clean and sanitary environment. What is most important about this perception of cleanliness is that the housekeepers complete their job without interfering with the guest's stay. Their presence—and perceived lack thereof—is critical. People rarely comment on housekeeping after they stay at hotels, unless they experience their room as unkempt. They mention the design of their rooms, talk about the service (usually focusing on things like the front desk), and may describe other amenities at the hotel like restaurants and gym facilities, but housekeeping is an invisible given. It is axiomatic that housekeeping will do its work, but it is even more important that the labor completed by housekeeping gets done without our awareness that any work is actually transpiring.

The connection between design and the concealment of housekeepers' work is particularly significant, since it is design that manipulates our perceptions about what does or does not occur at a hotel. Several scholars have discussed the notion that design delineates how we construe space. For instance, Dell Upton claims that architectural historians have been too beholden to a history of style—a fetish for the surface—that ignores the critical fact that humans engage with architecture through the act of construing space. In other words, those of us who think about design (and here I am extrapolating from and extending Upton's engagement with architecture) need to think more about how society *uses* spaces and objects within them instead of focusing only on the form or stylistic impulse visible on a design's surface.[1] Making a similar observation, Neil Maycroft argues that "academic fascination with designed objects has tended to emphasize their semiotic and symbolic attributes."[2] One of the classic examples of Maycroft's premise in relation to hotels is Fredric Jameson's discussion of Los Angeles's Westin Bonaventure Hotel as a signifier of postmodern space.[3] Instead of only formulating an analysis bound to design's surface, Maycroft and Upton want design to be assessed from a point of view that gets beyond the veneer, which enables questions about how people actually experience design.

Part of what design does, of course, is reify power dynamics. As Marx pointedly explained, the production of things and the manner in which those goods are sold in the world produce and reproduce economic inequalities. Labor creates things in a way that enhances the bourgeoisie's (to use Marxian terminology) financial advantages, and when designed products enter the marketplace, these objects, experiences, and environments become fetishized as consumable things. This process further distances those buying these products from the labor of production, while concomitantly adding to the class stratification that consumption promotes.[4] This commodity fetishism must be taken into account as we assess how guests, management, and workers construe hotel spaces, which are some of the most obsessively designed spaces found in our neoliberal epoch. Following a Marxist understanding of labor, Harry Braverman and others have contended that under capitalism it is very difficult for workers to have any agency over production, as they follow the orders put forth under management's rules. Braverman's 1974 book *Labor and Monopoly Capital* initiated an entire subfield of sociology that fostered a critique about work's dehumanizing conditions in the modern era.[5] *Housekeeping by Design* does, to some extent, adhere to this Marxist perspective, but I am also interested in understanding the dynamic and often-fluid relationships that exist among guests, workers, and managers. There are instances I describe in detail where management sets the agenda and their choices can negatively affect the lives of workers, but there are other moments I explore when workers' voices have been heard in the wake of bad design decisions that overlooked those who had to live with, maintain, and circumnavigate the designed spaces and service design systems found at hotels.[6]

Using Marx and Upton as a springboard, I am interested in expanding the definition of design. Instead of being concerned only with material culture, or those objects, things, and fetishes that provide cultural information, I have become increasingly fascinated with the realm of service design. The manner in which the hotel industry plans, manages, and arranges the perceptions through which both guests and labor experience hotels is essential to my study. How customers and workers encounter workflows and the organization of a service is a design issue that frequently gets overlooked and needs to be considered. Many scholars in the field of service design contend that through a careful consideration of these "touchpoints" we can improve the way we construe our world.[7]

The problem is that most practitioners and thinkers who engage with service design and physical design choices focus their attention on the experience of the customer while ignoring the realities, voices, and bodies of workers.[8] Industry designers, for instance, will inevitably spend time thinking about the ways in which guests will move through the process of checking into a hotel. The service designer—who, in the case of most hotels, is the property's manager—will assess how the guest enters the hotel, goes to the front desk to exchange payment information for a key, and then makes his or her way to the guest room. Alternatively, the interior designer and architect will be more interested in how the front desk looks and how the guest perceives the reception area's materials and appearance. This hypothetical team of designers will consider questions about the lobby's appearance, the hotel's software system, the training of the hotel's employees, and the workflow that enables a smooth check-in—but all through the lens of the paying customer. Since the fiscal bottom line often drives hotel design, the customer-centric focus is not all that surprising.

Offering a new perspective, *Housekeeping by Design* asserts that hotel workers, and by extension all workers, need to be considered as more than just facilitators of the consumer experience. Workers need to be integrated into the design process. Their labor can make or break the guest's stay at a hotel, but when management disregards employees' needs, especially in the context of their interactions with interior and service design, the ramifications on individual workers' lives and bodies can become catastrophic, and the impact on business can lead to unintended disadvantages. Thus, my book argues that if line workers (hotel employees who are not management) had more say about design, the industry would change for the better, instances of labor strife would be less frequent, the physical consequences of hotel work would be less harmful, and hotels would become even more cost effective for their owners.

Let's turn briefly to my critique of sustainability at Starwood Hotels and Resorts in Hawaii, which my fifth chapter elaborates on, to explain how the housekeepers I interviewed described the ways in which an unwillingness to discuss design causes hardship. In 2009, Starwood Hotels introduced a program called Make a Green Choice to several of its properties in Hawaii. Starwood is a major player in the hotel industry, as it manages brands such as W Hotels, Sheraton, St. Regis, and Westin. The green program allowed guests to opt out of housekeeping for a small bonus, such as Starwood Preferred Guest points (which lead to free stays at hotels) or a meal voucher. The relationship between the tourism industry and ecology has been well documented, as washing linens and using toxic cleaning chemicals does adversely affect the environment. And, in fact, many hotel guests expect the hotel industry to respond to these issues.[9] Thus, Make a Green Choice appears, at least on the surface, to be an ameliorative effort on Starwood's part to mitigate the correlation between hotels and the planet's ecological health.

However, the lived experiences of Make a Green Choice were quite different from its progressive ethos. Guests did utilize the program, and it was not difficult to get them to embrace the idea of not having their rooms cleaned. As a result, Starwood could point to the ways in which the program led to a reduction in the use of laundry, electricity, and cleaning solvents. On the other hand, Make a Green Choice had two consequences that made the housekeepers' lives difficult. First, as the housekeepers I spoke with made clear, the hotel rooms' physical design elements became degraded as a result of rooms not being cleaned for multiple days. Mold built up on the surfaces of these Hawaiian guest rooms, and several of the housekeepers described these rooms as "hurricanes," since guests scattered their belongings everywhere, as if tossed up by a cyclone, after not being visited by housekeeping for several days. In addition, housekeepers noted how myriad service design issues arose. Usually housekeepers clean a specific set number of rooms that are close together, to allow for the easy movement of what can be heavy equipment, such as a housekeeping cart. Now that certain rooms had to be "skipped" as a result of the program, this typical navigation of a well-delineated group of rooms was disrupted. In fact, housekeepers I spoke with on the island of Kauai described having to move their carts to multiple buildings across a large property to fulfill their quota of fifteen rooms. Additionally, green guests still asked housekeepers for help with things like towel changes and trash removal. Consequently, housekeepers now had to clean their allotment of rooms and deal with additional guests who still wanted some level of service, even though they had opted into Make a Green Choice. These realities made Starwood's sustainable efforts a service design nightmare, as they interrupted and hindered housekeeping's orchestrated efforts.

Having fewer rooms to clean also led to housekeepers losing work hours while waiting to be called into work, undoubtedly the most profound consequence of these unfortunate design choices that did not account for workers' lives. Even though the politics of Make a Green Choice appeared progressive, the program's implementation meant lower pay, decreased benefits, and other significant design-related costs for many of the housekeepers I interviewed. Learning about this program forced me to contemplate whether Starwood's management had shrewdly devised a service design plan that would save money on labor while promoting their efforts as aligning with the enlightened ideology of climate change activists. Part of this complicated conundrum, a knot of issues where labor, design, and finances become entangled, can be unraveled by engaging the theoretical writing of Bruno Latour, the French sociologist whose ideas about the relationship between design and people have asked scholars to rethink their understanding of our artificial world.[10] If design is, as Herbert Simon has contended, "changing existing situations into preferred ones," then we must grapple with the fact that this "transformation" is always reliant on nonhuman actors, as Latour explains.[11] Humans have, of course, designed these inanimate things, but the repercussions of design's presence in our lives is too frequently overlooked or taken for granted in a manner that ignores the political freight that design carries. By allowing the workers who must participate in the daily maintenance of design choices to become active in the design process, some of design's unintended ramifications could be mitigated.

While most of this book focuses on contemporary hotels in the United States, and the ways in which design affects housekeepers, the history of hotels needs to be considered.[12] To explicate part of this history, the second chapter of *Housekeeping by Design* assesses a book written in 1900, entitled *The Practical Hotel Housekeeper*.[13] What becomes clear in Mary Bresnan's rather didactic text is that guest room attendants (whom Bresnan calls chambermaids) have historically been managed, and that the management of emotions and bodies takes place through service design. For instance, Bresnan spends ample time describing how the chambermaid must be flexible if she wants to attend to all of her allotted rooms, as guests often remain in their rooms, leaving almost no opportunity to enter and properly clean. In a rather humorous set of vignettes, Bresnan relates how the chambermaid can assiduously shuffle her cleaning schedule to accommodate all of her guests' temporal particularities, making certain that she gets her job done, all the while ensuring that the guests remain happy. This management of emotions may require that the housekeeper explain to one guest why she must clean another guest room first because that guest is expecting company, or it may mean completing part of one guest's suite and then returning to tidy the bedroom after finishing up another room, but a well-orchestrated plan leads to success. Bresnan helps us understand that successful service design has always translated into a type of flexibility that requires labor's complete attention to both physical and emotional needs.[14] When hotel managers and workers focus only on the maintenance of space, and disregard the critical nature of service design, problems arise that foster conflict among guests, employees, and management. Extrapolating beyond the world of the material, my book argues that the seemingly invisible realm of service design—the decisions about issues related to workflow, customer service, and the delivery of experiences—also needs to be unpacked to understand just how critical all facets of design are to our everyday lives.

To reveal such facets of design, this book looks at several moments within the world of hotels when the tension between design and labor comes to the fore and when a form of co-design could have improved work conditions. To tighten this study's focus, most of my examples come from the realm of housekeeping. This may strike some readers as peculiar, as housekeeping is usually not the first aspect of hotels that people want to discuss. And, in part, this is why I do discuss housekeeping. When I have shared my research on "hotels" with interested listeners over the past several years, the most common reaction—from scholars of design to people who consider themselves hotel aficionados—is that I must be considering specific, well-known designers who have worked on hotel projects. And although this book does briefly mention such instances, I have concentrated on housekeeping because it is the housekeepers who have the responsibility of maintaining the design choices that have been made at hotels. Moreover, the industry's most thought-provoking aspects of service design can be found in the context of housekeeping.

My intention is not to discount the role of designers; rather, I hope to encourage the larger fields of design studies, design history, and design praxis to consider the ways in which the workforce can potentially help with the design process, since they must construe design choices. Housekeeping provides a unique window into understanding labor—and individual workers have been long overlooked in relation to design. Although the category of labor has entered the discourse of design studies, it is usually discussed in terms of the design process and the work of designers. Perhaps the most widely cited scholarly example in this category is Donald Schön's essay "Designing: Rules, Types and Worlds," which appeared in the journal *Design Studies* in 1988 and describes how designers both use and conform to patterns as they think through specific design problems. Thinking certainly is a form of labor, and Schön examines how and why designers think about typology in the ways they do.[15] However, my questions about labor not only include the design process but also make suggestions about this process, while calling attention to physical labor and the ways in which design choices—those intellectualized practices that Schön and others explicate—affect physical work. For instance, if a hotel designer is beholden to a specific typology while designing a hotel room, then how does that typology hinder or ease the physical labor required to clean that space? And how does the design of workflow within hotels, certainly an act that falls under Schön's notion of the work of design thinking, change the nature of physical labor at hotels? These questions about how design produces different outcomes sit at the center of my book.

Since housekeepers play such an integral role in *Housekeeping by Design*, it is important to get a sense of who performs this work. What is apparent—and this will be obvious to any reader who has stayed at a hotel or motel in the United States—is that the overwhelming majority of housekeepers are women. Furthermore, it is women of color who usually serve as guest room attendants in hotels.[16] Men may be the ones in housekeeping who get called on to move furniture or stock linens, but the individuals who actually clean hotel rooms are almost never men, and rarely are they Caucasian.[17] In the wake of the Dominique Strauss-Kahn scandal of 2011, the gendered nature of this work briefly sparked an international conversation about the perils of housekeepers who have to contend with sexually aggressive guests. Even though *Housekeeping by Design* briefly assesses Strauss-Kahn and Nafissatou Diallo, the housekeeper who accused Strauss-Kahn of sexual assault and attempted rape at the Sofitel Hotel in Manhattan, it is important to recognize from the outset that this was one of the few times when the racial and gender dynamics that define housekeeping became topical within the mass media.[18]

By focusing on questions about design and housekeeping I want to change the conversation about hotels and labor, and several previous studies have helped me frame my argument. For example, Sarah Chaplin, Barbara Penner, and Jilly Traganou have each written books that assess how the business of travel deploys design as a way of creating a specific type of touristic experience. Miodrag Mitrašinović has also explored the role of design, and questions about the hidden notion of labor, in theme park spaces.[19] Sociologist Rachel Sherman has completed one of the most provocative ethnographic studies of hotels. Sherman spent time working at two different luxury hotels, and her book *Class Acts: Service and Inequality in Luxury Hotels* considers a variety of topics that influence the way in which employees and guests construe design. Sherman asks her reader to think about service, separate spheres of work, and games around employee-employer-guest interrelationships, which have greatly influenced my own research.[20]

The fields of tourism and leisure studies have also guided *Housekeeping by Design*. Scholars such as Dean MacCannell and Orvar Löfgren have described the ways in which Western culture devises touristic pursuits that define our sense of self in the modern world. Löfgren views vacationing as "a cultural laboratory where people have been able to experiment with new aspects of their identities, their social relations, or their interaction with nature and also to use the important cultural skills of daydreaming and mindtraveling."[21] Löfgren and MacCannell take their readers on a journey into the tourist's quest for adventure where a multibillion-dollar industry—replete with themed hotels—has devised ways to capture and define our imaginations. MacCannell and Löfgren offer a valuable perspective, but my project is more invested in looking at how hotels reinscribe the inequities of class, race, and gender dynamics that delimit the lives of hotel workers in our neoliberal era. Scholars such as Karl Spracklen have looked at leisure as a "hegemonic but invisible power relation that privileges (and normalizes) the culture and position of white people."[22] Spracklen also describes the ways in which cultural conceptions about gender and class further the privilege of "whiteness," especially in our leisure pursuits. Indeed, each chapter of my book investigates how the complex interface between design and workers at hotels is contingent on cultural constructions of race and gender that reify unfair labor practices.

The first chapter of my book was inspired by Wayne Koestenbaum's *Hotel Theory*, which approaches hotels as a very personal and theoretical conundrum. Theory defines the parameters of my study, and my initial chapter turns to Karl Marx, Henri Lefebvre, and Thorstein Veblen to initiate a larger discussion about design, hotels, and labor.[23] Marx sets the stage for my inquiry into labor and how hotels often obfuscate reality through the veneer of design. Lefebvre was one of the first to consider space as a product of capitalism, which, in places like resorts and hotels, manifests the fantasy of an escape from reality. Veblen spoke to the notion of display and the manners of consumption, which are imperative to many guests' experiences at hotels. Moreover, Veblen published his famous text, *The Theory of the Leisure Class* (1899), within a year of Mary Bresnan's *The Practical Hotel Housekeeper* (1900), and there are connections between Veblen's exploration of manners and Bresnan's obsessive interest with propriety. Each of these theorists provides insight into hotels as carefully designed and highly orchestrated spaces where workers' voices are far from paramount.

After this foray into theory, I establish that the connection between design and labor at hotels can be traced historically. As discussed before in terms of service design, my second chapter looks at Bresnan's *The Practical Hotel Housekeeper*. Bresnan's tone in this book is pedantic. She is full of advice and does not shy away from stereotyping chambermaids and describing their shortcomings. What most interests me about Bresnan, and the other period sources that I connect to her text, is the way in which her concerns from over 110 years ago remain relevant in the twenty-first-century hotel industry. Her ideas about timing, workflow, and the management and silencing of labor in relation to design lead to my discussion of E. M. Statler's development of regimented systems of service design that defined the experiences of guests, workers, and managers at his important hotels built at the beginning of the twentieth century. Statler devised methods of efficiency that seem closely tied to Frederick Winslow Taylor's conception of scientific management, where labor could be streamlined to make business more lucrative.[24] Statler's forward-thinking notions about service design remained committed to a gendered conception of labor and domesticity, where women did the work of housekeeping at his hotels. As Ruth Schwartz Cowan, Grace Lees-Maffei, and others have contended, the work of housekeeping, even in the wake of modern technological change, remained women's work in the twentieth century.²⁵

The third chapter of my book turns to contemporary hotels and the management of housekeeping as well as the labor required to maintain design features found at these sites. Here, I examine how the academic discipline of hospitality management defines the discipline of house-keeping and elides the voices of housekeepers. Specifically, I look at hotel management textbooks to assess the complicated world of housekeeping as discussed in hotel management courses at universities.²⁶ I argue that design plays a key role in how these textbooks, and the larger field, circumscribe the housekeeper's role. These textbooks use graphics and photography to detail the importance of creating a well-designed system of work where tasks get accomplished without hindering a guest's experience at a hotel. This careful attention to design allows the guest to feel as though he or she is not being disturbed.

The fourth chapter of *Housekeeping by Design* turns from the academic sphere of textbooks to the realm of well-edited popular culture and the Travel Channel's humorously titled reality show *Hotel Impossible*. The program's premise is that hotels can be saved by quick and invasive inter-vention. Each week, the show's host, hotel guru Anthony Melchiorri, travels to different hotels that face fiscal distress. Through a management, labor, and decorative makeover, Melchiorri saves these hotels in one (commercial-laden) hour. The show follows the typical narrative of reality television, where subjects who have not been living up to the neoliberal dream (of taking care of the self in our capitalist-driven marketplace) find salvation. Beyond analyzing the show's narrative arc, I look at *Hotel Impossible* to better understand how popular culture represents design's im-pact on housekeepers. Several of the show's episodes from its first season (2012) focus on housekeeping, and I consider how Melchiorri and his team improve their perceptions of housekeeping's presumed short-comings without listening to ideas from housekeepers, who remain the show's reticent soldiers, completing their tasks in silence.

Management's assessment and standardizing of housekeeping leads to my investigation of two separate instances when housekeepers became design activists and challenged management's mishandling of specific design decisions. My fifth chapter looks at a set of housekeeping con-cerns that arose, as discussed above, in Hawaii. The housekeepers I spoke with clearly detailed how the economics and design of Starwood's Make a Green Choice program made their workday unbearable. My analysis critiques the myth that sustainable design choices only ameliorate exist-ing conditions, as "going green," in this instance, led to personal hardship for the housekeepers I interviewed. My final chapter then draws on interviews I conducted at the Hyatt Regency Chicago to describe how housekeepers responded to the renovation, completed in 2011, of this enormous hotel's more than two thousand rooms. Having the opportunity to speak directly with housekeepers, to get beyond corporate press releases' rhetoric and management's canned responses, was a revelation. I quickly discovered how these workers' day-to-day lives had been adversely affected by the Hyatt management's unilateral design decisions, which led to the housekeepers' physical pain and emotional duress. As in Hawaii, the housekeepers in Chicago did not sit idly by and allow these design choices to change their lives without raising their voices against these decrees. Through various union-led actions, these workers fought against these corporately driven choices.

These housekeepers' activism, especially when it came to changing design-related dogma, could be extended if hotel managers and owners willingly adopted a co-design policy. Co-design fosters a design process that includes contributions from myriad constituents who inevitably have to contend with design decisions.[27] One important way in which workers can have a voice in the hotel industry's approach to design is through unionization. As Dan Zuberi has argued, "Union membership confers substantial advantages on hotel workers," and even though such advantages do not always hold for wages, unionization is often effective in improving job "stability and benefits."[28] In the case studies I explore in *Housekeeping by Design*, the union's strength did empower labor to act. Yet I contend that with the implementation of co-design, the opinions of individual workers would become even more influential and the adversities associated with housekeeping would lessen. Co-design could, I assert, reveal the benefits of listening to workers' voices while both improving hotel design for everyone (guests, management, and workers) and decreasing the friction between unions and management.

The economic and physical difficulties related to housekeeping have been well documented. According to the Bureau of Labor Statistics, the average pay for "maids and housekeeping cleaners" who work in "traveler accommodations" in the United States was $21,800 in 2012, far below the mean national salary in the same year, which was $46,440.[29] Additionally, a variety of studies have documented work-related pain among hotel housekeepers, including one of the most thorough analyses in this field, by Niklas Krause, Teresa Scherzer, and Reiner Rugulies. Out of more than nine hundred Las Vegas hotel housekeepers they surveyed, just 5 percent reported "no bodily pain," while 27 percent reported either "severe" or "very severe" pain. The respondents explained that the hotel room's design (including elements like "heavy bedspreads, or comforters") and equipment (including things like heavy carts and cumbersome vacuum cleaners) accounted, in part, for these outcomes.[30] Moreover, connections have been made between gender, race, and ethnicity in relation to injuries among hotel workers. As Susan Buchanan and her coauthors assert, women who work at hotels face injuries far more often than men, and "an alarming injury rate among housekeepers in general and Hispanic housekeepers in particular" could be identified within the large cohort they studied.[31]

The measured nature of statistics can help us understand the importance of considering design, but I also begin each of the following chapters with a personal vignette to highlight the pressing issues I explore in *Housekeeping by Design*. With each year that I teach, conduct research, and write I am further impressed that what we study is integral to our lives and experiences outside scholarship. This impression grows even stronger when it comes to hotels. As Molly Berger writes in the introduction to her important book *Hotel Dreams*, "*everyone* has a hotel story."[32] Our hotel stays—and, as I argue throughout this book, our fantasies about hotels— often define who we are and how we think of ourselves. The chapters' personal vignettes expose my own racial, gender, and class-bound hotel experiences within the context of the larger themes found in *Housekeeping by Design*. I hope these vignettes will provoke readers to think about the often-subtle ways in which hotels define cultural issues related to privilege.

Several chapters of my book, especially the case studies in chapters 5 and 6, include interviews with housekeepers that provide a perspective on design and labor that has not been previously explored. My earlier academic work dealt with deceased subjects who could not talk back and whose lives could not be adversely affected by my research. To make certain I understood the rules of fieldwork, I applied for Institutional Review Board (IRB) approval and carefully weighed questions about anonymity and compensation for my subjects.[33] I offered all of these subjects anonymity if they requested it and asked them to sign informed consent forms, specifying that I could use their names in my research unless they objected. I also spent time before each interview explaining the nature of academic publishing and made certain that each subject understood how I would use their names if they gave me permission. Finally, I debated and discussed the idea of anonymity with several colleagues who were more experienced with fieldwork than I. However, as I spoke with the women who work on the front lines of housekeeping, what came through was that they wanted to be heard. Most of these women wanted their stories told and did not want their identities obscured under an alternative name or the moniker of "Anonymous."[34]

I connected with many guest room attendants I interviewed through their union, as my numerous attempts to recruit housekeepers on my own had failed. Thus, it is important to recognize that a number of these women were already enmeshed in union activity and did not shy away from controversy. In fact, the interviews I conducted in Honolulu occurred at the offices of UNITE HERE, one of the most powerful hotel unions, whose efforts to attain better working conditions for hotel workers have been well documented.[35] Even though I spoke to these women in a room where other subjects and union organizers could not overhear our conversations, being at this site, which made it easier for me to conduct numerous interviews in succession, must have influenced the housekeepers' responses, as we were at a location that supported several of my subjects' efforts in organizing guest room attendants—through strikes, walkouts, and other types of protests—in an effort to attain a better work environment.[36] Management eventually had, for the most part, heard the voices of these women, who were far from anonymous or reticent, in their workplace.

I should clarify a few other issues about interviewing these women. A few subjects did ask to see their quotes before I used them, and I complied with their requests. When I followed up with these interviewees, the language shifted only slightly, but it is important to acknowledge this postinterview dynamic. Moreover, on a few occasions an interviewee made remarks that, in my estimation, put his or her job at risk. Specifically, these individuals might not have wanted to be identified in print with their derogatory comments about a specific manager or property. Therefore, in some instances, after careful consideration, I made the subject anonymous. Finally, I also offered most of my subjects twenty dollars in compensation for speaking with me. Although a debate in the field of qualitative research questions the appropriateness of compensating interviewees, in entering a world where fiscal compensation for labor was already hotly contested, it seemed unfair—and unwise—to ask for individuals' time without offering something in return. Not one individual in management ever accepted compensation, but several housekeepers did take my offer of twenty dollars, and I am confident that this financial exchange did not compromise our conversations. I consistently discussed the payment before the interview began and before each subject signed the consent form, which also included details about this remuneration. I never used this financial arrangement as a way to extract further information in the middle of an interview.[37]

Including housekeepers' voices and perspectives will enable my readers to think about hotels, and their own experiences of them, as something richer than a fantasy or an escape from day-to-day reality. If the reader rethinks his or her own hotel stories, this may lead—as some of my readers have already admitted—to a reconsideration of past, present, and future hotel stays, and perhaps to a sense of responsibility when staying at a hotel. For as much as this book attempts to expand the field of design-related scholarship, it is also my intention to shift the way we imagine and engage with the realities of labor in our daily lives. This will, it is my hope, make visible the individuals whose invisibility renders our own lives so comfortable, while offering design interventions that could improve these workers' lives.

BOOKING A ROOM

Barrie Selesko was one of my mother's closest friends from high school. I can still recall Barrie and my mom gossiping about mutual friends and laughing together on the phone, but I also remember Barrie's infinite wisdom about travel and the merits of different hotels. Barrie was my family's go-to travel aficionado; she knew everything about the business. She could describe in great detail the pros and cons of myriad destinations and various hotel options in far-flung places. Barrie was, until in her untimely death from cancer in 2002, a travel expert. She was the quintessential travel agent before online booking became the norm: she spoke with you on the phone, booked your tickets, made your hotel reservations, and then sent you a thick packet of information, via mail, that included each and every detail of a carefully planned itinerary. I have a clear memory of our family arriving in Greece in August of 1977, and my brother and I being delighted at the size of the pool at the Athens Hilton. Barrie knew about that pool; she knew what suggestions to make for a family of four who would be traveling with restless children.

In the twenty-first century, there are very few travel agents, as the business has changed. Now we can go online and research travel in a way that Barrie could never have imagined when she was mailing paper tickets, printed with a dot matrix printer, in the twentieth century. Moreover, we are now able to get a perspective about experiences from like-minded travelers who offer details about their adventures on websites that rate, review, critique, and laud different travel options. For instance, we can now go to Seatguru.com to help us choose the best airplane seat on a 737-900, or we can look at Kayak.com to compare prices for various travel options, including hotels, airfares, car rentals, and vacation packages. One of my favorite sites, which I always go to while looking at hotels, is TripAdvisor .com, which offers reviews of everything from tourist attractions to specific hotels. It is TripAdvisor's hotel reviews that I find particularly fascinating in terms of the issues related to design that I am concerned with in *Housekeeping by Design*.

TripAdvisor launched during the heady days of the Internet start-up boom in February of 2000. The idea of the site has always been to proffer user-generated content about travel. After visiting a hotel, a restaurant, an attraction, or any other travel-related destination, one can easily go on the site, post details, and leave a rating. The hotel appraisals are particularly rich, as reviews include a written evaluation, a series of star-rated assessments, and, if one is feeling particularly ambitious, photos and videos. TripAdvisor is also in the business of making money, so along with the reviews comes the opportunity to book flights and reserve hotel rooms, using the different search engines that have paid to be embedded within TripAdvisor's site. Thus, TripAdvisor.com serves as a remarkably helpful search aggregator. In other words, when you make a hotel reservation on the site you are able to see results from a number of different search engines, permitting a level of comparison shopping that we have come to expect in the age of Internet commerce.

For all of its benefits, TripAdvisor does have drawbacks. The travel press has recently revealed instances in which hotels have asked employees and others to post fake reviews to get their ratings to climb. Given the lack of detailed oversight, these deceitful reviews can easily change the ratings of a particular hotel. The watchdog blog TripAdvisorWatch has exposed several examples of abuses, including a 2010 story about the Clare Inn in Ireland where hotel managers wrote to seven employees and asked them to help mitigate a recent spate of bad reviews on TripAdvisor by fabricating their own reviews. Management told the staff to do this from their home computers, or an Internet café, so that they could avoid detection. One email from management to a Clare Inn employee noted, "I'd rather you didn't discuss this with your team. This is not something we would normally endorse but the reviews of the Clare Inn at the moment leave us with no choice. Please do not use hotel language or else our plan will backfire."[1] TripAdvisor responded to the situation quickly and took down the fake reviews, but for a site that has millions of monthly visitors, each searching for the best travel options, the Clare Inn's shenanigans are a telling tale about how easy it is to manipulate perception.[2]

Beyond the mischief of bogus reviews, TripAdvisor is a confusing place; I have spent many hours trying to decipher a schizophrenic set of reviews about a particular hotel. For instance, let's briefly look at a few reviews that focus on the subject of the sixth chapter of this book, the Hyatt Regency Chicago. GrandmaBecky, a frequent TripAdvisor contributor, titled her August 2013 review of the hotel "Nice place, courteous staff and centrally located to all attractions with in [*sic*] walking distance." Outside of complaining about her room's location as being too close to an elevator shaft, she noted, "Hotel was nice, centrally located to downtown and most attractions. Walking was our choice of travel as we felt we could see the most of Chicago! We were so right! Love Chicago."[3] Shawn W, another frequent contributor to TripAdvisor, was not impressed with the Regency. He complained in his 2013 review, "The lady that checked us in almost seemed as though we were a burden to her. My wife was basically handed keys and sent on her way. We had to ask how to get to our room . . . expected more."[4] What can we make of this strange disparity and the lack of consistency in the over twenty-eight hundred reviews of the Regency posted on TripAdvisor? Where is Barrie Selesko when you need her to make sense of this morass of confusing content? Did these guests all stay in the same hotel?

Most of the reviews of business and luxury hotels on TripAdvisor ignore issues related to housekeeping. Likewise, I imagine that the conversations that my mother and Barrie Selesko had about hotels also ignored housekeeping, as they both understood it as an unspoken given. As I discuss in each chapter of this book, guests contend that rooms should be clean without thinking about how the details of housekeeping transpire. Think about the last time you chose a hotel: Did you actually look for details about previous guests' responses to housekeeping? Before starting this book, I certainly did not ponder the intricacies of housekeeping. The only hotels where apprehensions related to housekeeping repeatedly arise on TripAdvisor are those that are filthy. And, in these cases, guests often post series of similar photos, revealing everything from stained carpets to mildewed bathrooms.[5] PeggyKate, a noted "senior contributor" on the site with over twenty reviews and several "helpful" votes, posted one of the few reviews of the Hyatt Regency Chicago that mentions concerns about housekeeping. Peggy's tale of woe, from September of 2011, is fascinating, as it is one of the rare moments where a labor dispute enters into a narrative found on TripAdvisor. She explains how she and her husband checked into the hotel and the "speedy check-in" and "beautiful" room made a terrific first impression. Then they went outside and she describes how they "walked around the hotel and noticed there were people picketing. . . . We were handed a flier and read that the housekeeping staff of the hotel were all on strike!" According to Peggy, the strike meant that her room would not be cleaned during her visit. While giving the room the lowest rating possible for cleanliness, she explains, "I was very disappointed that the hotel had such a poor response to their housekeeping staff being out on strike and feel that a better effort should have been made to keep the rooms clean."[6] As my chapter on the Hyatt Regency Chicago details, a housekeeping strike did take place that coincides with Peggy's disappointing stay. In fact, the strike was, as I explore, part of a protracted dispute between Hyatt and the hotel workers' union, UNITE HERE.

I want to highlight the unusual nature of Peggy's review, as it is the anomalous nature of her narrative that I find particularly intriguing. Over and over again, the reviews written on TripAdvisor offer details about hotels that further the fantasy that labor, and especially housekeeping, should happen in a seamless, unnoticeable way. That rooms should be clean is axiomatic, but the work and organization of workflow that it takes to maintain these "beautiful" rooms (to use Peggy's words) gets obscured by other details that reviewers offer while assessing a particular hotel stay. Location, overall aesthetics, and feelings about overt service usually get mentioned, while details about housekeeping rarely appear. And the concerns of housekeepers are almost never raised in guests' reviews.

TripAdvisor should be understood as another voice in a larger hotel industry that all too often refuses to account for the reality of work, especially in relation to questions about maintaining design and the complexity of service design systems that allow housekeeping to function. To unpack this issue further, the following chapter reinserts the importance of labor through various theoretical interventions. It is this engagement with theory that I hope will start to elucidate how labor repeatedly gets asked to hide itself in a way that defers to guest satisfaction, while eliding the cumbersome and sometimes painful work required to attain the guest's approval.

1
THEORETICALLY CHECKING IN

Margie Garay, the director of housekeeping at the Four Seasons Hotel in New York City, becomes very excited while discussing turndown service. Turndown is the nightly ritual that occurs in luxury hotels throughout the world when guest room attendants transform the hotel room into a cocoon of comfort for the evening. Garay explains, "When you check into a hotel, it's understood that you are going to get a clean room." However, at the Four Seasons "everyone gets turndown and that's the experience. That's when you come in after dinner, after the show, after the meeting, and your room light is dimmed, your drapes are drawn closed, your music is on classical, your turndown mat is on the floor, your slippers are placed. That's an experience" (fig. 1). She smiles and continues, "You walk in and you say, and no matter how hard your day was, you don't say nothing other than home, 'wow, home, I'm home.' That's the experience!"[1]

Garay's notion of an "experience," and how design plays an integral role in that experience, is what I explore in my investigation of the complicated relationship between design and labor. While Garay proudly describes the end result of the turndown process, the individual who worked to make that service occur in a seamless manner is absent from her description. Furthermore, note that the guest is not part of her narrative until she returns at the end of a long day. Suddenly, the guest enters into a magical space where the design of the room has been altered and her visual and aural senses are overwhelmed. The design of the larger system of housekeeping that makes this room presentable encapsulates a highly orchestrated, hidden process of management and labor, a scenario where work is invisible and surface appearances are paramount to the guest's sense of domestic comfort and well-being.[2]

In what follows, I assess design and hotels by offering a theoretical perspective about the way in which workers create Garay's notion of

FIGURE 1 Turndown service at Four Seasons Hotel, New York. Permission by
Four Seasons Hotel New York. Photo by author.

"the experience." This chapter introduces several concerns that my book
raises about the dialogue between labor and hotel design. I will define
several of the theoretical parameters and conundrums that have surfaced
in my study, and it is my hope that some of the ideas presented here will
incite initial thoughts about design's role in the guest's experience, the
hotel management's decision making, and the amount of labor required
to maintain these properties. Moreover, I hope to set the stage for my discussion about the need for hotel workers, and specifically housekeepers,
to be included in the design process.

Unpacking

Hotels temporarily house guests who check in for either business or pleasure. The business guest wants convenience in terms of location, food,
and an overall experience that does not hinder productivity. The vaca-
tioner also wants convenience, but in this instance the traveler focuses
on spending time on activities outside work and engaging in tourism.
Hotels, for both types of guests, promise an escape from the everyday,

where daily stresses can be alleviated. As a putative escape, the design of hotels offers a liminal space where ideas about home become conflated with a space that clearly signifies that which is not home. The hotel can be homey, but contrary to Garay's assessment above, it cannot be too domestic, since that would obscure the promise of diversion that the hotel industry is predicated upon. One does not have to do the everyday activities of home-related work in a hotel. Food is delivered, activities outside the hotel are reserved, beds are made (sometimes twice a day), and rooms are cleaned. By paying a fee, the hotel guest buys into the promise of being able to check everyday cares at the front desk and venture into a realm of coddling where labor seemingly vanishes.

Wayne Koestenbaum has theorized that when we check in and arrive at a hotel "existence uncannily suspends us above groundedness. To be in hotel is to float." A hotel is a space that permits a "turn away from work as a means of 'taking care.' . . . To check into a hotel: this, too, may be a mode of taking care, of refusal."[3] Koestenbaum's notion of floating above reality, based on his reading of Heidegger, is an ideal metaphor for thinking about what it means to envelop oneself within a hotel, where we are neither here nor there; we are neither home, nor away. For instance, part of what the guest embraces at a luxury hotel chain brand, such as the Four Seasons, is that whether she is in Hong Kong, New York, or Costa Rica, the marble bathroom, the oversized mirrors, and the enormous bathtub are guaranteed amenities that bring her back to an impermanent home at different properties throughout the world that signify familiarity, yet that offer just enough difference. Hence, much of a hotel stay is meant to emulate that which guests can, in a sentient way, latch on to as part of an experience that has become integral to globalization. The hotel brings us outside the banal and into the transcendent by creating a fantastical world that functions, through design, as a site that attempts to meet expectations that remind the guest that she is back "home," safely ensconced by, in the case of the Four Seasons, a luxury brand that promises familiarity.

How does the work of hospitality get done in the liminal space of a hotel? The actual labor of moving items through hotels and getting guests what they want is not easy. Even more labor intensive is the less-talked-about concern of cleaning the hotel. The heavy lifting, which often occurs within what the hotel industry describes as the back of the house, becomes a performance that, when done well, is a seamless act involving, as one employee described to me, "smoke and mirrors."[4] In hotels, work takes on a peculiar duality where it is both seen and hidden. Things happen—again, food is delivered and beds are made—but the imagined lack of an agent in these passive acts of doing is exactly what many hotels want to highlight. Work should be noticed, but not overtly seen by the guest.[5]

This obfuscation of labor, which gets heightened by management's consistent lack of interest in their workers' ideas about design, creates an approach to commodities (things, places, experiences) that fetishize their value, distorting our sense of what something is worth.

Marx details how capitalist societies obscure the actualities of labor, relegating commodities to the class of things that we exchange without an understanding of the work that has transpired to make these goods. Because of this disconnect from labor, we transform the natural state of commodities into objects (and experiences) that take on special coded significance. Using the example of altering wood to form (or design) a table, Marx claims that the table is, in essence, a "common, every-day thing. . . . But, so soon as it steps forth as a commodity, it is changed into something transcendent. It not only stands with its feet on the ground, but, in relation to all other commodities, it stands on its head, and evolves out of its wooden brain grotesque ideas, far more wonderful than 'table-turning' ever was."[6] Here Marx defines a critical aspect of the design process. Design takes a natural or artificial resource and makes a product. For instance, the designer will use the possibilities of wood—its sturdiness, its pliability, its beauty—to create a table. Since the advent of industrialization, workers who follow the specifications devised by the designer manufacture the table. The finished table leaves the factory and then enters the marketplace. In this movement away from the actuality of work, the table becomes a commodity transmuted by consumers into something else, something outside the realm of work that enhances its meaning through the process of fetishization. No longer is the table merely a table, but now it has a "mystical character" devoid of the manpower that gave it life.[7]

This sense of mysticism that surrounds certain commodities becomes almost religious in nature. In its formulation of commodified desire that abstracts value and moves meaning away from the logistics of labor, the capitalist marketplace is, according to Marx, analogous to modern religion, where ideas about the divine and people's place in a larger cosmological order become dependent on abstractions. In other words, we believe that which we do not see and, unlike other cultures that continue to worship the natural world that they can witness firsthand, capitalism rouses our faith in the intangible. This faith in the abstraction of meaning "is but the reflex of the real world," where capitalism asks us to do in the marketplace what has been done in churches.[8] We do not actually see the work, but we believe in value as if we had a type of blind faith in that which is being sold. For instance, Bulgari bath products appear on the marble counter in the bathrooms at many Four Seasons hotels, but the guest is left with this fetishized aftermath of labor; the actual work that went into creating the bathroom amenity and building the marble counter has been elided.[9] Furthermore, the housekeeper who places the amenities and takes the products in and out of the room is often ignored. And what do we actually know about the labor that went into cleaning the bathroom and making the surfaces gleam so that the Bulgari product, with its radiant green glow, can appear especially alluring? And did the housekeeper have a say in the materials used to design that bathroom? And, if not, why has her voice not been heard?

In the world of hotels this elision becomes even more pronounced, since the ineffable nature of work usually functions as part of the back-of-the-house dance of service design, which is part of a complex system of exposing the end products of labor while concealing the difficult tasks that occur behind the veneer of what gets termed "good service." In the luxury hotel, where service is, according to the Ritz Carlton's website, about being "responsive to the expressed and unexpressed wishes and needs of . . . guests," the imperative for work is abundant. Not only does that possible task need to be predicted, but also, of course, it should be executed in a manner that fosters "memorable and personal experiences." Memories should appear without effort, and luxury simply happens with a smile and gesture that always embraces "anticipatory service."[10] This waiting in the wings to make things happen, to create the "wow," gets accomplished through design, which mediates the encounter between the guest's experience and the putatively invisible hotel employees.

Checking into a Four Seasons hotel during the day exemplifies this emphasis on how design helps to disguise the presence of housekeepers, as guests do not see what most other hotel patrons throughout the world observe as they walk from the elevator bank to their rooms. What is absent from the Four Seasons' hallways is the housekeeping cart. The housekeepers use carts—in fact, Four Seasons properties often have two different types of carts, one for morning service and another for turndown—but the carts remain in a service room hidden on each floor. The carts are not in the hall; thus, housekeepers must go back and forth from the service room to the guest rooms while making certain that high levels of standards are met. This lack of a cart does, many would contend, make the guests' stay more pleasurable. Navigating around cumbersome carts and seeing stacks of towels and linens put a dent in the pretense of service. However, what seems more important, rather than the overt aesthetic concerns, is the cart's relationship to showcasing work. If guests must face the labor required to make their rooms the perfect cocoons that Margie Garay describes at the start of this chapter, their sense of pleasure, their delight in the physical appearance of the well-designed and well-maintained room, may fade.[11]

Marx and Marxist scholars, such as Harry Braverman, suggest a clear power dynamic where labor lacks a voice in capitalist societies, but scholarship on hotels has critiqued the limitations of this perspective, claiming that hotel workers have been able to negotiate authority within the hierarchical hospitality industry.[12] Rachel Sherman claims that Marxist readings of labor tend to "focus on managerial dictates rather than on workplace relations." She further notes that scholarship often looks at work "as a source of constraint on workers rather than as a source of enjoyment or alliance."[13] Additionally, Daniel Levinson Wilk urges us to assess hotels as places that encourage socioeconomic freedom, especially when we look at the service industry in relation to previous centuries' commitments to slavery and inequitable work environments. Wilk argues, as I noted in my introduction, "that the modern service sector was not only better to its workers than its masters and mistresses were to servants, but that it played a significant role in the decline of servitude in the United States."[14] In my study of hotels I have found instances where a hierarchy defines worker relations within hotels, but I have also seen how workers have created powerful positions within the industry through unions and, as Sherman clarifies, through ordinary exchanges with guests and management.

Even with these instances of empowerment, guests and management often do what they can to silence workers, especially housekeepers. Thus, another way of thinking about the power relationship found in hotels is to consider line workers, or those who are not management, as what Erving Goffman deems "non-persons."[15] The non-person is neither the "audience" in a setting nor the central "performer." He or she is metaphorically, and often literally, off to the side and not perceived as a viable entity during interactions. For instance, a training video the Four Seasons Corporation shows to select employees highlights exchanges between workers and guests. The dialogue on the video reveals ways to enact the standards of service that represent the Four Seasons brand. However, when it comes to representing standards through the example of housekeeping, the guest room attendant is silent. She cleans, she dusts, and she does her work with a slight smile, but she is Goffman's exemplary non-person; she works in silence.[16] Moreover, hotel guests admit that they often do not think about housekeeping. They take their room getting cleaned as a given, and when that service gets disrupted, they get upset at having to contend with that interruption. One guest I spoke with honestly noted, "I take housekeeping for granted."[17] While Marx and Braverman would most likely interpret the non-person worker as an obvious consequence of capitalism, something more complicated and nuanced is actually occurring. Again, and I want to stress the importance of this point, the negotiations that take place between unions and hotel management make it evident that the moniker of "non-person" is not quite accurate, as many workers do have agency in relation to the industry.[18] Guests may not be privy to these negotiations, and many workers, of course, do not have union representation, but these conversations about workload, safety, and, as I explore throughout this book, design are integral to the daily operations of many hotels. There are several moments in what follows, especially in my chapters on the Hyatt Regency Chicago and Starwood in Hawaii, where I further explore these complicated and fluid power dynamics.

As Yvonne Guerrier and Amel Adib have posited, race, class, and gender define work roles and hierarchies within the labor organization found at hotels.[19] Historically in the United States—and this trend is still very much a part of the industry—white staff tends to the front-of-the-house operations (front desk and concierge workers) whereas individuals of color often run the back of the house (guest room attendants, kitchen staff, etc.). This delineation can also be found outside the United States, where those from the country where the hotel is located are up front and on view for hotel guests, whereas those behind the scenes usually come from nations geographically distant from the hotel. These racial distinctions manifest themselves in power dynamics that enable guests, management, and line workers to code specific tasks as "invisible." Additionally, one does not have to look further than who is pushing housekeeping carts on the typical guest room floor to notice that the majority of these workers are women. This is in stark contrast to the line of men that usually staffs concierge desks at hotels. The gendered and racialized composition of the hotel staff, or who is doing what, is a significant issue.[20]

This gendered and racial divide becomes even more apparent if we think about how guests and management perceive the differences between back-of-the-house and front-of-the-house workers. It becomes easier, for instance, for guests to humanize workers they frequently see, such as bellhops, concierges, and front desk clerks, but back-of-the-house work, such as housekeeping, which must strive for invisibility, can more readily be dehumanized and fetishized as a result of the unseen nature of this labor.[21] This creates a divide between guests' perceptions and the delivery of service, since guests can be blissfully unaware of what is happening behind the scenes to make their stay comfortable. These back-of-the-house workers also must contend with stereotyping by the managers who supervise and discipline them. The author of one of the most widely used housekeeping management textbooks, for instance, explains that mangers must contend with the psychology and demography of housekeepers. Housekeepers, in this model of stereotypical thinking, often

struggle with English, are frequently uneducated, and come from difficult circumstances.[22] In short, these are women who have been concep-
tualized as defective; thus, their ideas about mitigating the difficult task of
housekeeping rarely get heard.

Even though my study focuses on workers' status within hotels, I also
highlight the guest perspective and why these spaces are so enticing. Marx
offers us a window into the alluring domain of commodity fetishism, but
Thorstein Veblen, who published *The Theory of the Leisure Class* in 1899,
elucidates the role of the wealthy consumer's mind-set in the age of what
Veblen defined as "conspicuous consumption." Veblen famously made the
distinction between the leisure and the working class and contended that
"the emergence of a leisure class coincides with the beginning of ownership."[23] This leisure class, according to Veblen, engages in a series of rituals where its financial status must be displayed in order to secure its sense
of status and to differentiate it from the working class.

Veblen explains that one of the sites where these class distinctions can
be made, via the act of conspicuous consumption, is a hotel. Being conspicuous about spending does not simply mean throwing one's money
around in a haphazard show of prodigality. Veblen identifies key rituals
that the refined classes engage in to display their wealth, so that "impress-
ing one's pecuniary ability" becomes possible. Thus, Veblen observes, "In
the modern community there is . . . a more frequent attendance at large
gatherings of people to whom one's everyday life is unknown; in such
places as churches, theatres, ballrooms, hotels, parks, shops, and the like."
These sites provide venues where "the utility of conspicuous consumption" can indicate "pecuniary strength."[24] Even though Veblen does not
go into depth about how this display of wealth could manifest itself at a
hotel, we can imagine how these acts of conspicuous consumption could
be enacted. Bettina Matthias explores this theme by connecting Veblen's
theoretical premise to the introduction of the tennis court at European
hotels in the late nineteenth century. She notes that hoteliers often placed
these courts near the hotel building, so that players could be seen engaging in conspicuous leisure. Moreover, Matthias cleverly notes that tennis
"dress itself became a sign of Veblen's 'conspicuous consumption' since
white is a very unforgiving color that shows any dirt, and one needs to
have many outfits, or someone cleaning them all the time, to be properly
dressed for the occasion." Tennis was the most popular sport at many of
these hotels, but other activities, such as golf and hunting, which also required vast expenditures of time and financial resources on equipment,
were also quite fashionable.[25]

Veblen identifies servants as a key component to the leisure class's
interest in conspicuous consumption. Although he keeps his discussion

of the servant to the domestic sphere, it is not difficult to imagine his conceptualization about the importance of servants in the context of the turn-of-the-century hotels that he would have been familiar with when he wrote *The Theory of the Leisure Class*, in the waning years of the nineteenth century. Indeed, while teaching at the University of Chicago during the late 1890s, Veblen would have certainly known about the city's famous "fancy" hotels, such as the Palmer House.[26] Homes, like hotels at the turn of the century, were incorporating more technological innovations that Veblen claims obviated the need for "body servants, or domestic servants of any kind," but the "canon of reputability carried over by tradition from earlier usage" the importance of having servants within specific contexts that would bolster the ability to consume conspicuously. Veblen also noted that even though "mechanical contrivances" mitigated the difficulty of labor, household servants were still employed in wealthy homes because "under the requirement of conspicuous consumption of goods, the apparatus of living has grown so elaborate and cumbrous, in the way of dwellings, furniture, bric-a-brac, wardrobe and meals, that the consumers of these things cannot make way with them in the required manner without help."[27] In other words, modern life had created less of a need for the typical servant's duties, yet the rise of new social mores and rituals ensured that the servant's labor was not becoming obsolete.

Calling to mind some of the issues of propriety that I identify in relation to hotel housekeeping, service design, and management supervision in this book, Veblen explained the duality between visibility and invisibility that defines the servant's role. Veblen writes:

> Personal contact with the hired persons whose aid is called in to fulfil the routine of decency is commonly distasteful to the occupants of the house, but their presence is endured and paid for, in order to delegate to them a share in this onerous consumption of household goods. The presence of domestic servants, and of the special class of body servants in an eminent degree, is a concession of physical comfort to the moral need of pecuniary decency.[28]

What is perhaps most telling about this passage is Veblen's understanding that there is a code of behaviors that defines this relationship. The members of the leisure class may not want to see individuals whose labor has become a requirement to keep up expectations and appearances, but there is no choice. Decency demands the servant's labor and the wealthy must concede and accept this unavoidable presence.

To Veblen, the "good servant" must "conspicuously know his place" to adhere to a specific model of decorum that the master must manage with great care. Veblen uses words like "form" and "skilful workmanship" to describe the importance of the servant's fastidiousness. The master's primary interest in the servant relates to his "ability to pay" for these services, but if the servant conducts his duties with "unformed style" then this indicates a shortcoming "on the master's part to procure the service of specially trained servants; that is to say, it would imply inability to pay for the consumption of time, effort, and instruction required to fit a trained servant for special service under an exacting code of forms."[29] This careful instruction or supervision, as will become evident in the following chapter, on Mary Bresnan's *The Practical Hotel Housekeeper*, were the watchwords that circumscribed the servant's role in a world where changing ideals about propriety led to anxieties about socioeconomic class, especially in the context of hotels, where the leisure class could be easily observed while engaging in conspicuous consumption.

Lefebvre's Reservations

Theorist Henri Lefebvre contends that capitalism is not just about the exchange of goods and the disenfranchisement of labor, as per Marx's assertion, but also about the yearning for specific spaces. The physicality of space, the actual places where we live, conduct business, and, critical to my project, vacation, can also be desired and exchanged within the capitalist system. Lefebvre notes that leisure spaces are often nonproductive and abstracted; they are the milieus that appear to be non-work-spaces. On the other hand, these leisure sites where vacations transpire are productive in that they function "in the spatial practice of neocapitalism (complete with air transport) . . . . [where] representations of space facilitate the manipulation of representational spaces (sun, sea, festival, waste, expenses)."[30] Leisure travelers go to these locations thinking that they are escaping the day-to-day logic of capitalism, as they enjoy the pleasures that accompany "all this seemingly non-productive expense," yet these spaces are, according to Lefebvre, another manifestation of capitalism.[31]

It is the hotel staff's primary function to make the guest feel as though he or she is in a carefully designed, nonproductive space where leisure can be enjoyed without the usual interruptions of consumption and work. Again, the hotel becomes a site where the chores that attend everyday domestic life—the making of beds, the vacuuming of floors, the washing of linens, the cooking of food—get done by line workers through a carefully planned system of service design. Lefebvre contends that this passage into the sphere of vacations can be understood as a "departure" from the "space of consumption" and a "move towards the consumption of space." As travelers transcend the everyday they "demand a qualitative space. The qualities they seek have names: sun, snow, sea. Whether these are natural or simulated matters little. Neither spectacle nor mere signs are acceptable. What is wanted is materiality and naturalness as such, rediscovered in their (apparent or real) immediacy."[32] Lefebvre's emphasis on the leisure traveler's attraction to nature, where the experience of the outdoors becomes the basis for the trip, leads to his notion that these trips involve the wanting and acquiring (both real and imagined) of space, where the hotel functions as the intermediary between the tourist and the ecological space he or she is consuming. Lefebvre notes how tourists crave hotels that are near the naturalistic wonders that they flock to while on vacation. The hotel, like the rest of the artifice that constitutes the "'vacationland festival,'" is "planned [designed] with the greatest care: centralized, organized, hierarchized, symbolized and programmed to the nth degree, it serves the interests of tour-operators, bankers and entrepreneurs."[33] Moreover, Lefebvre explains how the capitalist logic of leisure produces hotels where bodies are "piled one on top of another or jammed next to one another in rows."[34] There is something dehumanizing about being at leisure, while we "stay" in what Lefebvre notes are merely "'boxes for living in.'"[35] The irony is that the controlled body supposedly wants to be restored while on vacation, yet it has been placed in a position that is endemic to the machinations of capitalism that create these vacationlands. "Thus," Lefebvre warns, "the contradictions become more acute—and the urbanites continue to clamor for a certain 'quality of space.'"[36] Caught in a tautological circle of desire, the hotel guest searches for a space of renewal but only finds the very system of capitalism he or she is trying to escape through leisure.[37]

The hotel industry claims that quality space will move the guest into a restorative milieu. Travelers often have this expectation of hotels beyond the leisure sites Lefebvre mentions. Hotels everywhere—in urban centers, in suburban malls, on beaches, at ski resorts, and in every other possible locale—promise to deliver an experience that obfuscates the contradiction between nature and capitalism that Lefebvre explicates. And it is design, both in its overt material appearance and in its covert organization of invisible systems, which mediates the delivery of these putatively curative experiences.

∗

It is design that I am most interested in, as it is design that is all too often ignored or thought of only as an aesthetic concern that has little to do with the actuality of work at a hotel. As Bruno Latour has explained in his essay "Mixing Humans and Nonhumans Together: The Sociology of a

Door-Closer," it is the world of things, and how these things interact with humans, that we need to pay attention to. These designed objects, spaces, systems, and services affect our everyday lives in ways that we ignore; thus, we need to reinsert a study of these things, places, and concepts into our analyses of "social relations." This is, Latour claims, critical and will enable us to assess what nonhuman agents have to do with our social, cultural, and political milieu.[38] As I discuss throughout this book, we must engage with Latour's mandate so that we can attain a clearer understanding of both material design (actual, built environments) and service design (workflow systems that create, or sometimes hinder, various experiences). Design studies, in all its various forms and iterations, has done a remarkable job of asking us to think about design's complicated condition, especially in relation to production, consumption, discourse, theory, and what is often referred to as its particular type of thinking.[39] But scant attention has been paid to the ways in which design decisions and thought have created any type of dialogue with labor.

It is time to move beyond this limitation and to include the idea of labor in our conversations about design's place in the world. Perhaps one way of doing this is through a discussion about co-design. In co-design, as described by Elizabeth Sanders and Pieter Jan Stappers, the individuals "who will eventually be served" by design are given a role in the design process.[40] This does not mean that designers should no longer be critical to the process of designing, but it is those who can benefit or suffer the most from design choices that need to be integrated into the practice of design. While most hotel designers think about their imaginary consumer as a guest, *Housekeeping by Design* argues that those who work in hotels need to also be understood as the end users of the designed spaces and services that define the hotel experience. Without the input of labor, hotels may only appear like magical figments of our imagination, where Lefebvre's description of space and consumption takes hold and where this ignorance about labor will only lead to more beautifully designed spaces where workers will continue to be marginalized in ways that are inequitable. The process of co-design would foster changes for an industry that has been struggling with labor conflicts.[41]

Investigating the relationship between design and hotels helps to foreground larger questions about design's role in facilitating, expediting, and eliding labor. By exploring a range of sources, from the tools of housekeeping to union contracts to the insights of hotel workers and guests, it is feasible to ask questions about design's function in these spaces that house temporary visitors. And by looking at design beyond the general appearance of how things look, and analyzing the systems of labor that make design happen, we can begin to assess how culture(s) uses design, thinks about design, and maintains design. As Victor Margolin asserts, studying design expands our understanding of culture and history, and it is my contention that studying hotels further opens the possibilities of critiquing design from novel perspectives.[42] Indeed, the hotel industry provides a window onto these larger issues through the complex ways in which it creates experiences that continue to entice by making guests say "wow!"

Vignette Two
PLAZA MEMORIES

Hotels evoke memories. Although I was born in New York City, my family left when I was two. We relocated to suburban Maryland, where New York was spoken about in hushed tones and excitement about what once was. New York was always that magnetic force that could take us back for a wonderful visit even though we no longer lived there. For me, part of its allure was staying at hotels. We would travel to New York for two- or three-day visits twice a year. We would see my grandparents, who lived in Queens; we would go to museums, especially the Metropolitan; we would eat Italian food; we would sit through endless sporting events held at Madison Square Garden. But, most vivid in my mind are New York's famous hotels, those spaces that were such an unusual marvel to a child growing up in suburbia. Every three or so years the hotel of choice would change, but from the mid-1970s into the early 1980s we usually stayed at the Plaza.

My parents splurged on these trips, so while my brother and I would share a double room, they always had a one-bedroom suite. Unlike the hotels of today, where a sense of consistency marks all guest rooms, lest the traveler have to cope with any type of unpredictability while staying in Los Angeles, Hong Kong, or London, older hotels, like the Plaza in the 1970s, maintained an idiosyncratic charm. The differences between suites could be enormous. Furnishings were not uniform, and the spaces—at least from the vantage point of my distant memory—had not been delineated into a highly organized plan, where square footage is a corporately driven, rational pricing scheme. The Plaza seemed to thrive on these wonderful irregularities, and each suite provided its own special sense of wonder. What today would probably seem like dated versions of colonial revival furnishings (including huge mirrors, an unpredictable use of door hardware, and ornate lighting fixtures) became all I could think about for weeks before each of these trips. I was less entranced with the upcoming ventures to restaurants and sporting events, and much more interested with what the room at the Plaza would hold.

The design of these rooms offered possibilities. These varied decorative schemes fostered my lively imagination and enabled me to leave predictable suburban Maryland behind and embrace something different, a place where I felt oddly more at home. I could project a sense of fantasy onto these interiors and transcend the banal and often humiliating experiences of grade school. Most eleven-year-old boys do not carry books with titles such as *Great American Mansions and Their Stories* to play dates.[1] While other kids longed for recess and the blacktop reprieve of gym class, I only wanted to go through the pages of the dreamscape offered by my book of late nineteenth- and early twentieth-century homes. The Plaza reflected the possibilities of living in the pages of that book. The reality, of course, must have been that nothing at the Plaza was from the turn of the century, outside of its remarkable facade and a few of its public spaces in the lobby. The furnishings of these suites must have been loaded with all kinds of reproductions, so the phony nature of the colonial revival appeared in these rooms as a type of copy of a copy, a kind of decorative fun house of stylistic mirrors. Yet this decor and its faux opulence made me feel like I could pretend to be someone else. I could more easily fantasize, as I often did at that age, about living in an imaginary world far removed from suburbia. If, as David Lowenthal argues, "the past is a foreign country," here was a veneer of another time period that became a proscenium for my very vivid imagination.[2]

In 1907, Henry Janeway Hardenbergh designed the Plaza Hotel for these types of imaginary musings. Very much beholden to turn-of-the-century opulence, the French Renaissance revival building on Grand Army Plaza, at Fifth Avenue between 58th Street and Central Park South, cost approximately $12.5 million to construct. The limestone exterior, with its extensive terracotta sculptural work, must have been quite a sight in the early years of the twentieth century, as its heavily decorative elements, along with its Mansard roof, enormous height, and turrets at the corners, were designed to impress (fig. 2). When the hotel first opened, rooms were $2.50 a night, which was not a modest sum at the time. The interior also reflected an unrestrained opulence: bronze wall decorations, mosaic floors, and an abundance of marble pilasters and columns defined these grand public rooms. Not satisfied with one revival style, Hardenbergh and the designers who worked on the interior spaces, which included L. Alavoine & Co., Ferdinand Schaettler, and others, utilized the German Renaissance, the Jacobethan, the neoclassical, and countless

FIGURE 2 Plaza Hotel. Courtesy of Fairmont Hotels & Resorts.

other architectural tropes to foster guests' fantastical musings while wondering through the Plaza's luxurious rooms.[3]

The hotel has changed ownership many times, but it has remained a mythical enterprise. In 1988, Donald Trump purchased the property for a reported $407.5 million and, as usual, could not contain his enthusiasm for his latest real estate venture. As he declared in a letter he placed in *New York* magazine, "I haven't purchased a building, I have purchased a masterpiece—the Mona Lisa. For the first time in my life, I have knowingly made a deal which was not economic—for I can never justify the price I paid, no matter how successful the Plaza becomes."[4] Today's Plaza has been reconfigured into both a hotel, managed by Fairmont Hotels & Resorts, and private residences. The residences, as of this writing, sell for over $5,000 a square foot.[5]

It is this endlessly celebrated warren of luxury that I most remember from my trips to New York. We would come back to the hotel after a long day of sightseeing and endless eating, and my parents would enjoy some downtime in their suite while I would leave on adventures. I remember riding elevators, walking up and down various stairwells, and always keeping my eyes alert for an open door. An open door meant that I could peek inside, see another space, and become—as was often the case at the Plaza—visually overwhelmed with yet another fantastical interior. The possibility of finding the most luxurious and unique nook and cranny in this labyrinthine realm made me look more intently while on these journeys. Hardenbergh's structure, with its countless stairwells and what appeared to my young eyes as marvelous twists and turns, only heightened my sense that I could, and inevitably would, encounter something magical at the Plaza.

Of course, a child's sense of wonder at the Plaza has become entrenched in popular culture through the pages of Kay Thompson's *Eloise*. Published in the 1950s, the four books in the Eloise series describe the rather peculiar life of a young girl whose absent parents and wealth allow her to live a very eccentric—albeit lonely—life at the Plaza. As the first book in the series details, Eloise takes full advantage of her privilege. Her indulgent nanny and the hotel staff fulfill her every whim and fancy, including the rather exacting standards she demands of disembodied room service operators. The Plaza enables Eloise to enjoy a type of transgressive freedom. With minimal adult supervision, the Plaza becomes a stage for her active fantasy life and the possibilities of hotel living foster her own precocious brand of humor and entitlement. I found the Eloise books very appealing, as they illustrated, through Thompson's hilarious language and Hilary Knight's vivid drawings, a never-ending adventure without the looming reality of a checkout time.[6]

My nostalgia about Eloise's adventures with room service and hedonism writ large may seem quaint, but I want to return to the question of labor, the central concern of my book, to detail what I did not understand while staying at the Plaza as a child. Rachel Sherman, in her book *Class Acts*, opens her first chapter with an epigraph from *Eloise*. This is the famous and oft-cited moment when Eloise describes how she orders room service: "Then I pick up the telephone and call Room Service. Oooooooooo I absolutely love Room Service. They always know it's me and they say 'Yes, Eloise?'"[7] Sherman uses this bit of brattiness to begin her discussion about how guests want hotel workers to perform as an "idealized mother," so that the caring, empathy, and immediate understanding of one's needs can be attended to.[8] Besides the fact that Eloise makes her room service order rather onerous in a way that will require more work, as she demands that her meal include a bone for her dog, one raisin for herself, and seven spoons, it is Eloise's imperious tone, as she places her hand on her hip while telling this voice on the other end of the phone what she requires, that is most revealing. Reflecting on Eloise's haughty nature has forced me to rethink what I must have been imagining as I roamed the Plaza, believing I had free rein. The nostalgic character of the Plaza's design, the very way in which its interiors attempt to showcase a New York of days gone by, helped develop my own imaginings about getting psychically lost in the space of a hotel. Moreover, the Eloise books, and her wonderful portrait, which still hangs in the hotel's lobby, enhanced my own dreams of hotel living. Away from home, distant from the everyday, spaces like the Plaza permit guests to wistfully engage with the past, even though the realities of the work required to maintain this pretense of a bygone era may be overlooked, ignored, and misunderstood.

It was when I first read Mary Bresnan's *The Practical Hotel Housekeeper* that I began reminiscing about my experiences at the Plaza. Bresnan, as the next chapter details, offers us a window into the life of a turn-of-the-century urban hotel. Her discussion of parlors, her hyperbolic attention to propriety, her putative understanding about ethnic differences between staff, and her explanations about how "chambermaids" need to be attentive to the ongoing demands of guests give her book a decidedly historical and dated sensibility. Issues related to unionization, fair wages, and equitable work conditions are not how she frames her narrative. Yet it is this very air of the antique, this patina of a hotel experience from another epoch, which makes Bresnan's account and didactic tone so intriguing. While my own memories of the Plaza may have subconsciously sparked my initial interest in Bresnan's book, the following chapter uses Bresnan's ideas and the larger context of late nineteenth- and early twentieth-century American hotels, including an assessment of the remarkable properties built by E. M. Statler, to consider several issues related to housekeeping and design. And as we consider this, it becomes possible to understand how this history helps us better understand how design continues to shape and define the hotel industry today.

2
DESIGN AND THE CHAMBERMAID

Mary Bresnan's *The Practical Hotel Housekeeper*
and E. M. Statler's Service Code

An advertisement in the April 1897 issue of the magazine *Hotel Monthly* offered the services of "a young widow of refinement [who] wishes position as housekeeper in first-class hotel, club or southern winter resort; thoroughly competent and first-class references. Address ESC care of HOTEL MONTHLY."[1] Unlike a contemporary hotel, for which the term "housekeeper" denotes an individual who cleans hotel rooms, in 1897 a housekeeper meant the woman who managed the chambermaids (today's housekeepers), the supplies, and the overall orchestration of the hotel's upkeep. The housekeeper was a type of executive. She, much like the director of housekeeping today, did not scrub toilets or sweep floors, but she did everything she could to make certain that those engaged in these activities did their tasks well and kept guests happy. By letting her potential employer know that she was a "widow" (someone who could be trusted while not burdened by familial obligations), this woman hoped that she could attain a position at a "first-class" establishment that would be commensurate with her stature and refined sensibilities.

Hotel Monthly, the venue where this woman of distinction chose to advertise her talents, was a national magazine for those in the hotel business. Its audience included hotel managers, housekeepers, and owners. The pages of the journal contain notices for everything from dinnerware to boilers to employment opportunities. Throughout its run, which began in 1896, the magazine also offered advice. With a prudent eye on the bottom line, topics such as what to offer in restaurants and how to bill patrons were the editors' focus. Not surprisingly, a number of articles on the perils and successes of housekeeping found their way into this popular periodical. *Hotel Monthly* became so successful that it even branched out into publishing books related to the hospitality business.

One of these books, *The Practical Hotel Housekeeper*, by Mary Bresnan, is a fascinating example of *Hotel Monthly*'s book-publishing arm. This title appeared in 1900, but the essays in Bresnan's text first appeared in the pages of *Hotel Monthly* as a monthly column. In these installments, Bresnan wrote about the ins and outs of managing housekeeping operations: She explained how to supervise chambermaids; she noted the importance of keeping up with supplies; she expressed concern about how the housekeeping staff should deal with complicated guests; and, most important for my book, she wrote a great deal about hotels and design, in terms of the workflow of housekeeping and the material spaces found in both guest rooms and the service areas located at the back of the house.[2]

Bresnan's audience was managers of turn-of-the-century luxury hotels. Historian Molly Berger has helpfully defined nineteenth- and early twentieth-century luxury hotels as those properties that focused extensively on the guest's comfort, while at the same time offering an abundance of easy-to-read design tropes that guests and visitors could label as "fancy." Given the context of *Hotel Monthly*, and the topics she repeatedly turns to, it is clear that Bresnan was writing about those hotels that were large enough to house their chambermaids and wealthy enough to buy expensive furniture and cleaning equipment, all while providing a wide assortment of services to guests.[3]

Bresnan did everything she could to reinforce the supervising construct that separated management from labor at hotels, and she accomplished this, to a large extent, through a discussion about design. Bresnan did not set out to write a book about design. However, she continually referenced design—in both its material and invisible manifestations—throughout *The Practical Hotel Housekeeper*. As I detailed in my introduction, design needs to be understood as the shaping of the artificial world to provide, as Herbert Simon contends, "preferred" conditions.[4] Design should be understood as both the shaping of tangible things and the devising of those service experiences that we take for granted. Service design issues are ubiquitous at hotels, and this chapter, like the rest of my book, focuses on housekeeping and the ways in which it is a managed activity that requires fastidious attention to details in order to clean rooms and public spaces while concomitantly keeping guests happy and unaware of its presence. Moreover, service design has been devised at hotels in a way that rarely takes into account the workers who do the actual labor of maintaining the design integrity of hotels.

Bresnan's book historically contextualizes many of the arguments that I make about design throughout *Housekeeping by Design*. The late nineteenth and early twentieth century witnessed a dramatic shift in the way that guests, managers, and hotel workers viewed each other. During this period, workers began to reevaluate their relationship to labor. Instead of seeing themselves as mere "servants," more workers began to describe their positions as akin to professional "staff," which diminished "the stigma of servility" and led to changes in the affective labor that defined the triangular relationship between guests, workers, and management.[5] Design played an enormous role in these arrangements that relate closely to ideas about class and status. While there are moments when Bresnan mentions specifics about emotional labor, there are other instances when she is very clear about the importance of establishing and maintaining propriety, regardless of the psychic cost.

While Bresnan struggled with how to cope with these changes in the service industry at the turn of the century, E. M. Statler turned to a holistic form of service design in the first decades of the twentieth century, which included architecture and novel labor systems that helped implement his famous "service code," predicated on the idea that "the guest is always right."[6] Statler, who opened his first hotel in 1907, built hotels throughout the United States, and the company bearing his name (Statler Hotels) continued to construct several more properties after his death in 1928. The Statler name will also be forever linked with the famous Cornell University School of Hotel Administration, which received funding from the Statler Foundation after the hotelier's death and has set a number of industry standards in terms of best practices and how to instill managerial rigor. Statler, his managers, and his architects instituted a paradigm shift where technology and procedures were put into effect with workers in mind. Design ideas, such as using shared plumbing shafts in adjacent guest rooms, and ways of thinking about the division of labor between housekeepers, such as Statler's plan for a flexible housekeeping schedule, continue to affect the industry.

This chapter assesses Bresnan's late nineteenth-century struggle with this shifting landscape of hotel labor that ultimately led to the changes that Statler's service code fostered in the first quarter of the twentieth century. Even though Statler's redesign of the hotel industry epitomizes a shift away from the model of servitude that Bresnan devised, an air of anxiety permeates both his and Bresnan's ideas of what it meant to run a hotel and supervise hotel employees, including housekeepers. Reading Bresnan and Statler alongside other period sources reveals the ways in which their writing about design and hotel work reinforces the connections between design and labor, which frame, in the context of my book, larger debates about the hotel workplace and the inclusion of workers' voices that continue in the twenty-first century.[7]

Disciplining the Chambermaid

The importance of the chambermaid's reticent subservience appears early in *The Practical Hotel Housekeeper*. In her first chapter, titled "The House-keeper's Duties," Bresnan outlined how to make certain that guests receive proper treatment and attention. One subsection of this initial chapter, titled "Calling on Lady Guests," noted that the "housekeeper must be on the alert at all times and where there are ladies in rooms it is her duty to call on those ladies for a few minutes every day and ask them if they are waited on and their work done as they wish." According to Bresnan, this was the only way to tell if the chambermaid was doing her job. And, even more important, it ensured that the housekeeper—the manager of the chambermaids—had "not [been] misrepresented by any one that may feel inclined to do so." This qualifying visit to guests' quarters, which should conclude with "bowing," guaranteed that rooms had been cleaned, details had been attended to, and, perhaps most critically, nothing spurious had been said against the housekeeper as she supervised the guest's satisfaction.[8]

When it came to furnishings, however, the importance of attending to the "lady guest" could become a bit of a trap if the housekeeper was not vigilant. In another subsection of her first chapter, Bresnan related the story of "The Lady Guests Who Make Trouble." By giving small gifts to the chambermaid, some guests become very close to the woman who cleans their rooms. The chambermaid may, with a sense of obligation because of this bond, help the guest procure "a certain kind of chair or couch, or, perhaps, lace curtains." This exchange sounds innocent enough, but gossip traveled quickly in the halls of a turn-of-the-century hotel, and soon another guest would realize, because of her own gossiping chambermaid, "that her dear friend has such a lovely couch or reclining chair." Demands ensued, as the woman who had not been given these preferential furnishings wanted her own parlor suite upgraded. She got her husband involved and they even threatened management with an early departure unless decor restitution was made. Bresnan alleged that without "having good sensible girls for chambermaids" a woman of leisure can easily take charge and garner favors, exchange gossip, and promote general ill will in the confines of the hotel.[9]

A humorous article in the *Chicago Daily Tribune* supports Bresnan's claims about the perils of the disingenuous "lady guest." The sarcastic article notes that "a woman in a hotel is worth seeing. She rings the bell three times to a man's once." A litany of bad behavior follows along with a discussion about how these needy women treat the chambermaid: "The woman in a hotel expects the chambermaid to 'see to' this, that, and the other thing, sewing on a button, taking a stitch, hanging up her dresses, and helping her to put them on. The chambermaid is only a poor human being who has a lot of work to do and the housekeeper to keep an eye on her. But what of that?" Indeed, the guest all too often ignores the chambermaid's plight and "asks her just the same: 'Iron these out for me, Mary, there's a good girl,' or to 'face up my dress, there's a dear,' or to 'put me in a few extra towels.'" These endless demands exasperate hotel workers and lead to "a whole line of impatient men waiting for rooms," while the women command all of the staff's attention.[10] As Bresnan recognized, these types of impertinent female guests needed to be monitored and supervised with frequent visits to prevent the potential abuse of chambermaids, supervisors, and fellow guests.[11]

Even with these warnings about difficult guests, Bresnan repeatedly detailed why the chambermaid needed to be managed, and, in part, this requisite supervision was the product of the chambermaids' abilities to deceive at the expense of the housekeeper's reputation. Bresnan included the story of the guest "who told me she left a first class house because her rooms were so poorly tended to." When Bresnan asked this woman what she saw as the cause of this neglect, she was told that the housekeeper overworked her chambermaids and "should be removed, she has no mercy on the girls." Bresnan eventually "became well acquainted with the housekeeper referred too [*sic*], and found her to be anything but severe. [She] was grossly misrepresented." Bresnan wanted to put an end to this seemingly duplicitous distortion of the housekeeper's talents, spread by a hostile chambermaid who raised her concerns with guests. It was only through "governing help" that this deception could be stopped.[12]

Church attendance and staying away from vice were key components to the chambermaid's success, since this enforced a type of regulatory control that ensured compliance. Bresnan suggested that religion could inspire more tractable employees. Sunday was often a quiet day at hotels, when guests slept in and the routine cleaning happened later in the day. Thus, "the housekeeper," in Bresnan's estimation, "should give all the girls in her department to understand that as far as she was concerned they might all go to church." Bresnan observed that "it is a well known fact that such girls [who attend church] work better and are more faithful." Going to church could mitigate the chambermaid's amoral leanings, and then after sitting in church "they can go and get back [to the hotel] long before their rooms are open for them" to clean.[13] Beyond gossip and a type of perverse pleasure in undermining the housekeeper, chambermaids also had the propensity to stay out late and possibly get into compromising situations. Bresnan pronounced "another important duty[,] and one that requires firmness, kindness, patience, concealment and great charity in the true housekeeper[,]" was the prevention of "her help from staying out late at night."[14]

Intertwined with the chambermaid's propriety were her interactions with male guests, especially when it came to cleaning guest rooms. Bresnan described how important it was to make certain "that no maid should on any account go into a gentleman's room to put it in order while the gentleman is in his room." The morality of the chambermaid should not be compromised; therefore, while cleaning a man's room the "maid should always keep the door of such rooms open while she is putting them in order. If he comes back before she has finished she must then keep it open." If the gentleman had to be in his room because of illness, "even the bell boy is better than to let the maid go alone."[15] Was Bresnan faulting the licentious nature of men or the weak moral compass of her chambermaids? This is unclear, but the idea that the maid's behavior had to be managed, in fact, scrutinized through open doors, was the central premise that she repeatedly returned to throughout her prescriptive book.

Bresnan's fixation about what made an ideal chambermaid speaks to the breakdown in power dynamics between servants and employers that occurred in the late nineteenth and early twentieth centuries. As mentioned earlier, this new paradigm was, in part, the result of changes to the affective component of work life, where society began to question the traditional view that labor should only be silent servants, and many cultural critics saw these radical shifts as disruptive to the status quo. Bresnan tackled this shifting ground. Instead of embracing this changing paradigm, she gave guidance that solidified traditional notions of supervision. She refused to back away from her premise that chambermaids needed to understand the appropriate way to do their jobs. And when modern life tested the boundaries of class and decency, she offered solutions that repaired these breaches in decorum. Let's next turn to Bresnan's discussion of design, where her unbending conceptions about hotel labor become even more apparent.

The Pragmatics of Workflow and Inventory

A housekeeper's board, or the number of rooms that she must clean per day, is often hotly contested. Changes in a hotel room's design, or in the programs offered by a hotel, can affect this number. Even less obvious, but equally important, is how a guest's use, or abuse, of the room also affects this quota.[16] Bresnan's book does not mention labor disputes, but questions about how work should be distributed and sequenced throughout hotels are paramount to her study. She also includes numerous examples of the hotel industry's attempts to design workflow systems that could codify and reinforce the structure of service design in turn-of-the-century hotels. These early attempts at service design further circumscribed what workers could do and not do in the context of the hotel.

Under a subsection titled "Number of Rooms a Chambermaid Can Do in a Day," Bresnan explained how this number is somewhat elusive, since it "depends altogether on circumstances." She detailed how this quota is contingent on design choices, so "when the rooms are large and have a full set of heavy plush or velvet furniture, such as there is at the Tremont House in Chicago . . . then fifteen rooms are sufficient when all are occupied." On the other hand, in certain desert locations, chambermaids "could do twenty and even more with perfect ease, as there [is] neither soot nor sand to sweep or dust in any of those rooms."[17] The hotel's housekeeper, or, again, what we would today call the director of housekeeping, should, according to Bresnan, make these decisions about local conditions; it is then the chambermaid's task to follow the quota as set by her supervisor.

In the late nineteenth century, the hotel industry started to offer proprietors new methods to help calculate and understand the importance of how guests utilized hotels, thus further connecting management's decisions to ideas about workflow. In 1897, *Hotel Monthly* advertised "Preston's Hotel Time Chart," which divided the guest's stay into segments so that charges would be appropriate and in line with industry standards (fig. 3). In a culture that was becoming increasingly invested in how increments of time could be divided into fiscal success, as the following two decades would witness the introduction of Frederick Winslow Taylor's scientific studies of physical labor and Henry Ford's assembly line, Preston's chart must have been a welcome addition.[18] The advertisement includes a sample of the chart along with copy that explains how easy it is to use:

> A section of the chart is herewith illustrated. A glance will show its usefulness to one who is not a ready reckoner, or who is apt to make mistakes in calculating the fractions of a day. A guest arrives, for instance, on Monday, before supper. If he stays until after breakfast on Wednesday, his bill would be for 1 3/4 days. This is shown by following the Monday supper line across the page to where it meets the Wednesday breakfast column. The calculating is simplified by having a new 'arrivals' line for each day of the week.[19]

Rather than charge guests for entire days, which is common practice at contemporary hotels, Preston delineated the day based on meals. Guests would only be charged the portion of the day that corresponded to the number of meals they ate. This would alleviate some of the concerns

PRESTON'S HOTEL TIME CHART.
Copyrighted 1895 by ALBERT L. PRESTON.

TIME OF DEPARTURE.

Time of ARRIVAL	MONDAY				TUESDAY				WEDNESDAY				THURSDAY		
	Bk.	Din.	Sup.	Log.	Bk.	Din.	Sup.	Log.	Bk.	Din.	Sup.	Log.	Bk.	Din.	Sup.
	DAYS	DAYS	DAYS	DAYS	DAYS	DAYS	DAYS	DAYS	DAYS	DAYS	DAYS	DAYS	DAYS	DAYS	DAYS
MONDAY Bk.	¼	½	¾	1	1¼	1½	1¾	2	2¼	2½	2¾	3	3¼	3½	3¾
Din		¼	½	¾	1	1¼	1½	1¾	2	2¼	2½	2¾	3	3¼	3½
Sup			¼	½	¾	1	1¼	1½	1¾	2	2¼	2½	2¾	3	3¼
Log				¼	½	¾	1	1¼	1½	1¾	2	2¼	2½	2¾	3

Time of ARRIVAL	TUESDAY			
	Bk.	Din.	Sup.	Log.
	DAYS	DAYS	DAYS	DAYS
TUESDAY Bk.	¼	½	¾	1
Din		¼	½	¾
Sup			¼	½
Log				¼

Time of ARRIVAL	WEDNESDAY			
	Bk.	Din.	Sup.	Log.
	DAYS	DAYS	DAYS	DAYS
WEDNESDAY Bk.	¼	½	¾	1
Din		¼	½	¾
Sup			¼	½
Log				¼

PRESTON'S HOTEL TIME CHART.

TELLS LENGTH OF TIME BETWEEN ARRIVAL AND DEPARTURE OF THE GUEST.

Albert L. Preston, author of Preston's Hotel Calculator, illustrated in the HOTEL MONTHLY of August 1897, has designed and copyrighted Preston's Hotel Time Chart, the object of which is to tell correctly, on the instant, the length of time between the arrival and departure of the guest.

A section of the chart is herewith illustrated. A glance will show its usefulness to one who is not a ready reckoner, or who is apt to make mistakes in calculating the fractions of a day. A guest arrives, for instance, on Monday, before supper. If he stays until after breakfast on Wednesday, his bill would be for 1¾ days. This is shown by following the Monday supper line across the page to where it meets the Wednesday breakfast column The calculating is simplified by having a new "arrivals" line for each day of the week.

The charts are marketed in two sizes to suit the convenience of the hotel using them, and are suitable either for tacking up on the wall or putting into a frame, or placing under a glass on the desk. The smallest size, measuring 10½x15 inches, gives seven arrival and eight departure days. The large sheet measures 15½x19½ inches and gives seven arrival and fifteen departure days. These charts retail at fifty cents each and can be obtained of the HOTEL MONTHLY.

FIGURE 3 "Preston's Hotel Time Chart," *Hotel Monthly* 5 (1897): 27. General Research Division, New York Public Library, Astor, Lenox and Tilden Foundations.

about late checkout, which is a common practice that continues to haunt hotel proprietors. The pictured chart is straightforward and uses simple graphics, such as bold lines that separate days of the week and thinner lines that separate meal columns, to ensure ease of use. This ability to tell "on the instant . . . the length of time between the arrival and departure of the guest" would have furthered the industry's move toward an understanding of time as that which could be apportioned to better appreciate how workflow, in relation to guest behavior, could lead to new models of compensation.

Closely related to workflow and the organization of hotel space was, according to Bresnan's logic, keeping a close watch over each hotel room's inventory of objects. Bresnan saw inventory as so critical that she opened

WEEKLY REPORT of LINEN ROOM -								Week Ending July 7 1899			
	TOTAL LAST COUNT	PLUS NEW STOCK	GRAND TOTAL	IN SERVICE	COUNT of LINEN ROOM SAT. P.M. SHOULD BE	ACTUAL COUNT of LINEN am IS	MISSING	MISSING ACCOUNTED FOR			REMARKS
								IN LAUNDRY	CONDEM?	LOST	
Linen Sheets	650	*30	680	320	360	340	20	5	15		*In. F.YC.#36
Linen Slips	702			320	382	377	5	5			
Cotton Sheets	216			96	120	119	1	1			
Cotton Slips	300			96	204	204					
Counterpanes	210			205	5	4	1		1		
Splashers	250			220	30	29	1			1	
Face Towels	1200			615	685	360	325	304	17	*4	*from Room 37. July 5
Bath Towels	150			75	75	53	22	22			

FIGURE 4 Mary Bresnan, *The Practical Hotel Housekeeper* (Chicago: Hotel Monthly, 1900). Courtesy of Hagley Museum and Library.

her book with several foldout pages that contained examples of linen inventory charts and then her subsection titled "The Inventory" appears on the first page of her book, under the heading "The Housekeeper's Duties." Like Preston's time charts, the inventory tables are counting devices that provide exacting standards, so that the location of linens within the hotel can be assessed. For instance, her first chart lists dates and the precise count for everything from "linen sheets" to "bath towels" under the title "Weekly Report of Linen" (fig. 4). Her other charts include the linen inventory in specific rooms of the hotel, such as the individual guest rooms, "dining room and pantries," and the "kitchen" (fig. 5). Bresnan wanted every item to be accounted for, and tracking linen, which often seemed to get misplaced as it went in and out of the hotel's laundry, was one of her pressing concerns.[20] Bresnan's description follows, and her language is particularly inflexible and unyielding. Here she cataloged items that every hotel room must have, such as a soap dish, pitcher, match safe, and slop jar. Bresnan claimed that "it is a disgrace to the housekeeper to have a chambermaid work for her, who knows she has in her division a room" that does not have a cover for the slop jar. The maid must "report to the housekeeper" when a cover to such an important item is broken or misplaced. Moreover, when any items go missing the housekeeper "jots them down in her book and, as soon as she possibly can, she replaces the missing articles."[21] Often the chambermaid will not be as fastidious about inventory, but while the "maid's memory may fail . . . the housekeeper's must not."[22] In Bresnan's calculus of hotel management, the housekeeper needed to be alert.

Replacing inventory required precision and could inundate the hotel

List of Linen Sent to and Returned from Laundry.---By use of Parallel Columns One Book Serves for Both Purposes.

FIGURE 5 Mary Bresnan, *The Practical Hotel Housekeeper* (Chicago: Hotel Monthly, 1900). Courtesy of Hagley Museum and Library.

housekeeper's already full schedule, but the realities of cleaning a hotel room without interfering with the guest's sense of entitlement—a service design conundrum—plagued chambermaids. The balance between serving a guest and completing work in a timely fashion required a delicate sense of diplomacy. To illustrate how awkward these scenarios could become, Bresnan offered the hypothetical example of three hotel guests: Mrs. Winslow, Mrs. Hamilton, and Mrs. Sheridan, who all want their rooms cleaned at the same time. The reality, which Bresnan was keenly aware of, was that these women each have different types of rooms and each paid a different rate for these rooms. Mrs. Hamilton "has only one room and cheap at that," while the "Sheridans have the finest rooms on the floor" and Mrs. Winslow has "rooms," indicating to the reader that her status within the hierarchy of the hotel is somewhat middling. Each of these guests has indicated, in a rather unfortunate moment of synchronicity, that she wants her space cleaned immediately. What should the chambermaid do? Bresnan came up with a clever plan. The maid can explain to Mrs. Sheridan that Mrs. Hamilton only has the one room and Mrs. Sheridan, Bresnan believes, "wouldn't for the world compel any lady to sit in a room with the work undone until all her rooms in her suite were finished." Then, Bresnan suggested that the maid tell Mrs. Winslow that "the Sheridans are expecting company." Again, Bresnan was certain that Mrs. Winslow would understand this predicament and agree that the chambermaid can attend to the Sheridan's parlor before returning to her rooms. In a rather dizzying game of musical hotel rooms, the chambermaid is able to complete her work "without giving offense to any lady or causing the housekeeper any trouble."[23] Through the careful art of negotiation, the chambermaid could emotionally manage her guests' expectations with efficient and shrewd service.

The ability to navigate this division of work and the importance of inventory note taking speaks to Bresnan's hypervigilant management style and her early fascination with service design. Remember, service design is specifically about arranging and systematizing both the material and immaterial aspects of a physical space or experience to enable workflow to facilitate both the customer's experience and labor's delivery of various services. Bresnan's routinization of housekeeping—as revealed in her charts and her demanding tone—addresses how the industry was turning to new ideas about the ways in which an early version of service design could solve the problems that attended demanding guests and, most significantly, chambermaids who were beginning to question their role in the workplace. While ideas about service design are often understood as contemporary, cross-disciplinary, and imaginative in a way that leads to better outcomes, Bresnan engaged in a service-design-like activity without exactly naming it as such.[24] Her ideas were more often than not about preserving a way of life that subjugated workers in the face of changing ideals about labor. As chambermaids had more distractions (think of Bresnan's anxieties about gentlemen in guest rooms), she felt the need to delineate a system of work—what I am referencing as a type of service design strategy—that would thwart many of the changes she understood as encroaching on traditional boundaries that delimited the distinctions between guests and workers.

Bresnan's lessons about how to manage the seamless delivery of service within a hotel speak to the emerging ideas about modern efficiency that were becoming more important to the growing industry. And along with these views about how to design services that would please the guest came a growing interest in the physical design of hotels. As Bresnan and other period writers detailed, a hotel could not function without a clear understanding of how to plan and devise physical space.

Designing for "A Better Class of Help"

In July of 1900, Edward F. Clark wrote an article for *Hotel Monthly* about designing a "plan of the Help's Quarters." Clark, a noted hotelier, explained that "providing suitable quarters for the employes of a hotel the proprietor is at once performing a duty towards others and gaining a profit for himself." He went on to detail that these rooms should be "clean" and "cheerful . . . with good light and ventilation," as this will "impart a self-respecting influence to the occupants, create a feeling of content in their minds and cause them to become attached to the house as their home." This domestication of hotel workers, in Clark's estimation, fostered "a better class of help . . . who will be more permanent and reliable, will attend to their duties cheerfully and, in all, render better service."[25] By housing hotel workers, the distinction between home and work could be abolished and employees would obediently go about their duties as a result of living in-house.

Clark provided the reader with a floor plan of the hotel staff's quarters. The individual rooms, as delineated in his scaled drawing, are twelve by eighteen feet and include a location for a bed and a closet (fig. 6). Much like the regimented rows of rooms found on a typical guest room floor, this space was designed to get the maximum amount of use out of the U-shaped floor. These rooms have plenty of light and several even include two windows. The floor's north elevation, marked "Dead Wall to The North," includes an "open court," a linen room, and a shared bath. Next to the linen room is a space that Clark designated a "Visiting Room." In his accompanying text, he noted, "A visiting room is provided wherein

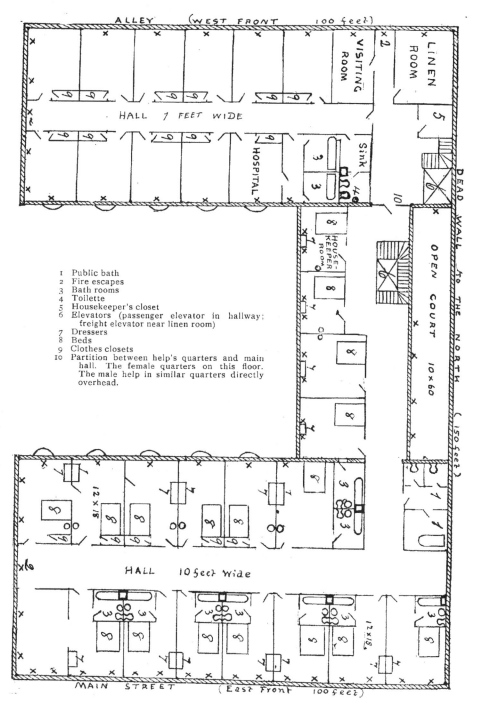

FIGURE 6 Edward F. Clark, "Plan of the Help's Quarters," *Hotel Monthly*
8 (1900): 14. General Research Division, New York Public Library, Astor,
Lenox and Tilden Foundations.

the women may receive their callers at certain hours. This room will have no doors and will be open for the convenience and pleasure of all women employees."[26] This space may have been designated for leisure, but its design allowed for easy surveillance.

In *The Practical Hotel Housekeeper*, Bresnan also included a discussion about "the help's" quarters. She explained that "hotel employes accept as part of their hire, their board and room; and the one should be wholesome and the other comfortable enough to satisfy any man or woman." These workers "don't expect luxuries or delicacies," yet they should be given "enough" so that they will not "grumble."[27] While Bresnan's book does not detail the way that the hotel's staff quarters should be designed, it does include information about how best to treat the sick chambermaid who lives at the hotel. Like Clark, Bresnan promoted the idea of keeping hotel employees in-house: "When any girl in the housekeeper's department is sick, don't send her to the hospital for a day or two, but treat her kindly, compassionately and with the respect that is due to all women from their own kind." In keeping with her mandate for supervising labor, Bresnan advised that women with similar jobs should wait on each other when ill: "If a maid, then one or two of the maids should cheerfully wait on her; if a scrub or paint girl, the same rule holds good." The housekeeper should also check in on the sick girl to make certain she is "comfortable," but by having one or two "girls" regularly "bring [the sick worker] a drink now and then and look in occasionally at her no time is lost, and the girl does not suffer for any lack of care." Once again, efficiency is paramount, but here a tone of sensitivity, a feeling of empathy, creeps into Bresnan's narrative. According to Bresnan, "There are few things sadder than a lonely neglected sick girl in the servants quarters of a large hotel."[28] Thinking back to Clark's floor plan, and the monotonous corridors of rooms that he designed for "the help," being stuck in a small and sterile room while indisposed would not have been an appealing prospect.

Clark also offered details about the design and use of the infirmary for the staff in his prototypical hotel. He explained: "The 'hospital room' is intended to be used for the sick only. It is connected with the bath, supplied with hot and cold water, proper ventilation, light, heat, etc. Any woman who is too ill to work should be placed in this room, given proper service and care and charged one dollar per day while she remains. Practical hotel keepers will discern the wisdom and justice of this idea."[29] Clark's description is much more clinical and pragmatic than Bresnan's putatively sensitive tone. Rather than provide a type of familial care for the sick, he thought it was best for the sick worker to be separated and charged a fee. In fact, by making the "hospital" next to the bath, and almost catty-corner to the visiting and linen rooms, Clark enhanced the visibility of the unwell. Could this have been understood as a type of visual warning about the way in which illness could lead to separation and seclusion? Unlike Bresnan, Clark did not seem to care about the potential "loneliness" that attended poor health. He promoted this segregation and even included, within his paradigm of "wisdom and justice," a dollar-a-day charge as a type of incentive for getting well.

Bresnan further articulated the need for good back-of-the-house design in her discussion about laundry rooms. She dedicated several pages to the laundry and offered very detailed criticism about existing laundry rooms and what could be done to improve what she understood as "one of the most important and profitable of all the departments connected with a hotel."[30] In order to provide an accurate understanding of these spaces, Bresnan visited numerous laundry facilities at the best hotels and came to the realization that cheap labor becomes "the most expensive in the end."[31] In other words, you get what you pay for, and in the case of hotels it is always recommended that the housekeeper find women who know how to navigate the complicated process of laundry with skill. Bresnan claimed, "Laundry help when well treated rarely change places, often spending the best years of their lives in one laundry. Unlike other parts of the hotel there is no caste among the people in the laundry of a good hotel." The laundry employees "very seldom mingle with the other help. They might almost be called a community."[32]

Poor design could, however, hinder the delivery of service in laundry rooms. Bresnan included a lengthy explanation of a service design predicament where a lack of training and a paucity of professionalism led to ripped linens, a harried staff, and an inability to replace soiled tablecloths in the hotel's dining room. Proper training, according to Bresnan, would have ensured that these failures never occurred.[33] She further explained that "hotel proprietors are neither architects nor builders," so the practice of placing the laundry in the "basement" of hotels, since they cannot be in front-of-the-house spaces, leads to laundry rooms that are "low and deep and dark or ill ventilated."[34] In short, Bresnan addressed a central concern of my book, specifically, how can designers devise spaces that are conducive to work? After providing further details about the poor quality of these laundries, she observed:

> This goes to show that the architects when drawing their plans for the building of those hotels gave very little thought to the laundries—in fact we found one hotel in which the laundry was completely ignored, and this, too, in a modern ten-story structure. But as this is now being remodeled and an addition being built, this addition when finished will contain one of the finest laundries in the country, and then the propri-

etor will be able to accommodate his patrons, while at the present time he has considerable difficulty in having the house cloths done in a corner of the basement.[35]

When attention is paid to these critical spaces the result is beneficial to business. Bresnan's reaction to the Hollenden Hotel in Cleveland is telling. Here she found that the hotel's laundry room's "light and fresh air" led to "perfectly smooth hems and square napkins and table cloths and towels."[36] A well-designed laundry cultivated a better work ethic and content guests.

Bresnan's stereotypes about gender and ethnicity affected her assessment of laundry room design, especially in relation to hotel management. She warned her reader about the European immigrant who comes to the United States in search of a job at the hotel's laundry department. With this immigrant population, the laundry can become like a vocational school, and when the European immigrant has "graduated, without waiting for a diploma [she may] leave for more profitable and congenial quarters." Bresnan asked, "how much has it cost" hotels to engage in these training practices?[37] Beyond her suspicion of amateur European workers who take advantage of their employers, Bresnan also described the perils of having women in laundry rooms who use steam machines. She reported on one incident she witnessed while visiting hotels for her book: "In one [steam] laundry a young girl without thought of fear or danger went so near one of the belts that it caught just a little bit of a few loose hairs and before anybody knew what happened she was carried screaming up the belt, which was stopped just before she reached the ceiling." This terrifying event resulted in this woman "lying in one of the best rooms in the house, having, at the expense of the house, the best doctors in city." This incident "convinced" Bresnan "of the danger that threatens women attempting to fill men's positions in steam laundries."[38]

In Bresnan's opinion, hotel work was gender and ethnic specific. Bresnan may have explained the plight of the young girl who got her hair stuck in the steam laundry conveyor with a bit of sympathy, but, like so much of her book, she asked hotel proprietors to pay attention to economics. She questioned the expense associated with the "best doctors" instead of asking questions about worker safety. While discussing the architecture of these spaces earlier in her book she mentioned light and ventilation, but avoiding potential accidents for the sake of the worker did not appear to be Bresnan's concern. The girl's plight as she headed up the conveyor was, in Bresnan's estimation, not the fault of bad design, but of poor management decisions when it came to embracing gendered notions of labor.

The Statler Service Code

As the twentieth century progressed, more hotels focused on how the careful planning of services and delivering of those services could enhance profits, keep staff vigilant, and create more loyal customers. The most famous name in the hotel world during the first half of the twentieth century was Ellsworth Milton Statler. Over his lifetime, Statler would build numerous hotels across the United States; the first one was the Statler Hotel in Buffalo, which opened to the public in 1907. Several other hotels would follow, including Statler Hotels in Cleveland (1912), Detroit (1915), and St. Louis (1917). These properties had between 450 and 800 rooms, which changed the nature of the hotel business.[39]

Statler learned the hotel trade at a young age through his initial experiences at the McLure House, a hotel in Wheeling, West Virginia. Here Statler, as was widely reported, worked very hard and "developed a passion for service, for doing a little more than the guest expected. His tips were plentiful. In a year and a half he had saved one hundred and fifty dollars, which he turned over proudly to his mother."[40] Over time, Statler worked his way from bellboy to check clerk to night clerk, and finally he became a day clerk. This job at McLure House led to Statler's initial investments in hospitality, such as running a billiard room and a bowling alley, and thus his legend as the businessman who changed the nature of the service industry was born.[41]

Statler's watchword during the development of his hotels was service. Mary Bresnan was also, of course, invested in the concept of service, but to her it was more of a top-down ideal. In other words, Bresnan extolled the virtues of supervision and a strict adherence to discipline. In Statler's conception of service, workers gained further control over interactions with guests, and in his estimation his workers' ability to function as a team became a key component to making the guests happy during their stay at one of his hotels. This does not mean that Statler could ever be understood as prolabor, but his service-design-dependent credo, "The guest is always right," placed a new type of responsibility on his workers.[42]

Statler described service as a commodity that could be sold to guests. Using the position of bellboy as an example, perhaps as a result of his own start in this position at the McLure in Wheeling, Statler highlighted the virtues of meeting the guest at the door and making a good impression from the start. Statler, in an article in the business magazine *System*, noted, "If the doorman is not alert or if the bellboy who is there to relieve them of their grips performs his job in an unmannerly or an ungracious way," then this would, inevitably, detract from the guest's stay. Statler further implored employees to "smile readily," and he explained that the supervisor was a type of "'superintendent of service' whose job it is to see that all of the employees under him who come in contact with guests meet them . . . graciously, courteously, and cheerfully."[43] Statler's focus on the affective qualities of service was a theme found in all his writing, as he claimed, "We try never to hire a man who cannot smile." In this article from *System*, Statler quoted from a missive he had recently sent to his managers: "You are instructed to hire only good nature people, cheerful and pleasant, who smile easily and often." He further admonished his managers to "get rid of the grouches." Personality became the key ingredient to service, and a smile, in Statler's estimation, would "make the guest feel friendly and 'at home.'"[44]

Even though this interest in affective service and maintaining a pleasant demeanor placed a new emphasis on the hotel staff that empowered their actions and offered them agency in the hospitality business, there were moments when Statler's obsessions with service sounded very similar to Bresnan's punitive voice. Statler would, for instance, have a physician examine his employees to make certain that each worker was healthy. He realized that "the healthier an employee is, we believe, the more apt he is to serve our guests as we insist he shall." This scrutiny of employees' bodies also entailed Statler's surveillance of their actions while interacting with guests. "Every day the manager of each hotel," according to Statler, "sends me a typewritten report . . . on which are listed the various kinds of complaints received in his hotel that day." The reports helped Statler keep tabs on what was happening at his properties across the county, and he admitted that many of the issues at his hotels could be chalked up to "a shortage of labor or some trouble that we know about and are working on."[45] However, there were matters that required more attention, and to make certain he maintained his vigilance, he kept these complaint slips on his desk in a loose-leaf file. This form of carefully orchestrated service design would need something more to guarantee that Statler's "code" was followed, and it was the great hotel proprietor's turn toward product and architectural design that made his efforts stand out.

In 1918, *Hotel Monthly* published an article about Hotel Statler's new property in St. Louis, where technology was changing the nature of service design, making the hotel into what the architect W. Sydney Wagner (who designed hotels for Statler) described as a "service machine."[46] By the late teens, Statler had become, as Molly Berger explains, a business legend because of his ability to use standardization and clever design ideas to maximize profits.[47] His St. Louis property was a case in point. According to *Hotel Monthly*, the hotel's architects "had to keep in mind the overhead—how, in this or that department, labor could be conserved and the pay roll minimized—how this or that device . . . could be installed so that the atmosphere of the working department would not intrude upon the front of the house, and the service be swift, silent, and pleasing."[48] One device that was integral to the workflow of the Statler, in relation to what the press praised as its well-designed service spaces, was the telautograph. This machine utilized electricity to transmit messages from one location to another and allowed the hotel's housekeeping department to receive messages about what guests wanted. *Hotel Monthly* gives an example: "If the room clerk wants to send special instructions, he writes them on the telautograph, as '1338, please make up extra bed,' which means that the housekeeper is requested to put an extra bed in room 1338." Without skipping a beat, "immediately this is done, it is reported to her, and she notifies the clerk that it has been done." In this instance, the guests' needs and workers' responses operate in a seamless fashion, creating a form of service design that ensures satisfaction. In keeping with a tone that is similar to Bresnan's disciplinary style, *Hotel Monthly* concludes by noting that with the telautograph every transaction leaves a paper trail, and "in this way there is a written record of every transaction, even to the time, and there is no chance for an excuse."[49] This reliance on technology made certain that labor performed efficiently.

Statler's most famous technological intervention was having his architects revolutionize the design of hotel bathrooms, which made the delivery of guest services easier. Indeed, Statler initiated the idea of each guest room having its own bathroom.[50] Not surprisingly, Sydney Wagner became the point person who promoted these new plans. At properties like Hotel Statler–Cleveland (1912) and the Hotel Statler–St. Louis (1917), Wagner modified the typical orientation of hotel bathrooms so that instead of being perpendicular to the hallway, they would now be parallel with the hallway. This made the rooms wider and also made guest rooms quieter, since the bathroom now separated the sleeping area from the corridor outside the room (fig. 7). Finally, and perhaps most significantly, Wagner connected the water and drainage of pairs of bathrooms running down each floor's corridor. This saved money on infrastructure. Moreover, the regimented rows of paired plumbing allowed Statler to repeat identical mirror placement in each bathroom and behind each mirror was a hidden entry point that gave plumbers access to these plumbing shafts (fig. 8).[51]

Other period inventions enhanced the hotel experience through design, sometimes saving on labor and at other times helping the hotel's guests negotiate complex interactions with workers. Statler, for instance, purchased a device called the Servidor for many of his properties beginning in 1919. This ingenious design created a storage compartment inside

HOTEL STATLER ST LOUIS MO.   4TH TO 15TH FLOOR PLAN

FIGURE 7 "Hotel Statler–St. Louis, 4th to 15th Floor Plan." Image and caption from "Fourth Hotel Statler Is Located in St. Louis," *Hotel Monthly* 26 (1918): 50. General Research Division, New York Public Library, Astor, Lenox and Tilden Foundations.

the guest room door and allowed for a trouble-free exchange of items that the guest wanted serviced (fig. 9). With the Servidor, the guest room door could be opened and closed as usual, but there was another opening accessed from outside the room and inside the room, where the guest placed shoes to be shined or clothes to be pressed. The design ensured that the service space could not be accessed simultaneously from both sides. Thus, service would occur in what appeared to be a seamless fashion that would also limit the need for interactions between guests and hotel workers. As one architectural journal from 1919 described: "The purpose of the Servidor is to add to the comfort, convenience and privacy of guests. It also adds to hotel profits . . . it eliminates the delaying of

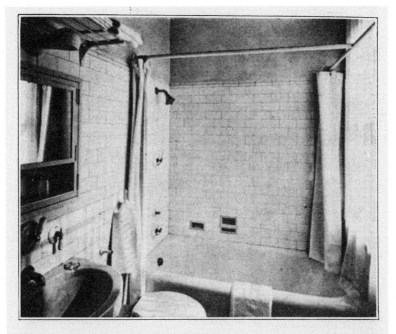

Typical bathroom in Hotel Statler-St. Louis, showing tub, shower, seat, lavatory, mirror, light, towel rack, and shower curtain; also recessed handrail and recessed soap receptacle alongside bath. The faucets for hot and cold water show the style of dial indicator and the lever for indicating desired temperature; also the lever for opening and closing waste is shown. The running ice water faucet (not shown in illustration) is to the left of the lavatory faucet. It is push-button type, the water flowing thru main faucet into bowl

FIGURE 8 "Typical Bathroom in Hotel Statler–St. Louis." Image and caption from "Fourth Hotel Statler Is Located in St. Louis," *Hotel Monthly* 26 (1918): 49. General Research Division, New York Public Library, Astor, Lenox and Tilden Foundations.

messengers and repeated calls to deliver goods when guests are absent." The device incorporated a sleek design made from walnut that did "not project beyond the door jamb," so it would not interfere with the aesthetics of the guest room floor.[52]

The Servidor not only looked good but also obviated the need for excessive labor and unwanted tipping. Statler's concern about disgruntled employees, who might reveal their upset over a meager tip through facial expressions or other overt affect, was infamous. While the Servidor appeared to facilitate the industry's growing interest in service design,

FIGURE 9 "Typical Room Corridor, Showing "Servidor," Hotel Pennsylvania, New York City (Note absence of transoms due to Servidor ventilating features)." Image and caption from "Hotel Pennsylvania New York," *Architecture and Building* 51 (1919): 21.

where guests could experience deliveries without having a physical exchange with labor, it also mitigated Statler's impression that individual workers could interfere with the graceful interface of service by signaling an awkward desire for a gratuity.[53] The economic imperative built into the Servidor is not surprising, since its inventor, Frank J. Matchette, started his career in hotels as a bookkeeper who devised what *Hotel Monthly* described in 1921 as the Matchette system, a careful accounting method from the late nineteenth century that utilized a "monthly statement sheet" to keep fastidious track of expenditures.[54] The Matchette accounting system, like the Servidor, relied on the conceit that costs, whether worker related or inventory based, could be controlled and restrained through prudent service design.

Statler made other important design decisions that directly affected the housekeeping staff's workload. For instance, he had his hotels use bed sheets that had a uniform hem all the way around. This meant that the maid would not "lose time in making a bed, if she happened to throw the sheet on the bed with the bottom of the sheet at the head of the bed." He went even further by using different hems to make a clear and obvious distinction between sheets for double and single beds. Rufus Jarman explains, Statler "had the hems for double beds made two inches wide at top and bottom and those for single beds made one inch wide. This enabled a housemaid to glance at a folded sheet and know immediately whether it was for a single or a double bed." To make things even quicker for housekeeping, Statler was also supposedly "the first hotel operator to build a linen chute opening from each floor, and emptying into the laundry."[55] In Statler's calculus of hotel management, these details led to a machinelike group of workers and, of course, happy guests whose service experience would be flawless.

Statler also made specific decisions about workflow systems and house-keeping room assignments that further exemplify his passion for service-related efficiency. Jarman explains that the Statler Hotels had a number of infamous maid-related tales that involved strange happenstances and lapses in sexual propriety. Today these stories read like lawsuits waiting to happen, but in the mid-twentieth century stories about maids ending up in bed (fully clothed) with guests or finding guests sleeping naked in linen closets would have been the source of jokes. Outside of these anecdotes, Jarman claims that maids are often a difficult lot, since "hotels have more trouble keeping maids than any other type of employee, except dish-washers." Thus, Statler "once conducted a scientific study to determine what type of woman made the most desirable housemaid, and found that, in general, they are women in their forties or fifties, who have had some experience such as practical nursing and who are married or have been." Statler putatively paid his maids well, and typically these women were "assigned a block of sixteen rooms to put in order during her eight-hour day." Like all aspects of his hotels, Statler preferred a nimble form of ser-vice design that permitted flexibility. During those periods when the hotel was not fully occupied, "the management can usually cut down the size of its staff of maids in a painless way by suggesting that any maids who would like to take a few weeks off without pay may do so." This "rather fluid working arrangement is one of the appeals" of a maid's job, but "manage-ment" was making these decisions, and in light of some of the other labor disputes discussed in *Housekeeping by Design*, one has to wonder about the appealing nature of this "working arrangement."[56]

By creating a "service-machine," Statler devised a new type of hotel design that continued to implement the organizational surveillance found in the late nineteenth and early twentieth centuries, yet he used novel conceptions of service design thinking that ushered in a Fordist model of hotel management. Additionally, his management style appears to be connected to the influence of early twentieth-century studies of physical work and human potential, such as those found in Frederick Taylor's 1911 treatise *The Principles of Scientific Management*.[57] Bresnan could never have imagined the scale of Statler's operation, as she seemed intent on the small details that plagued her hotel. In contrast, "Statler's methods," as Molly Berger explains, "drew on Fordist principles that featured com-plex production systems (in this case, the hotel as a machine for service), extensive division of labor, massive economies of scale . . . and, price management." However, Statler was also trying to attend to "individualized personal needs," which Henry Ford famously fought against in the context of the limited options that came with the first Ford cars.[58] This stress on the ways in which design could inform the realm of service would continue to change the hotel industry. The rise of hotel management schools, the professionalization of the industry, and the development of an enormous sector that caters to the hotel business demonstrate the significant imprint Statler had on the modern hotel. It is impossible to walk down the corridor of a contemporary hotel and not think of Statler's ideas about plumbing shafts, efficient labor, and affective service that should arrive — the guest continues to believe — with a smile.

As hotel design continued to incorporate novel methods to satisfy the customer, Statler's ideals, his "service code," remained influential in the twentieth century, even though this focus on service design was giving way to more of a corporatized sense of management where stock prices, new methods of scientific supervision, and an obsession with the globalization of hotel brands began to take hold. As Annabel Jane Wharton explains, this mid-century "McDonaldization" of hotels, where Fordist ideals extended, increasing the speed of production and consumption through deskilled labor, further changed the industry.[59] Cornell University's School of Hotel Administration was a critical site where this more corporate emphasis thrived, and Statler was instrumental in funding the famous school, both during its inception and through the vast holdings of the Statler Foundation that gave Cornell millions of dollars after his death in 1928. In fact, an enormous part of the foundation's wealth came from the sale of Statler Hotels to Hilton Hotels, which, led by Conrad Hilton, was one of the leaders in the development of the corporate era of hotels.[60] The sale of Statler Hotels for $111 million to Hilton, which occurred in 1954, was a key moment in the ever-increasing consolidation of what had become, by the mid-twentieth century, a global industry.[61]

A telling article in the 1969 volume of the *Cornell Hotel and Restaurant Administration Quarterly*, the journal of record for the eminent school, reveals this emphasis on a corporately driven ethos. The article is a chapter of a new management book written by Herbert Witzky, who was the first director of planning and administration for the globally oriented Intercontinental Hotels. Witzky traces the history of the hotel industry during the twentieth century and explains how the Depression led to economic turmoil, including a high percentage of properties having to either reorganize or enter into receivership. The Second World War helped hotels for several years, but by the late 1940s inconsistency plagued the sector again, until the minds of great entrepreneurs like Conrad Hilton "began to realize the benefits of modern management methods."[62] This renaissance in

management included, according to Witzky, innovative ideas from the social sciences. What is telling from reading this overview about the changing world of hotels is that by the mid-twentieth century managers had to
cope with individual workers in relation to a larger company's goals. By
1947 Hilton had been listed on the New York Stock Exchange and suddenly managers had to face the wrath of shareholders who seemed far
removed from the day-to-day operations of hotels and more interested
in profit margins, revenue streams, and ways in which to maximize efficiency well beyond what Statler could have ever imagined.[63] Witzky raises
a number of questions that this new generation of managers must ask and
tellingly he includes, "Do managers have a primary responsibility to society, shareholders, consumers, workers, and the community?"[64] The
twentieth-century fascination with stock prices, which came at the cost
of individual workers, had arrived. And tellingly, Witzky, like so many
other examples I explore, ignores the critical relationship between design
and workers. This obviation portends the rising influence of unions and
the increased emphasis on workers' rights that have defined the industry
from the mid-twentieth century to today.[65]

∗

In 1915, *Ladies' Home Journal* published an article by Gerald Mygatt that
details how the requirements for efficiency in modern hotels had created
a world of misery for chambermaids. In an industry where hoteliers like
Statler were becoming the norm, Mygatt explains how the "modern hotel
must be efficient above all else. Its prosperity, its success, its very life, de-
pend more on efficiency than on any other quality." This demand for economic leanness required "reliable chambermaids" who, Mygatt woefully
notes, are difficult to find, and this dearth of good help has made "the
lot of the manager . . . an unhappy one." While Mygatt starts his article
by remaining true to the need for supervision found in Bresnan's book,
and the nascent ideal of corporatized prudence urged by Statler and later
solidified by Hilton, his exposé takes an unexpected turn that blames the
hotel guest for the chambermaid's tragic life. It is the guest who often
unwittingly calls upon the hotel manager to complain about a personal
belonging—a piece of jewelry, let's say, or a small amount of money—that
has gone missing. The hotel's management does not want to fire the maid
and blame her for this mishap, especially "if the girl's record is good," but
even if the guest misplaced her own belongings, the fault descends upon
the chambermaid and the hotel must take action or risk an unhappy customer.[66] Remember, this is the beginning of the age of Statler's premise
that "the guest is always right," so the chambermaid is let go and, as My-

gatt reveals, she follows in the long wake of others who have been wrongfully dismissed before her.

If we return to Edward Clark's floor plan, which in theory offers ample room for chambermaids, we can get a better sense of Mygatt's understanding of the difficult work conditions that chambermaids faced in the first decades of the twentieth century.[67] In Clark's schematic, the regimented rooms, the infirmary, the bath, and the visiting room all articulate a meticulously designed living space where workers can be monitored. We can imagine a housekeeper, like Bresnan, walking down these halls and assessing the physical and emotional condition of her charges: Are the rooms in order? How many girls are sick? Who is visiting whom? In a type of Foucauldian power paradigm, the housekeeper's disciplinary control would be facilitated by design.[68] And, most significant, she would have no say over this design. Additionally, the physical space of Clark's hypothetical floor plan would have functioned in tandem with the overall goal of refining a space where work occurred seamlessly. In fact, if we can envisage this space as being run by Statler, after the first decade of the twentieth century, we could envision a telautograph machine, perhaps positioned in a central location on this floor, delivering assorted work orders that these women would have had to execute to make certain they were working toward the goal of efficiency.

Perhaps most intriguing about Clark is his approbation of the idea that "the help" should be living at their place of employment. This typical arrangement, where staff could be monitored both while working and after work hours, gave hotel managers a sense of additional control, since their charges would be restricted within, as one article in *Woman's Home Companion* described in 1910, "less agreeable quarters."[69] Intriguingly, in 1899 Thorstein Veblen pointed to the potential improvement of these "spacious servants' quarters" as a mark of vicarious consumption, where the owner derives some satisfaction by providing more ample quarters to his servants.[70] Yet, the reality of these spaces must have been difficult, since a lack of privacy and an inability to escape from the gaze of management must have been overwhelming. As Elizabeth Clark-Lewis has described in relation to live-in maids in the early twentieth-century domestic sphere, the practice of residing within the work environment meant there were enormous pressures in terms of expectations and availability.[71] Bresnan, remember, also wrote about how best to care for and manage employees who live at the hotel. She repeatedly indicated the need for a type of paternalistic presence where her chambermaids' actions could not be trusted, and where the chambermaid had to be surveyed and regulated to ensure her commitment to serving the guests' wishes. Following in Bresnan's supervisory model was Statler, who may have devised novel ways to increase efficiency that offered his employees some agency in the delivery of affective service, but who continued to be adamant about the need for workers to remain at the ready, always uneasy under the threat of having a complaint filed against them by a demanding guest.[72]

Bresnan and Statler were, of course, interested in economics, but with the rise multinational corporations, which became more focused on a mode of management that moved away from the individualized concerns articulated earlier in the twentieth century, hotels had an increasingly difficult time negotiating between shareholder concerns and service design. Herbert Witzky points to this and explains in his article from 1969, "Managers will be required to establish new yardsticks for measuring the effectiveness and the true potential of people, particularly in deciding what workers are to accomplish, and how they can be motivated towards such accomplishment."[73] The conundrum about what exactly that "yardstick" would measure continues to foster a remarkable divide among workers, managers, and guests. These disputed opinions about what should be assessed and by whom define the contested realm of labor at the corporately driven hotels that constitute the industry in the twenty-first century. And it is this need to manage hotel workers, and silence their ideas about design, which the following chapters explore.

Vignette Three

"FOR YOUR SAFETY"

Design features at hotels are not supposed to blow up. I had just gone for a run through the Los Angeles neighborhood of Bel-Air, and the hilly terrain had exhausted me. There was a slight chill in the air, and returning to my guest room, I thought about how pleasant it would be to light a small fire in room 378's hearth, especially since I was going to have to leave this haven of luxury in a couple of hours. The renovated Hotel Bel-Air on the west side of Los Angeles prides itself on luxury design. Each guest room includes the latest in technology—from iPads to light sensors in bathrooms to an array of service call buttons—and the fabrics, abundant windows, marble floors, high-thread-count sheets, and gas fireplaces are all design details that make staying there a pleasure (fig. 10).

I opened the fireplace screen, lit a match, and followed the directions I had received two days before when I had checked in. I slowly turned the gas knob on the wall in a clockwise direction and held the match to the logs. Nothing happened. I lit a new match and turned the knob again, a bit more aggressively. Suddenly, a large fireball emerged; it blew open the glass screen and made a jarring sound that, in retrospect, was akin to the whoosh of flames heard in cartoons that try to imitate, through onomatopoeia, the sound of combustion. The explosion knocked me back, and something flew out of the fireplace and hit the side of my head, forcing my glasses off of my face and onto the marble floor.

I lifted myself to my knees. A delayed yell emerged from my open mouth. I could feel blood coming down the side of my face, and in that moment all I could think of was that I must have been terribly hurt. A few more seconds went by and I slowly started to get up. There were ashes and a bit of crumbled plaster in front of me; I smelled something rather awful, noticing that the abundant hair on my left leg, especially by my shins, was a bit thinner and slightly singed at the ends. These were, fortu-

FIGURE 10 Grace Kelly Suite, living room, Hotel Bel-Air, Los Angeles, CA.
Courtesy of Hotel Bel-Air.

nately, very small injuries. I stood up and quickly headed out of the room, running down the hotel's storied outdoor, pink passageways toward the front desk.

I must have radically disrupted the calm of the reception area as I ran into the tranquil space while yelling, "My fireplace exploded!" I was still shaking and the cut on the side of my head must have caused some alarm. Moreover, I was still without my glasses, so I was not terribly balanced or focused. The front desk attendant and concierge came toward me and calmed me down. They sent security to my room to make certain that the fire was out and that no further damage could occur as a result of the mishap. A few minutes later security came back toward reception explaining that everything was "fine." There had clearly been a small explosion, but it was safe to return to my room. I went back to room 378, escorted by a small entourage of the hotel's staff.

The moment we entered the room, the head of security offered an apology and, as a token for my troubles, a "breakfast on us." I remember glaring at him as I noted that I would have to think about his strangely timed—and rather meager—offer. In retrospect, was I upset with what I perceived as a paucity of what Arlie Hochschild refers to as "emotional labor"? Did his performance lack affective panache? Just what did I expect from this hotel employee?[1]

All this happened on a Sunday, so the hotel's general manager was not in that day, and it was getting late; I had to leave for the airport to catch my flight. I gathered my glasses and showered, and by this point the small cut on the side of my head had stopped bleeding. The hotel promised that the general manager would be in touch the next day, and I settled the bill. I was only charged for the first night; the Bel-Air had comped the second night of my visit.

The complications of the hotel business, especially when these nuances involve design, are limitless. In the research I did for the following chapter on hotel management textbooks, it became obvious that specific situations arise that *are* typical. For instance, guests making requests for a specific type of extra service, like having their room cleaned an additional time, or guests' occasional obdurate behavior, such as an unwillingness to vacate a room after they have supposedly checked out, happens frequently. The way in which these issues get resolved are often the mark of a good hotel. The Bel-Air, for instance, will make every accommodation for a late checkout, and repeated visits by housekeeping occur frequently. What interests me is the way in which these types of scenarios are closely tied to the service design concerns I discuss throughout this book, since they involve shifts in workflow and an unexpected recalculation of labor required by the hotel's staff.

There are also, of course, instances when the atypical occurs, which goes beyond an additional visit by housekeeping or a guest's reluctance to leave. The gas fireplace explosion that I encountered is not a standard event, and situations like this require management to respond in a way that cannot always rely on best practices—as described in a textbook or other type of best-practice guide. The flexibility of a hotel's workforce is often dependent on precedent when it comes to service and guest satisfaction, but fortunately explosions do not occur regularly at hotels. The head of security's awkward reaction and suggestion of a free breakfast, which I definitely took as insulting as I looked at my dented glasses on the floor, had happened—I am convinced—because he did not know what else to say. He was, understandably, at a loss for words. This was not, I was certain, anything he had encountered before. And this was not a situation in which a textbook could provide a simple resolution.

The next day, safely back in New York, I spoke with the Bel-Air's general manager via phone and her comforting tone helped. She agreed to pay my doctor's bills (I was examined later in the week to make certain everything was fine, and it was) and she also offered two additional free nights at the hotel. These gestures, coupled with her sympathy (and abundance of what I perceived as arduous "emotional labor"), went a long way.[2] But in the immediate aftermath of the explosion, the day before, the hotel management's inability to respond in a way that I found caring is telling about the limitations found in places like management courses and in the textbooks I explore in the following chapter. A textbook, I contend, is a like a playbook, yet it is impossible to define and solve every circumstance in the pages of a textbook or during a management training program. While much of the hotel industry appears beholden to the precarious balance of awareness about cost and attention to customer service, this business ideal is not easy to maintain. And breakfast, to state the obvious, does not quite compensate for an exploding fireplace.

Upon my return to the Hotel Bel-Air several months later, the manager did everything she could to make the visit special. I received an upgraded room, the front desk was more than gracious upon check-in, and my request for a late checkout was honored graciously. But my favorite touch, the thing that made me feel especially grateful, was the new sign that sat on the fireplace mantle in the room: "*For your safety*, do not attempt to light the fireplace on your own." This command, italicized for emphasis by the hotel, is a rare thing at a luxury hotel that prides itself on allowing guests to do whatever they want, whenever they want. My little incident from the previous year had changed the hotel's policy. Thus, in the end, there were specific actions taken after my fireplace episode that seemed exemplary, especially when the hotel had time to consider its options. And yet, in the moment, directly after the unpleasant incident, when the head of security offered breakfast, I was left hoping for a more sympathetic reaction.[3]

As the following chapter explores, the notion that there is a "correct" way, or a perfectly designed service solution in an industry where an endless array of odd situations can arise, will be exposed as a myth. The dialogue and negotiations among guests, labor, and management are simply too complicated to arrive consistently at the right response and the ideal resolution. In a world where guests can get their hands on matches, things happen that test the resolve of committed employees who try to contend with a variety of strange happenstances that hinder the flow of service design at even the most iconic of luxury hotels.

expanded on the subject: Grace Brigham's 1955 *Housekeeping for Hotels, Motels, Hospitals, Clubs, Schools,* Georgina Tucker, Madelin Schneider, and Mary Scoviak's 1982 *The Professional Housekeeper,* and Thomas Jones's more recent *Professional Management of Housekeeping Operations* have been teaching future managers how to train, develop, and organize the complex operations of housekeeping within the hospitality industry.[3] An in-depth look at a few of the more popular textbooks in this field provides insight into how the industry conceptualizes the function, management, and design of housekeeping. While American presses have published the books that I look at, and many of the examples I consider are from an American perspective, the questions I raise are applicable to what has become the global hotel business, where chains and management companies run multinational corporations. This is especially the case as the hotel has become a type of uniform-design object, where cultural differences are often obfuscated for the supposed comfort of the demanding guest.

While this chapter discusses some of the ways these textbooks define housekeeping from a holistic perspective, I am more interested in how these books, especially Jones's popular *Professional Management of Housekeeping Operations,* characterize issues related to the designed management of housekeeping. Again, I am using the term "design" in two distinct yet interrelated ways that will enable scholars from a variety of fields, including design studies, labor studies, and tourism studies, to learn more about the integral role that design plays in hotels. First, by "design" I mean the planning of housekeeping workflows and how the conceptualization and use of space and equipment within hotels define and mediate labor through service design. In other words, housekeeping, as an operation, is a designed, labor-intensive activity; without the design of that workflow the guest's pleasure would not be possible, since the timing of housekeeping operations, as Mary Bresnan showed us, is critical.[4] This notion of designed management should be understood in the context of the burgeoning school of thought that looks to the problem-solving techniques deployed by designers to increase efficiencies in various settings. While scholars such as Richard Boland and Fred Collopy have called for the implementation of a type of managerial design thinking that relies on the notion of flexibility, where novel ideas can shift and improve practices in corporate and artistic settings, the textbooks that I focus on reveal that a more rigid sensibility about a designed system of labor is fundamental to the hotel industry. This inflexible approach is more in line with what Boland and Collopy identify as a "decision attitude," where managers decree edicts based on current conditions rather than designing novel possibilities. It is my contention that a "decision attitude" way of thinking is still reliant on and mediated by a designed configuration, even though it does not carry the open-ended promise of "the design attitude" that Boland and Collopy advocate.[5] Moreover, it is this very "decision attitude" that obfuscates the voices of workers. Second, housekeeping is, at its core, about caring for the hotel's interior design, which without housekeeping's upkeep would become untidy and not presentable. Thus, I also discuss how these books assess housekeeping's task of making certain that the integrity of a hotel, in terms of its design and public presentation, is maintained. This notion of maintenance closely relates to what Elizabeth Shove portrays as our mandate to design environments where a culturally constructed sense of "cleanliness" becomes de rigueur. More than simply expected, this hyperbolic sense of cleanliness has become normative.[6]

As I explore throughout this book, it has become a cultural given that women are more often than not in charge of maintaining cleanliness. As Ruth Schwartz Cowan and others have revealed, women have historically had to cope with the technological changes and cultural expectations that accompany the hard work of housekeeping.[7] Guests at hotels insist that rooms be spotless, and they do not want the discomfort of watching women (or anyone else, for that matter) engaged in the difficult labor of cleaning their room. Part of the guest's sense of order demands that objects—both the guest's personal effects and those that are part of the hotel room's design—evoke a type of rigor, where chairs and fixtures line up, clothes are folded, and beds are made in a manner that makes the guest perceive tidiness. It is my contention that this is the attention to detail that makes Garay's imagined guest say "wow" after entering a hotel room that has been prepared in that guest's absence. This is also the attention to detail that involves heavy lifting and complicated maneuvers that are part of the daily tasks of maintaining the objects and spaces that make up a hotel's interior.

To get a better sense of how the maintenance of interior design necessitates housekeeping I also discuss the design of housekeeping equipment and include information from both hospitality textbooks and interviews I have done with hotel guests and professionals who work in the industry. I use the conclusion of this chapter as a space to delve into worker's rights and the agency of individual housekeepers within the industry, a topic that I return to repeatedly in *Housekeeping by Design*, since I contend that it is this agency that would, if permitted, create better working conditions. Thus, I ask why both interior designers and those managers who implement the designed processes of housekeeping sometimes choose to overlook the realities of labor. As I explain throughout this book, the industry demands that hotels be designed with guests in mind, while the labor necessary to maintain these design choices becomes an afterthought.

Designing, Inscribing, and Managing Labor

These university textbooks that focus on the management of hotel workers enact a type of inscription onto the larger field of housekeeping and its relationship to a fastidiously designed supervisory structure. Textbooks are authoritative voices of accepted norms in given fields.[8] Textbooks attempt to redact knowledge so that it can be imparted in the classroom, and then students carry this information into the world. However, textbooks have limitations, and while they attempt to communicate best practices and accepted ways of learning, they often hinder the very instruction they are trying to facilitate. Claire Kramsch has discussed the limitations of the textbook in relation to the foreign language classroom. She notes that foreign language textbooks often make assumptions about the link between language and culture.[9] Kramsch explores how textbooks allow students to gather information passively from an educational rubric, rather than engage in the benefits that attend real-life experiences.[10] Textbooks falsely promise a window into authenticity. As Wiley, the publisher of Thomas Jones's *Professional Management of Housekeeping Operations*, claims on its website, Jones's "industry standard . . . includes new case studies that help readers grasp concepts in a real-world setting."[11] Here the real-world setting is the carefully designed management of housekeeping operations that can be delineated and mapped within the pages of a book. Textbooks represent the fantasy that there is an axiomatic body of facts about a given field, yet they have obvious liabilities that keep "learners unaware of the multiple facets of the target group's cultural identity."[12] In short, textbooks impede a student's potential for understanding the culture he or she is studying.

Clifford Geertz notes that inscription requires "setting down the meaning particular social actions have for the actors whose actions they are."[13] Geertz's interest is in ethnographic fieldwork; hence, the act of writing down meaning, or engaging in observation and putting that observation into the context of a written document, is an inscriptive practice that turns an event "into an account."[14] Once an act becomes inscribed, it can be "reconsulted," and it then takes on a type of power through the very process of providing meaning for that act within the framework of writing. This is why textbooks on topics like housekeeping are critical to study, as they reconstitute and represent what appears to many as mundane—often even invisible—tasks that are taken for granted and turns them into inscribed acts filled with meaning that defines and delineates these jobs through discourse. In spite of this, many facets of the designed aspects of housekeeping are absent from these industry textbooks. While issues related to workflow design and design maintenance get addressed, the complexities of labor relations and the consequences of physical work, which could have been shared by actual housekeepers, get overshadowed.

Issues covered in university courses that teach housekeeping management include how to schedule staff, how to properly manage housekeeping employees, how to keep hotels clean and sanitary, how to make certain that the consumer is kept at the forefront, and how, in short, housekeeping can be, and should be, a designed activity. For instance, a course titled "Housekeeping" at Philadelphia's Walnut Hill College, taught by Professor David Morrow, had students look at "effective staffing and scheduling," "training motivating & evaluating staff," and "managing the care of interior design."[15] While Morrow's class used the fourth edition of Tucker and Schneider's book *The Professional Housekeeper* (1998), many housekeeping classes make reference to various editions of Thomas Jones's *Professional Management of Housekeeping Operations*, which appears to be the industry-wide favorite text and the one that has the most updated editions available.[16] What these courses stress is management, as they claim, in the words of another syllabus from Wor-Wic Community College in Salisbury, Maryland, to give students "an understanding of the organization, duties, and administration of a typical hotel housekeeping department."[17] These college courses are not for actual housekeepers, but instead they are for future managers who will be in charge of hiring practices and designing a system of housekeeping workflows that will enable hotels to appear clean, presentable, and acceptable for guests.

These textbooks written for college courses spend pages defining the concept of hospitality and how best to manage housekeeping operations. According to Jones, "Hospitality is the cordial and generous reception and entertainment of guests or strangers, either socially or commercially." He goes on to note that when "people go to a home away from home, they will need care. They will need a clean and comfortable place to rest or sleep."[18] With this concept of creating a domestic-like setting for guests comes the necessity of housekeeping, which "is responsible for setting the scene and for maintaining the quality of the scenery."[19] This mandate is explicitly linked to the realm of interior design. While guests observe the superficiality of a room's design or a lobby's appearance, they usually ignore how their experience is tied to the way in which housekeeping maintains these spaces. Guests spend money to enjoy what they assume will be perfect settings, where a sense of cleanliness and having everything in its "proper" place is integral to their overall pleasure.

To facilitate the ideal housekeeping operation, Jones, who taught at the hotel administration school of the University of Nevada in Las Vegas, catalogs different styles of management. He starts with the scientific management ideas of Frederick Taylor, who claimed in the early twentieth century that a set of work tasks could be expedited by coming up with a clear template of action where one task logically leads to the next.[20] Jones covers other theories, as well, such as the behavioral school of psychology, which claims that workers need to be taken care of and their psychological state should be nurtured. In the behavioral school, workers are not simply the mechanistic means to an end that Taylor lauded, but, instead, they are human beings with emotions who should be tended to by management. Jones also mentions more current thinking about management, such as ideas about leadership and participant management, where workers take part in decision making.[21] All of these methods of managing a staff are, according to Jones, critical to housekeeping, where "creating proper attitudes" leads to a sense of "pride" and "concern for guests, which will make the guests want to return—the basic ingredient for growth in occupancy and success in the hotel business."[22]

At the core of his discussion about good management, Jones calls for a well-designed system that will control housekeeping and the multitude of "uneducated" women who makeup housekeeping staffs, fostering an environment where the ideas put forth by housekeepers become understood as superfluous and uninformed. He quotes R. Alec Mackenzie, who broke the task of management into five categories: planning, organizing, staffing, directing, and controlling. Each of these interconnected roles should be performed in a sequential manner. In other words, a good manager will start with planning and end with controlling. Since the daily operations of many hotels involve housing hundreds to thousands of guests, it is critical that this management of staff becomes a highly regimented function, where there is little room for variation and where each task becomes part of the overall experience that the hotel is trying to impart to its guests. Jones's reliance on MacKenzie's understanding that everything leads to "controlling" is telling, since this is the step where standards, results, action, and rewards formulate the core values that hotel managers refer to in conversations about their hotel's operations.[23] As Jones further details, "In order to more effectively manage housekeeping employees, we must understand their demographic and psychographic characteristics." The housekeepers in Jones's model often speak other languages besides English, can have "little or no formal education," "may come from lower socioeconomic backgrounds," and can "have emotional or economic problems, or may even have a dependency problem."[24] Even though Jones does not focus on the fact that most housekeepers are women, the images that fill his book make it obvious that having a male room attendant is an anomaly. While his typing of staff may be accurate in some instances, it is revealing of the industry's desire to control these workers that Jones mentions these supposed complexities directly after providing

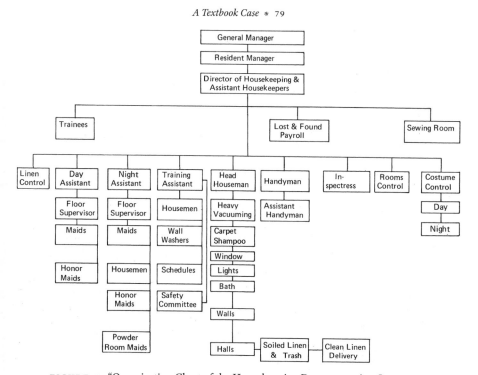

FIGURE 11 "Organization Chart of the Housekeeping Department in a Large Property." Image and caption from Georgina Tucker, Madelin Schneider, and Mary Scoviak, *The Professional Housekeeper* (New York: CBI, 1982), 74. This image can also be found in Georgina Tucker, Madelin Schneider, and Mary Scoviak, *The Professional Housekeeper* (New York: Wiley & Sons, 1998), 30. Courtesy of John Wiley & Sons, Inc.

his students with details about how to manage these supposedly pathological housekeepers.[25]

Managing the typical housekeeping staff, as posited by these textbooks, relies on the representation of a clearly designed hierarchy.[26] Even in the twenty-first century, when ideas about participative management seem to be the new order of the day, these housekeeping textbooks prescribe a reporting structure (typical in corporate settings) so that work gets done and, even more critical to management, work gets supervised. Tucker and Schneider, for instance, provide several organizational charts where rectangular boxes serve as holding places for individual jobs (fig. 11). In the milieu of housekeeping, it is always the director of housekeeping who oversees a range of functions, from the lost-and-found department to the housemen who deal with lights and windows to, of course, maids, or guest room attendants, who do the daily cleaning of rooms. These charts contain a vertical and horizontal logic and stipulate that specific back-of-the-house roles all report to the director, yet there are a variety of functions that fall under the purview of the larger housekeeping department. Each of the separate functions focus on some aspect of maintenance and providing services that make the interior design of the property look clean and sanitary.[27] Even more than simply evoking a normalized sense of cleanliness, the designed organization of housekeeping ensures that the consistent, tidy look, which consumers expect, will remain uniform and predictable. These books also detail the enormous amount of physical labor required to maintain hotels.

Designing and Representing Work

Beyond the scope of hierarchy, these textbooks organize ways in which the work of housekeeping can flow as a result of service design. Hotel work necessitates an emphasis on profits, as rooms need to be cleaned expeditiously to allow guests to enjoy these interiors without interference. Jones provides his readers with a "House Breakout Plan" that is a "pictorial representation" detailing the layout of guest rooms inside a typical hotel. It is, as Jones explains, "a line drawing of the guestroom portion of the hotel, showing the relative position of guestrooms, corridors, service areas, and other areas significant to guestroom cleaning."[28] He offers several of these diagrams that subdivide rooms into sections to show how individual attendants can clean a set number of rooms, allowing for easy supervision. An explicit sense of flexibility is key to these schematic representations that Jones includes. For instance, in this drawing of the first floor of a model hotel there are four extra rooms (noted as section 7 in the drawing, which includes rooms 1023, 1025, 1027, and 1029) that do not fit in with the exact division of rooms between housekeepers, so a flexible shift structure must be put in place to ensure that these rooms get cleaned (fig. 12). By color-coding these regions, Jones notes that these extra rooms may need to be cleaned by an attendant from another floor to permit an even distribution of work. This idea of dividing work between floors and sometimes even buildings can lead to labor conflict, as I will discuss in my chapter on Starwood Hotels and Resorts in Hawaii. From the basis of these charts, "housekeeping teams may be formed. A housekeeping team consists of one supervisor (senior GRA [guest room attendant]) who is in charge and one section GRA for each section within a division."[29] By deploying simple graphics, the director of housekeeping can divide and subdivide tasks so that work gets done and can be checked by supervisors.

The division of labor also mandates that GRAs approach guest rooms in a specific way, so that the room can be cleaned to maintain the guest's privacy and the GRA's invisibility.[30] As I discussed in the previous chap-

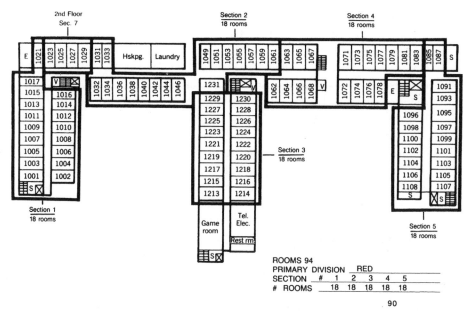

FIGURE 12 "House Breakout Plan of the model hotel; first floor." S, storage;
V, vending; E, electrical switch room; X, elevator; GL, guest laundry. Image
and caption from Thomas Jones, *Professional Management of Housekeeping
Operations* (Hoboken, NJ: John Wiley & Sons, 2005), 39. Courtesy of White
Lodging Services.

ter, choreographing movements around and through designed spaces
plays a key part in this unusual dance between guests who may still be in
rooms and housekeepers who are attempting to gain access to a space that
needs attention. Often the liminal position of being outside and inside
the rooms requires, according to Jones, ringing the doorbell or knocking
and waiting for up to fifteen seconds. Then, after not hearing a response,
the GRA should repeat her attempt at entrance and then "after another
five seconds, she should open the door announcing once again, 'Housekeeper, may I come in please?'" The issue of the door, the barrier between
the guest's privacy and the outside hallway, becomes even more complex
because, as Jones details, "under no circumstance should a GRA be in a
guestroom with a guest behind a closed door." This is for the protection
of both the guest and the GRA, since "GRAs and guests have both been
assaulted in guestrooms." The GRA should use either a doorstop wedge or
her housekeeping cart as a device that ensures an open door, if the guest
asks that the room be cleaned and refuses to vacate.[31] A Four Seasons
training video, titled *Sequence of Service for Cleaning a Guest Room Safely*,
also begins with the arduous steps required before the housekeeper enters

the room, where we see the GRA ringing the bell and eventually opening the door while just putting her head over the threshold.[32] The director of housekeeping at the Four Seasons in New York City, Margie Garay, relates that individual GRAs occasionally watch these DVDs, yet they are really for those exceptional housekeepers who train new staff. These trainers view the DVDs and use the carefully designed workflow prescribed by Four Seasons management as a model for their own lesson plans.[33]

The obsessive nature of these steps represented in this prescriptive literature is always couched in the language of safety, but part of this orchestration is, of course, about using service design solutions to try to hide the actual work of cleaning the room. Hotel guests enjoy having their rooms cleaned in an "invisible" manner. When they come back to their rooms, guests like that everything is perfect and that this transformation has occurred in their absence.[34] Guests do not want to be disturbed by the GRA, as this can interfere with their fantasy about how hotels take care of them without intrusion. So, the timing of how this transpires—the importance of temporality during the housekeeping process—is paramount to the guest's stay. If labor becomes an imposition, and the GRA does not respect the guest's sense of space, this can ruin the overall experience. The knocking, the waiting, and the poking her head into a small crack in the door all assure discretion, but it is also vital to the obfuscation of labor that is integral to the hotel industry.

The GRA's actual workload, as discussed in these textbooks, varies from property to property. Jones claims, "The national standard for numbers of rooms cleaned in one eight-hour shift by one person can vary from 13 to 20 rooms per day."[35] Some luxury properties, such as the Four Seasons in New York City, have GRAs carry a ten-room load.[36] Other sites differ even within hotels that are on the same resort property. At Walt Disney World in Orlando, Florida, the range of rooms to be cleaned per day varies from ten to eighteen, and this distinction correlates with how Disney advertises each hotel. According to the Disney union contract with their GRAs from 2004, the hotel that only requires ten rooms is their Fort Wilderness Resort, where the rooms are often larger, more expensive, and described as more luxurious.[37]

The work that goes into maintaining cleanliness and the interior design's integrity for guests is made very explicit in the industry's textbooks, but the details of that labor are put forth in a declarative manner that does not include the voices of the women actually doing this work. Since the bedroom is (except for people staying in suites) the initial encounter a guest has with a room, it often gets discussed first in the context of the cleaning procedure. Jones describes how bed linens should be shaken (in case of a lost-and-found situation), new sheets should be donned on each bed (he even goes so far as to describe the different layers of sheets), and then a bedspread should be put on top of the bed. Following this, "chairs, tables, dresser tops, windowsills and tracks, headboards, air conditioner, thermostats, hanging swag lamps, pictures, luggage racks, and closet shelves" should all be wiped with a wet cloth. Then all guest room amenities, such as literature, should be replaced and positioned. Drawers of those who have checked out should be checked, and then the desk area of each room needs to be dusted. Additionally, all lights and drapes must be repositioned, and the doorsill leading to the connecting room should also be wiped down. Finally, Jones mentions the need to vacuum, which "some hotels require . . . every day."[38] In a chart titled "Supervisor's Daily Work Report," he also details the importance of inspecting these rooms after the GRA has completed this and other work, such as the tedious and messy business of cleaning the bathroom. Tucker and Schneider also itemize a very lengthy inspection, which includes details ranging from making certain that amenities, such as bathroom products, are in order to "inspect[ing] beds to see that linen has been changed and beds properly made."[39]

The photographs that accompany the description of the housekeeping work in Jones's book appear perfunctory and documentary-like as visual descriptors, yet they reveal more about worker surveillance and the inspection procedure. They are black and white, often taken from an elevated perspective, slightly blurry, and shot with the intent of representing the work described in the text (fig. 13). Given that Jones taught in Nevada, many of the images of women GRAs were taken at Las Vegas hotels (according to their captions). However, the images are highly posed and we can imagine Jones, or someone else who is not a professional photographer, taking these photos over the course of a few days. The lack of careful lighting and the sheer number of pictures that fill *Professional Management of Housekeeping Operations* speaks to the rapid-fire intent to capture as many vignettes as possible. In all of the images of the housekeepers doing tasks, from dusting the television screen to scrubbing the toilet bowl, we witness GRAs in uniform who have a rather serious look. And, in keeping with industry statistics, most of the GRAs are non-Caucasian women, whereas the photographs of management often represent white men and women.[40]

Two images in this series of photographs of work from Jones's book are particularly striking because they include the GRA with another individual, highlighting the importance of managing housekeeping and further inscribing the imperative to obscure the overt presence of the GRA's labor. In figure 10-26 we see a GRA handing a seated guest a magazine (fig. 14). We get the sense that a small exchange of pleasantries is taking

FIGURE 13 "The GRA turns the spread back about 10 inches in preparation for rolling the pillows as a unit." Photo and caption from Thomas Jones, *Professional Management of Housekeeping Operations* (Hoboken, NJ: John Wiley & Sons, 2005), 216. Photo used with permission.

place, as the GRA smiles and both women make eye contact with each other. Jones captions the photo by noting, "Although GRAs should not be overly conversational with the guests, they should welcome the opportunity to provide simple amenities. Here, a GRA delivers a magazine to a guest with a smile." Jones's sensitivity about the GRA not being too comfortable with the guest speaks to the complicated narrative about the visibility and invisibility that pervades his textbook. The cheery GRA places the magazine directly in the hands of the guest without being too obtrusive and Jones assures us that she will sooner, rather than later, leave this interaction. Three pages after this image, we see a GRA hanging a tag in front of a bathrobe while a man in a suit watches her, his body leaning inward as if he is making a point while he holds a piece of paper (fig. 15). Jones explains, "The GRA is reminded that tags on guest bathrobes should show price information in case the guest would like to purchase one."[41] Both of these photographs visualize a pedantic tone of discipline toward the housekeeper, as management tells this nameless housekeeper how she should act and how she needs to be mindful of the guest's place as a customer. Jones offers hypothetical scenarios for future managers who will be in charge of reminding GRAs of their role within a rigid hierarchy that demands a type of panoptic surveillance along with a careful orchestration of both being seen and unseen, depending on the context.

FIGURE 14 "Although GRAs should not be overly conversational with the guests, they should welcome the opportunity to provide simple amenities. Here, a GRA delivers a magazine to a guest with a smile." Photo and caption from Thomas Jones, *Professional Management of Housekeeping Operations* (Hoboken, NJ: John Wiley & Sons, 2005), 220. Photo used with permission.

FIGURE 15 "The GRA is reminded that tags on guest bathrobes should show price information in case the guest would like to purchase one." Photo and caption from Thomas Jones, *Professional Management of Housekeeping Operations* (Hoboken, NJ: John Wiley & Sons, 2005), 223. Photo used with permission.

While labor theorists, such as Karl Marx and Harry Braverman, would critique these textbooks' sense of hierarchy as examples of worker disenfranchisement, these textbooks do contain references to unionization and other instances of worker empowerment.[42] In both Jones's and Tucker and Schneider's texts the union becomes an obstacle to new types of management tactics, such as flexible scheduling, where hours can be altered from week to week, and team cleaning efforts, where suddenly the number of rooms a GRA cleans jumps significantly. Jones contends that when "union contracts are in force, the executive housekeeper should work to ensure fairness to employees."[43] Tucker and Schneider offer similar words of advice about the need to be "careful" with scheduling, a critical component of designed labor activities. They conclude that when hotels change the way rooms are cleaned this becomes "a delicate management decision to be studied from all angles."[44] The union influence on major hotels, especially those in metropolitan areas, has forced management to become more aware of fair labor practices. Now that labor has venues to air grievances and devise contracts, management must learn how to comply with these details, even in the context of textbooks used in university-based courses.

Other sections of these textbooks focus on protecting workers from the dangers of poorly designed housekeeping equipment—from toxic cleaning supplies to heavy vacuum cleaners. Jones includes a section on the Hazard Communication Standard of the Occupational Safety and Health Administration (OSHA), which hotels have been forced to follow since 1988.[45] These standards set guidelines that management must put in place and cover the use of chemicals, the presence of body fluids, and other workplace hazards. On OSHA's website there are policy initiatives on a variety of hotel-related topics that help delineate what constitutes a safe work environment.[46] Jones also includes in his appendix an article by Chris Murray entitled "Ergonomics and Backpack Vacs." Murray is an engineer who works for a company (ProTeam Inc., based in Boise, Idaho) that makes a backpack vacuum system. He explains in this two-page article the importance of good design in creating an ergonomically sound vacuum that a GRA can wear to make housekeeping easier. The pack that his company manufactures fits on the back to help with carrying the machine to different spaces. Murray provides specifics that reveal how ProTeam's industrial design process utilized notes from field studies so that, for instance, "shoulder straps should be curved in a natural position that does not interfere with the motions associated with vacuuming." Additionally, while vacuuming, the housekeeper's "upper body should stay upright with little twisting during backpack vacuuming." Finally, Murray suggests that a regimen of physical fitness, instituted by the employer, can

FIGURE 16 "The Merit 2000 burnisher has a 2000 rpm speed and a 'smart handle' that eliminates the need for a front wheel. It also contains a dust control system." Photo and caption from Thomas Jones, *Professional Management of Housekeeping Operations* (Hoboken, NJ: John Wiley & Sons, 2005), 132. Courtesy of Kärcher North America.

help those using the backpack system. "A lack of physical fitness is often the problem. Blaming cleaning tools or tasks for fatigue and discomfort in poorly conditioned workers is like blaming the road for the breakdown of a poorly maintained automobile."[47]

Jones and other textbook authors represent the physicality of housekeeping work throughout their books, but they omit actual housekeeper's experiences. Jones mentions that a housekeeping cart can weigh "over 500 pounds when fully loaded."[48] He further details dimensions of different vacuum cleaners that make the onerous nature of this equipment obvious. It is, however, the photography in his textbook that elides the difficulty of maneuvering this equipment. The inclusion of a photograph of a woman with the Merit 2000 burnisher exemplifies this soft approach to arduous labor (fig. 16). Here a woman smiles broadly as she pushes the device forward with ease. Her arms appear relaxed and her body is devoid of any stress related to the task at hand.[49] Additionally, her lack of a uniform indicates that she is a model hired by Windsor Industries (the manufacturer of the Merit device), rather than a housekeeper who would have to use this apparatus. This burnisher, which weighs 113 or 116 pounds, depending on the exact model, is made to polish floors with hard surfaces, such as marble and tile.[50] A press release by Windsor promises that its "floating 'smart handle' simplifies operation and increases productivity by automatically adjusting to the height of the operator. The handle also eliminates the need for a front wheel and provides smooth operation for a consistent shine." The explicit message in both the photograph and the press release is that this product will make floors gleam with little effort, which will lead to more productivity and "a healthier work and customer environment."[51] The very equipment that the housekeeping staff uses promises to provide the cleanliness that has become fetishized by the lodging industry and its fastidious guests.

Rewards, Motivation, and Designing Workflows

There is a striking duality in these textbooks between representing housekeeping as a relatively agreeable undertaking and also admitting to the unpleasant and complicated tasks that accompany the work required to maintain and manage—through a designed process—the upkeep of a hotel's interior. The overall tenor of these books implies that this work can be enjoyable and rewarding for management, line workers, and hotel guests. An event known as the Annual Hospitality Competition, discussed by Jones in his first chapter under the subheading "Rewards and Motivation," is an example of the industry's efforts to make housekeeping appear pleasurable.[52] In a gray box titled "Motivational Tip," Jones reports that every year at the Las Vegas International Hotel and Restaurant Show twenty-two housekeeping departments compete in a number of events, including "the Bed-Making Competition, Vacuum Relay, Johnny Mop Toss, and Buffer Pad Toss." He notes that "each team has a cheering section" and that "the event is usually covered by the local news media, so contestants can see themselves on the evening news." He concludes, "Every state hospitality show should sponsor an event like this one."[53] According to a flyer that Jones has reproduced, the event offers prizes such as complimentary nights at hotels and free theater tickets and meals.[54]

YouTube offers an array of videos that showcase the housekeeping competitions Jones mentions. One video, titled *Bed Making Competition*, posted by a user named Splendid Video, documents an employee-appreciation event at the Embassy Suites in downtown Manhattan.[55] The video begins with a title slide that introduces International Housekeeping Week (a weeklong celebration that hotels and other organizations can utilize to celebrate their staff), and then another written announcement notes that this is the "Embassy Suites Battery Park, New York 2nd Annual Bed Making Contest." The first images reveal housekeepers smiling for the camera while eating. While a number of GRAs mug for the cameraman, we immediately get a sense that housekeepers and management have segregated themselves at this event, as uniformed housekeepers and individuals in suits sit at separate tables. The general mood of these images is fun and lighthearted, but Michael Jackson's song "Working Day and Night" plays in the background. The lyrics are about a man's overwhelming sexual desire for a woman, but many of Jackson's lines, such as the chorus "You got me workin', workin' day and night," seem to signify, when played over the images of bed making, the intense nature of housekeeping.[56] Then we read "1st. Round" on the screen, and Rimsky-Korsakov's "Flight of the Bumble Bee" comes on as the soundtrack to the bed-making competition, which appears timed and rushed, as groups of mostly female GRAs scramble to finish their beds. After these scenes of scurrying action, the video flashes the title of the next segment, "The Inspection." Here management (denoted by the suits the women and men wear) judges the GRAs' work. They check hospital corners and inspect pillowcases. The video concludes with prizes being given out to smiling housekeepers.[57]

Victor Margolin, in a short essay titled "Casualties of the Bedding Wars," argues that "beds are hardly a sweet dream for the housekeepers who make them. The combined weight of mattress, box spring, and duvet for a king-size hotel bed is 225 pounds. For a queen, the total weight is 183 pounds. As a result, housekeepers have been experiencing an increasing number of back and shoulder injuries." Studies have shown that "91 percent [of housekeepers] had back or shoulder injuries related to their jobs, 67 percent had visited a doctor because of the pain, and 66 percent took medication to relieve it."[58] As I explain further in other sections of my book, the job of a housekeeper requires enormous physical effort that can damage her body, and hotel guests are oblivious to this strain. Jones's inclusion of these events in his textbook and these YouTube videos raise a conundrum that sits uneasily at the center of the hotel industry. The difficult nature of hotel work and its relationship to design is explicit, as we read about and visually witness the labor that housekeepers engage in. Yet the larger ethical issue about how management treats and compensates these workers is not an easy matter to untangle. These competitions celebrate the housekeeping staff, and the fact that we witness prizes being awarded and joyous workers could easily be interpreted as a visual reassurance that everything is fine—housekeepers are happy, and management lauds hard work. However, the fact that these competitions focus on bed making is ironic, given the ongoing debate about the design of these beds and the physical burden required to make them.

With Margolin's critique in mind, what more can be said about the smiling housekeepers who appear to be enjoying the bed-making competition at these events? How do we correlate these images of pleasure with the contestation over workers' rights that is prevalent in the hotel industry? How do we reconcile these images with the cumbersome tasks that Jones and others describe in their textbooks? There are no easy answers to relieve the complicated tension that exists between what workers do and their economic and psychic compensation. These images of competition and prize winning can be read as exemplary of the industry's willingness to shower line workers with praise and, to use Jones's term, "rewards." They could also be seen as more overt examples of the types of games that fill the hotel industry, giving workers a sense of agency in relation to their difficult work.[59] Finally, these competitions could also be understood as another example of the hotel industry's intent on duping workers and offering them an outlet for play through a narrative that seems to repeat their daily work lives, as they make beds, get inspected, and listen to verdicts that judge their labor, all while rarely being given a voice to improve the design of this work.

The tension in these competitions is positioned uncomfortably between attempts to give workers a space where they can enjoy their work and the business model of hotels that is beholden to profits that are often made, to a large degree, through the hard labor of others. In these competitions the housekeepers do face the kind of surveillance that operates within their daily lives. Men and women with clipboards do follow these GRAs as they go about their tasks, cleaning their daily allotment of rooms and hearing criticism if their rooms are not deemed perfect. However, what the textbooks assessed in this chapter reveal is that the industry is also beginning to cope with workers' rights in a workplace that is traditionally laden with unfair labor practices. Jones's mentioning of union contracts, his inclusion of how ergonomic design affects housekeeping, and his periodic calls for fairness speak to this changing dynamic. Yet beyond the smiles and the apparent fun and games that are present in the YouTube videos, there is also the disenfranchisement of labor. These events do not showcase work transpiring in an actual hotel room, and the competitions usually take place around a larger series of events that complement International Housekeeping Week. By moving this labor outside an actual guest room, into the realm of a party-like atmosphere, this performance abstracts labor. The enormous effort of moving the heavy beds that Margolin mentions disappears as teams of GRAs easily maneuver through the task of housekeeping in record time, all while never being given a chance to voice their own insights into the highly orchestrated activities required to maintain the design integrity of hotels.

*

Director of Housekeeping Margie Garay explains that the Four Seasons in New York has its own in-house competition that occurs during International Housekeeping Week. "It's a lot of fun, it's motivating. . . . At the same time, it's energetic . . . [and] brings out the best in people, in our discipline of housekeeping. And, you're put on the spot, in front of everyone. And you want your bed to be done within the specified . . . time . . . you want that bed to be perfect."[60] Deploying these activities as a motivational tool may enhance the work environment, but it also hides the difficult tasks that are part of housekeeping. As the hotel workers' union UNITE HERE explains in research they have published about the hardships associated with cleaning rooms, unreasonable room quotas, heavy beds, and malfunctioning equipment cause enormous suffering. Hotel workers are, according to the union's estimates, 48 percent more likely to have an on-the-job injury than workers in other sectors of the service industry.[61] A designer of hotel spaces or equipment who ignores the realities of what is required to clean these rooms can unwittingly cause injuries and further pain. These competitions may create a sense of camaraderie and a fun atmosphere for a short period of time, but taking these tasks outside the realities of room cleaning, and putting them on the performative stage, obfuscates the difficulties of maintaining these ambitiously designed interiors.

As will become more apparent in my exploration of labor conflicts at several hotels in the following chapters, design and labor continue to be integral to hotels. As the work that goes into maintaining the design of hotel rooms increases, and as the demand for rooms with design elements that are more difficult to clean becomes de rigueur, labor issues have become more pronounced. It is critical for us to think further about how this labor has become a highly designed process where management creates workflows, rules, and regulations that require an enormous amount of labor from guest room attendants. This is a system of designed work inscribed through language, images, and charts in textbooks that train future managers. This is also a form of management that typically ignores the voices of the individuals completing this work. Through a close reading of these texts, I have offered a critique of these acts of inscription, where the bodies of GRAs are frequently treated as little more than mechanized possibilities that clean the interiors found in hotels. By presenting the human-centered critique that is at the core of this book, it is my hope that future designers of these management systems will begin to take the physical realities that attend housekeeping into account. Those who design workflows and interiors in hotels need to adhere to ideas put forth by actual housekeepers to help them conceive of spaces and labor practices that provide a sensible workspace for employees. Indeed, housekeeping cannot and should not simply be represented as fun and games, as real lives and actual bodies must contend with the design decisions made by the hotel industry.

THE HOTEL AS MISE-EN-SCÈNE

Hotels permit a type of fantastical transformation, and the transient nature of hotels allows guests to act, experiment, and temporarily change their lived experiences in ways that have been fodder for books, films, and television shows. In many of these instances, cultural stereotypes get highlighted during these short stays that make their way into popular culture. Movies, such as *Pretty Woman* (1990) and *Psycho* (1960), pathologize characters using predictable, Freudian tropes that seem almost more believable in the confines of a hotel. We watch and become titillated by these narratives because the hotel is the ideal setting that permits us to suspend belief. The story may rely on familiar conventions, but as an ideal mise-en-scène, the hotel facilitates the audience's escape.

One of my favorite hotel movies is *Plaza Suite*. Based on Neil Simon's 1968 Broadway play of the same name, the 1971 film, directed by Arthur Hiller and set in the famous hotel, comprises three separate acts within suite 719. In the film, Walter Matthau plays the leading man and deftly performs as the cheating husband, the cavorting producer, and the demanding father of a hysterical bride-to-be. Although the central plot twists of *Plaza Suite* involve infidelities, sordid affairs, and troubled families, the hotel is the star. At the end of the film, as the final act concludes with a newly married couple at the hotel's entrance being sent off by well-wishers, the camera pans up toward the Plaza's facade. Then Hiller cuts to a more distant and elevated shot of the hotel, which must have been taken from either a crane or a helicopter, before the camera returns us to the suite for the actors' final bows. While most contemporary movies based on dramas attempt to transcend the proscenium, Hiller embraced the play's original staging.[1]

Simon's and Hiller's devotion to the Plaza meant a great deal to me when I first saw the movie as a ten-year-old. While I am fairly confident that I did not completely understand all the sexual and adult themes at the core of *Plaza Suite*, I definitely appreciated the opening shots of the Plaza's lobby and the furnishings of suite 719. I wore down my father's VCR tape of the film as I repeatedly pressed the rewind button to revisit the marble and gilding that surround the check-in desk at the start of the film. My own memories of the Plaza, which I discussed earlier, seemed to be verified and somewhat legitimated by watching these ornately designed interiors memorialized on celluloid.

Even though *Plaza Suite* offers Simon's take on familial drama, his real interest is in memories. The first act focuses on the attempts of Karen Nash (Maureen Stapleton) to bring romance back to her failing marriage by booking what she contends is the very suite (719) where she and her husband, Sam Nash, honeymooned twenty-four years earlier to the day. At check-in we watch her in the Plaza's lavish lobby as she inquires about whether or not she will be given 719. Karen's efforts only lead to heartache when she learns that her husband is having an affair with his attractive secretary, Ms. McCormick (Louise Sorel). The second act continues its focus on awkward memories. A well-known Hollywood producer checks into 719, and we watch, somewhat uncomfortably, as he attempts to re-kindle—at least for the afternoon—an old flame with a woman he knew from childhood named Muriel (Barbara Harris). And finally, in the third act, we witness the nuptial disasters that befall the Hubley family (Lee Grant plays Mrs. Hubley) as their daughter resists attending her own wedding by locking herself in the bathroom of suite 719, out of fear that her marriage will replicate her parents' apparent unhappiness (fig. 17). Mimsy (Jenny Sullivan), as the daughter is playfully referred to by her parents as they plead for her to leave her perch on the toilet seat, becomes burdened by her own memories of familial discord and does not want to repeat the mistake of her rather despicable, and overly self-involved, parents.

The Plaza, as I noted in my second vignette, plays a mythical role in our collective memory, and in *Plaza Suite* the hotel becomes a venue where affective responses to these recollections get enacted in rather dramatic ways. Extreme emotional responses add to Simon's narrative tension in each of the three acts. Indeed, suite 719 seems to further these demonstrative displays, and, in fact, I would argue that the very idea of the Plaza—a site loaded with sentimental value within the larger fabric of New York—enhances this interpersonal mayhem.

Yet while representing this emotional turmoil, Simon's screenplay obscures labor. As in other examples in popular culture, the nature of hotel work is absent in *Plaza Suite*, and when it does surface, it only serves to further the characters' own affective display. For instance, during the film's first act Mrs. Nash sends a room service waiter back to the hotel

FIGURE 17 Still from *Plaza Suite*, 1971. © Paramount Pictures Corp.
All Rights Reserved.

kitchen to get her and her husband champagne in the midst of their ongoing fight. Mr. Nash raises his voice and explains that he does not want
champagne, but Karen persists. During the following scenes we watch
their marriage quickly fall apart as Sam discloses that he is having an affair with Ms. McCormick, and eventually he leaves the suite to return to
his office, where McCormick is waiting. After his departure, the unwit-
ting room service waiter returns with champagne and two glasses, "just
in case." In act two, Jesse Kiplinger, the rapacious Hollywood producer,
receives a phone call from housekeeping about when he wants his room
made up. He explains after four, but by this point we have learned that
Kiplinger is desperate to fill his afternoon, between the hours of two and
four, with a romantic rendezvous. Similar to the instance of the room service waiter serving as a punch line to the Nash's marital discord, the phone
call with housekeeping reminds the viewer of Kiplinger's own character
flaw. The guests, and their emotional struggles, are Simon's focus, and
the staff at the hotel enhances our understanding of these difficulties. The
complex nature of service (and service design) at the Plaza merely highlights Simon's characters' troubles; thus, labor remains oblique and surfaces to further the audience's assessment of the guests' circumstances
while otherwise remaining invisible.

It is popular culture's ability to erase labor, or twist it into another
plot device, that interests me in my next chapter, which focuses on the

4
LABORIOUSLY UNREAL
Design and *Hotel Impossible*

In episode 8 of the first season of the reality television program *Hotel Impossible*, Anthony Melchiorri, the show's host, encounters an anomaly. As he surveys the property and overall state of the Southern Oaks Inn in Branson, Missouri, he spots "someone who could also use a renovation." In the distance the camera focuses on a Caucasian man who appears near a housekeeping cart, but, as Melchiorri quickly reveals, "That's not a housekeeper." He looks, instead, like a "bum," with a hat turned backward and an overall appearance that "indicates an unprofessional housekeeping department." This "bum" ends up being a man named Jason who is, we soon learn, a housekeeper at the hotel. While Jason gets a makeover over the course of the show, which concludes with a renovated Jason, who becomes well groomed and ready to clean rooms, it is Melchiorri's initial reaction that is worth considering.[1] This is the only instance in the show's first season when we encounter a male housekeeper, and it is very rare in the hotel industry to find men who work as guest room attendants. Men work in housekeeping departments as runners of linens, or they may help with delivering extra furniture, such as rollaway beds, but they are rarely on the front lines when it comes to the daily servicing of guest rooms.

Things become even more peculiar when Melchiorri goes over to engage with Jason about his appearance. Melchiorri does not get far; he becomes distracted by a black-light device that he notices on Jason's cart, and he asks what it is for. Jason explains that he uses the black light to detect urine, blood, and semen that many guests leave behind, after they checkout. Jason then brings Melchiorri into a room and shows him urine stains on the toilet by shining the black light on the toilet seat. He notes that semen and urine are the most popular stains, at which point Melchiorri enthusiastically chimes in, while pointing to the light, "This is your semen detector." Jason's proactive and invasive techniques make Melchiorri very happy, and what ensues is a hearty round of laughter, as we witness the two men bonding in a way that is unusual, especially when compared with Melchiorri's interactions with other housekeepers during the program's first season, where his conversations can be stilted, abrupt, and hostile. At the Southern Oaks Inn something different occurs. At first Melchiorri does not read Jason as a guest room attendant because of his gender and slovenly appearance, but then Jason's strengths become apparent, as he is able to do what many nonwhite women fail to do each week on *Hotel Impossible*: he can find the most undesirable and undetectable substances in guest rooms and cleanup these messes. Melchiorri, at the end of this episode, tells us that he "almost called the police" when he first saw Jason: the combination of his unusual gender and his unfortunate sartorial choices made Jason seem like another problem in a long list of issues that needed to be fixed at the inn. However, Jason's keen sense of sight—aided with his trusty black light—gives Melchiorri a heightened sense of respect for this housekeeper.

Jason's unlikely presence perplexes Melchiorri, but his cameo speaks to reality television's obsession with personal transformation achieved through the close management of bodies and attitudes.[2] Moreover, Jason's ability to uncover what is hidden, namely, bodily fluids, reveals reality television's peculiar obsession with exposing what many believe is lurking behind a dangerous disguise. The camera and voice-overs on *Hotel Impossible* take on a documentary posture that makes it appear as though we, the viewers, are gaining access to a world that is usually unseen. While the editing, camera angles, and dialogue suggest that unseemly discoveries are constantly being unveiled, the reality of this reality television show, like others in this ever-expanding genre, is dubious at best and fictitious in most instances.

This chapter unpacks some of the themes that Jason's appearance in the Southern Oaks Inn episode raises in relation to how design affects the management, training, and surveillance of employees at hotels. Moreover, this chapter reveals several instances where, once again, housekeepers who do this difficult work are not heard or given any agency in the design choices made at hotels. What makes *Hotel Impossible* such an unusual case study for this book is its popularity. It is, after all, a reality television series.[3] Thus, this chapter is not about a textbook or one particular hotel property, but, instead, looks at an example of popular culture to assess how the mass media, and by extension the larger public, represent—and think about—hotels. What emerges after watching the first season of *Hotel Impossible* is that like the other examples explored in *Housekeeping by Design*, the representation of hotels and housekeeping in this television show focuses on the premise that management should keep close tabs on employees to ensure a compliant staff that follows and anticipates guests' wishes all while remaining reticent.[4] Even more significant for my study is the way in which this management of employees' actions and bodies becomes entangled with the complexities of design issues, including the physical presentation of guest rooms and the seemingly immaterial manifestations of service design.

"I'm Anthony Melchiorri"

Each episode of the first season of *Hotel Impossible* opens with Anthony Melchiorri's words: "When hotels are in trouble, they call me." After this dramatic statement, the show uses a montage of images and words to introduce the troubled property of the week. Sound and image bites offer a range of problems, from disgruntled workers to poor management to an abundance of guest-room-related filth. The introductory setup, the Travel Channel hopes, will keep the viewer tuned in while helping to frame the significant challenge that Melchiorri faces during that week's installment. The introduction also serves as a contrast to the upbeat ending of each episode, when all of the hotel-of-the-week's problems have been resolved in a magical transition that happens right before our eyes.[5]

Hotel Impossible first aired on April 9, 2012, and, as of this writing, has completed its sixth season. Like many other networks, the Travel Channel has turned to reality television because of its popularity and inexpensive production costs. Gone are the days of hiring expensive writers and actors. Instead, the camera putatively documents real-life interactions, which are then edited and aired very quickly, without needing too much postproduction care. Like other reality television programming, *Hotel Impossible* follows a formulaic structure where banal problems get heightened for their entertainment value and then solved in a manner that is satisfying because nothing is left open ended and issues get resolved. Every episode of *Hotel Impossible* follows this pattern where intemperate emotional states get sorted out, leading to narrative closure. American viewers have been conditioned to watch and learn from this televisual model. Reality TV has become akin to a form of government retraining, where weekly episodes police, discipline, and supposedly make subjects better through myriad situations that are all suspiciously similar. Laurie Ouellette and James Hay claim that reality television "simultaneously diffuses and amplifies the government of everyday life, utilizing the cultural power of television . . . to assess and guide the ethics, behaviors, aspirations, and routines of ordinary people." They further contend that reality television propounds "guidelines for living."[6] These parameters facilitate participation in neoliberal society, where citizens need to be retaught to cope with the ever-changing economy. This is especially the case in makeover shows, where individuals who have suffered economically, socially, and aesthetically under neoliberal conditions learn how to manage and ultimately thrive. But in order to prosper, these subjects have to be coached—in the very public venue of mass media—about how to work on their physical and psychic selves. After embracing this hard work through crises that are made "real" through affective responses (for instance, the abundance of tears that are shed during these shows), participants seem ready for fiscal and emotional success.[7] These well-edited vignettes drive reality television's expanding audience, since viewers have come to expect that the difficulties and turnarounds promised by these shows will only become more extreme, more entertaining, and more representative of what culture needs to teach its citizen viewers.

On the reality makeover show, an expert is necessary to convince the viewer that a well-educated transformation is underway. As Brenda Weber argues, in order "to be empowered, one must fully surrender to experts" within the context of makeover television.[8] Anthony Melchiorri is the ideal expert who puts troubled proprietors and employees through their paces so that they can effectively and affectively perform and, more important, reconcile their past transgressions. As the undisputed authority on *Hotel Impossible*, Melchiorri dresses well and is more presentable than the hotel workers, managers, and owners he visits. His direct tone and military-like shaved head give him an air of conviction that makes his role as the ultimate consultant more believable. In short, Melchiorri adheres to the role of the expert perfectly on *Hotel Impossible*. Once the episode's challenging hotel-of-the-week has been presented, he glides through a revolving door as he defends his expertise in the show's introduction, declaring:

> I'm Anthony Melchiorri. Outstanding hotels are my world, and after 20 years in the hotel business, there's no problem I can't fix. All around America, there are hotels that are hurting. They're understaffed, mismanaged, and in desperate need of a facelift. That's where I come in. I've turned around some of the most famous properties in America, from boutique hotels to big-city landmarks. I'm on a mission, and I won't stop until every hotel you check into is perfect.[9]

The notion of perfection, Melchiorri's ultimate goal, becomes apparent as he states these introductory remarks over a montage of the various properties that have been "transformed" over the course of the show's first season. Melchiorri is confident; there is no hesitation in his voice. He is always willing to explain the details of the problem with great specificity, and his manicured appearance and overly confident tone make it apparent that with Melchiorri around perfection is the only solution.

So, just who is Anthony Melchiorri? Melchiorri has aided in developing and renovating many hotels, such as the Algonquin Hotel in New York and the Nickelodeon Hotel and Resort in Orlando. He began in the hotel business as the director of front office operations at the Plaza in New York. His work at the Plaza led to several other positions in hotel operations, and at the young age of twenty-nine he became the general manager of New York's Hotel Lucerne. After he left the Lucerne, Melchiorri became the general manager of the Algonquin Hotel, where he oversaw a $4 million renovation of the property's restaurants as well as its back-of-house operations. He went on to other jobs in the business, including work for Tishman Hotels, and he served as the senior vice president of the New York Hotel Management Company. Today, Melchiorri has his own hotel consulting company, Argeo Hospitality, and, of course, he hosts the Travel Channel's *Hotel Impossible*.[10]

Melchiorri's entire career has been focused on management. As he relates on the homepage for Argeo, "Argeo hospitality is built on the premise that the 'devil is in the details' and every problem is merely a minor obstacle to be overcome." Filled with images from *Hotel Impossible*, which highlight his role as the hotel fixer with a heart, Melchiorri explains that his "consulting services team works on eliminating inefficiencies and developing plans to increase productivity." They "fix what is not functioning properly and put fail-safe systems in place to enable the client to remain in control of the problem solving process."[11] This complicated process, and the machinations required to turn around problem hotels that are in crisis, is the narrative that drives *Hotel Impossible*. Melchiorri has built a professional practice around coming into bedeviled spaces and devising solutions that will enable troubled properties to thrive.

"My Favorite, Favorite Department"

On reality TV, the expert arrives to transform bodies, places, and situations with a flourish. The failure of a person or place needs to be identified quickly, so often the camera and the voice-over, provided by the expert, homes in on deficiencies. A critical aspect of the expert's mission is to help those who have become less-than-desirable neoliberal citizens. Programs like *Hotel Impossible* not only expose problematic spaces and individuals but also hunt for scenarios where potential participants are having an economic crisis and need to change their behaviors so that they can contribute to the capitalist order of things in a way that can be deemed productive.[12]

On *Hotel Impossible*, the need for renovating bodies and spaces blatantly appears in the series's first episode, when Melchiorri takes us to Gurney's Inn in Montauk, New York. This seaside resort has 109 rooms, and, as Melchiorri declares, the "view is ridiculous."[13] However, his initial enthusiasm about the property "quickly goes down from there." The beauty of the ocean gives way to an overall appearance that makes it seem "that no one cares," as the hotel's interior design has deteriorated. As he does during all of his hotel makeovers, Melchiorri looks at guest rooms early in his visit, and here he finds dirt under the toilet rim, dirty air conditioning filters, and fans that need to be cleaned. Directly after this inspection, he comes across members of the housekeeping staff who are in the midst of cleaning a room. He starts with a rather formal welcome, declaring, "Good morning, ladies," and then proceeds to detail all of the issues in the room he has inspected. He focuses a lot of his energy on the need for a checklist that housekeeping can use to make certain that details do not get left unattended.

The second episode of *Hotel Impossible* is where Melchiorri's focus on housekeeping and design becomes even more explicit, during his visit to the Penguin Hotel in Miami Beach. After entering the hotel and giving his typical litany of complaints—ranging from a lack of a car attendant to a poorly maintained lobby—Melchiorri asks for a "master key" to "see how housekeeping staff cleans."[14] Upon entering the room, he immediately points out the poor quality of the sheets and also notices other design flaws, such as the aging mattress pads. Then, while inspecting the sheets further, he notices a pubic hair on the bedding. Mugging for the camera with exaggerated facial expressions, Melchiorri declares, "Dirty rooms are not only unsightly; they're unhealthy." He adds, "Thoroughly cleaning every room is critical." During his inspection of the bathroom, Melchiorri becomes more alarmed about the condition of the room and he shifts his blame away from the individual housekeeper to the hotel's lack of proper management. The physical state of the guest room's design has deteriorated beyond the point where a housekeeper can make a difference. Here he finds mold and filthy grout. The bathroom is unsanitary, and, as he did at Gurney's, Melchiorri explains that "we need to put a system in place." He then reveals what becomes an ongoing theme throughout *Hotel Impossible*: "This is not the housekeeper. This is the supervisor, this is the manager not helping the housekeeper."

In response to finding these design flaws, Melchiorri raises, as he does so often in his show, the emotional tenor of the situation by haranguing the hotel's owners. According to each episode's narrative, he first talks to owners, instead of attempting to hear issues raised by individual housekeepers and other hotel line workers. We watch as Melchiorri sits down with the Penguin's proprietors, Giada Rocca and her husband, Markus Friedli, and details what he has uncovered in their unkempt rooms. To make his point clearer, he also shows Friedli and Rocca comments that other guests and hotel reviewers have made about the Penguin at Oyster .com and TripAdvisor.com, two online venues that offer guest reviews of hotels. Exposing the hidden truth — the dirty little secret — is a critical moment in the reality television plot, and here Melchiorri does not hold back. He tells Friedli and Rocca, "When you are 102 on TripAdvisor [referring to the Penguin's rank on the site's Miami Beach list of hotels], it's not just a couple of people that don't like your hotel." Friedli and Rocca contend that "the challenge is staff," but Melchiorri refuses to let the couple's blame fall on their employees, and instead reinforces his contention that the only thing that has led to the hotel's problems is poor management. It is, once again, the management of staff and having a system in place that Melchiorri focuses on as the key ingredient to a hotel's success. His accusations lead to Friedli and Rocca's overly emotional reaction. Friedli walks off and Rocca appears distraught, but the viewer has become entranced. Reality television demands this type of affective response, as it signals that change is in the air. Melchiorri has hit a nerve, and now the real work of transformation can begin.

To initiate change, Melchiorri meets with the Penguin's housekeeping director, Chris, to assess her staff's upkeep of the hotel's interiors. Again, he starts with management in an accusatory way, but one wonders: what would happen if he began by speaking with the women who are struggling to complete this work? Together, Chris and Melchiorri go to the hotel's most expensive room, a $250-a-night space on the top floor of the property that has sweeping views of Miami Beach's South Beach. Melchiorri makes the claim that 80 percent of the director of housekeeping's job should be spent overseeing the cleaning of rooms and making certain that the guest room attendants are working efficiently, so he wants to see how Chris conducts her inspections. They open the door to the room and he points out the issues: "Look at that filth . . . this tile floor, okay, is really dirty." He also takes her toward the balcony and notes the rotting wood around the door. Chris claims that everything appears in order and she has no problem with a guest staying in this particular room, but Melchiorri is resolute: "This is just absolute negligence," he retorts as his eyes dart around the space looking for other examples of inattention to the room's design features. Later in the episode, he repeats his overall claim about the importance of management: "Housekeepers work very very hard, but they can't see everything." This additional sight, or extra surveillance, can only come through supervision, and Chris is falling short.

After berating Chris, Melchiorri talks with the guest room attendants so that he can "take charge" of the situation at the Penguin. He stands in front of the housekeeping staff and smiles at these nameless charges as he proclaims, "My favorite, favorite department in a hotel is housekeeping." Then, to make certain they understand his position, he continues, "Housekeeping is the most important department in a hotel." However, there is, as the viewer has already witnessed, a problem. When I "inspected the room, it didn't look clean. I saw dirt, dust. . . . I know you are very dedicated, but it's about being more focused." He acknowledges that housekeeping does not have what it needs. The missing checklists and the overall lack of supervision is a setup for failure, and this confrontation makes it evident that housekeeping "needs better supervision."

In the context of reality television, Melchiorri only has forty-two minutes to rectify the dire challenges that he has identified in relation to the upkeep of the Penguin's interior design. And in the case of the Penguin, Melchiorri, as he does every week, works miracles. After confronting the housekeeping staff about their nonexistent focus, Melchiorri shortly thereafter engages in the "reveal," that point in the reality show when the viewer gets to witness how the makeover has physically altered that which had been found wanting.[15] In this case, Melchiorri walks into a room where Chris, the head of housekeeping, is supervising the work of a guest room attendant. The space seems lighter and cleaner, as the housekeeper joyfully wipes the glass shower, wipes the walls, and dusts by the room's window; this room is ready for guests, and Melchiorri's delight is obvious as he gives the housekeeper a fist bump to celebrate her success and to create an implied pact about how this and other rooms will be cleaned differently moving forward. Chris watches as the housekeeper's latex-covered hand hits Melchiorri's fist; smiles abound in a way that guarantees to the viewer that a transformation has taken place.[16]

The episode at the Penguin highlights the ever-present power of "before" and "after" that defines reality television and its unrealistic representation of labor, further distancing the actualities of work from this fetishized transformation. In the case of *Hotel Impossible*, before and after must happen to both individuals and to the hotel's design. It is not enough that the hotel can become something new, something unexpected, and, most important, something profitable, but its staff—both management and workers—need to change along with the decor. The scene of Melchiorri in the room with Chris and the housekeeper speaks to the power of this dual transformation. The space looks clean, and Melchiorri wants us to understand this, so he rubs a white towel on the grout between the tiles to reveal the absence of dirt, but at the same time the camera focuses on the faces of the hotel's staff, and Melchiorri's relief makes these women beam. The actual intensity of the work required by the housekeepers has been avoided by the camera as Melchiorri has, in a very brief period of carefully edited time, modified the Penguin and made it into a potentially profitable business. Yes, we see women working, yet their brief on-camera efforts very quickly lead to their sheer pleasure—their affective display of satisfaction—that attends their acknowledgment that they have made Melchiorri (the expert) happy. To ensure the viewer's understanding about how dramatically effective these changes have been, as the credits run at the end of the show we learn that business at the Penguin has increased by 10 percent since Melchiorri's visit. The nameless housekeepers have done their job, even though their individual voices and opinions have not been aired during the forty-two-minute episode.

"There's Got to Be Procedures in Place"

One of the most heart-wrenching episodes of *Hotel Impossible* focuses on another Miami property, the New Yorker. The New Yorker is in a section of Miami that is slightly off the beaten path. Unlike the Penguin, which sits on Ocean Drive in popular South Beach, the New Yorker is not on the beach. It is on a busy north-south thoroughfare called Biscayne Boulevard, and other hotels and motels surround the New Yorker. Like many of its neighbors, the New Yorker falls into the architectural category referred to as MiMo, or Miami Modern. Designed by the architect Norman Giller, the 1953 building has a streamlined facade, and its white and light blue colors speak to this particular Miami-based aesthetic.[17] Shirley and Walter Figueroa have owned the property since 2009, and the Travel Channel's editors make this couple lovable. The owners of other properties on the show often wear on the viewer's patience, only to then be turned around by Melchiorri's magic, but the Figueroas are different. Because of their economic difficulties, they live in the hotel. They appear hard working and kind. To raise the emotional tenor, we learn that Shirley has been recently diagnosed with multiple sclerosis. Melchiorri notes that helping the New Yorker is about "more than just saving a business; this is saving a family." The problem, however, is that the hotel is $1 million in debt and the low $70-per-night rates are dragging the Figueroas into bankruptcy.

At the New Yorker, Melchiorri initially addresses physical design issues, such as the hotel's signage and the rather pathetic breakfast area, but he quickly realizes that the hotel's most pressing challenge relates to service design. The Figueroas and their staff have no system in place to work through the scenarios that arise when guests do not follow typical patterns or expected protocol. When Melchiorri inspects a room at the New Yorker the problems related to this inflexibility become apparent. After entering the guest room, Melchiorri makes positive comments about its overall appearance, but then enters the bathroom where, to his dismay, he discovers excrement in the toilet. He finds Shirley and alerts her that for the most part the rooms were very clean, but "in the toilet there was human feces." Shirley relates a sad tale of hotel woe: a guest, in this instance, had already left the room, but he returned after his check-out. Housekeeping had assumed that the room was ready for the next guest, since the room had already been serviced. This is where the gap— the blind spot—in service took place. Melchiorri's face contorts to project a sense of empathy, but he explains that this is what the industry describes as a "pick-up room," a room that needs to be revisited by the housekeeper because of a guest's unexpected return. It is critical that housekeeping "check a room any time someone has been inside." He further explains that "mistakes happen, but there's got to be procedures in place to make sure it doesn't happen again." He declares, in a typical reality television makeover moment, "I need a level of commitment that really rises beyond the norm."

To signify the importance of the new "system," where this additional "commitment" will transform the hotel, Melchiorri, after detailing the critical nature of the situation to the New Yorker's owners and employees, has the staff jump into the hotel's pool. This act, akin to a type of reality show baptism, initiates the moment of change. With this leap of faith, the line workers at the New Yorker submerge their bodies and cleanse their pasts; they emerge renewed and ready for the challenges and successes that will follow. Karen Tice has insightfully connected makeover reality TV to a type of religious epiphany, or awakening. She explains, "In addition to . . . talk shows that pepper Christian themes such as testimony, conversion, resurrection and salvation throughout their narratives, numerous reality TV makeover shows use religion and revival as motivating principles for their makeover/conversion regimes."[18] To make certain the viewer grasps the significance of the conversion, Melchiorri asks each of the staff members if they "are committed" before he invites them to leap into the pool. He goes down the line of employees and then explains that they will "memorialize" this new dedication with each plunge. The staff shrieks, laughs, and some even cry as they stand in the pool revitalized and recommitted to the systems that Melchiorri has put into place.[19] And yet, we never hear from these individual employees, as they appear motivated thanks to Melchiorri's managerial sleight of hand, which occurs without any of their input.

Housekeeping's commitment to service and service design also surfaces in the *Hotel Impossible* episode about the Hotel Corpus Christi Bayfront in Corpus Christi, Texas. This 199-room property does not have the personal charm of the New Yorker. Here the owner, Gregory Markwardt, has abandoned his responsibilities. From the moment Melchiorri arrives at the Bayfront, the cameras reveal empty spaces that are in disrepair. Things go even further downhill after Melchiorri enters a room that the hotel is offering for a mere thirty-nine dollars per night. The space is, as Melchiorri declares, "a hotbed for germs."[20] He takes a bacterial measurement, with a special electronic device, and bacteria appear to be everywhere. Even more visually alarming are the bugs in the bathroom sink, and there are scores of dead bugs in the cabinet beneath the filthy basin. The room is a mess, and to make matters worse Melchiorri discovers that the hotel charges guests ten dollars per night if they want their rooms cleaned.

To get to the bottom of the bugs and filth, Melchiorri takes the viewer to the source of the problem, and so he finds Sylvia, who is the head of housekeeping at the Bayfront. He asks Sylvia how the housekeeping carts are set up, since he is curious about the hygienic issues he found in the room. The housekeeping cart, both its setup and design, is critical to the overall service design system found in hotel housekeeping departments. Without attention to carts, housekeeping becomes disorganized. What Melchiorri finds on the cart makes him cringe. He sees a prevalence of "cross-contamination." Brushes and sponges that should be kept separate for use on distinct surfaces are intermixing, creating an unhygienic morass. For instance, he learns that the housekeepers use the same rag to clean both the interior of the toilet and the toilet seat. Melchiorri emphatically explains, "You cannot take a rag from the toilet bowl and put it where someone will put their ass!" Sylvia looks taken aback, so Melchiorri adds, "I know you work hard; we got to do this the right way."

To rectify the situation, Melchiorri, once again, asks his charges—who are consistently management and not individual hotel workers—to think about labor and service design. He creates a color-coded system that marks the different cleaning supplies on the housekeeping cart. He also brings in carpet cleaners and demands that the hotel hire more housekeepers. Interestingly, he offers the viewer details about how long it takes to clean hotel rooms. "Typically hotels allot thirty minutes per room for housekeeping, but at this hotel [the Bayfront] they have under twenty minutes." He continues, "We are no longer asking these hard-working employees to clean twenty rooms in an eight-hour shift. It is not fair." He demands that the hotel institute a policy of fifteen rooms per day, per housekeeper. Moreover, Melchiorri is adamant that "once I train her, I'm very confident Sylvia will train her team properly."

This prolabor segment of *Hotel Impossible* is important to think about in the context of reality television. Is it possible to implement changes in worker equity and service design? Reality television, as I have mentioned, trains "us" how to live, work, and, perhaps most important, consume. In this didactic moment, Melchiorri steps in and assures his viewers that beyond management and the fiscal bottom line, there are people and real employees. In this case, there are housekeepers who have been overworked and who need to be given the time to clean rooms in a way that is fair to them and their guests. But there is no way of knowing if Melchiorri's demands have been met. At the end of the episode, he revisits a guest room and does a follow-up reading of the bacterial level. The issue has been resolved and the bacterial reading is now negligible; the room's design elements have been tidied and made safe. Melchiorri claims that he can "lick" the stick he used to do the reading and "not get sick." The episode's conclusion also reveals that one of the hotel's more likable employees, Dee Dee Perez, has become the general manager, which removes some of the burden from the hotel's owner (Markwardt) and fosters a higher level of professionalism. There is also the written text that offers more information during the episode's final moments, which assures us that "since Anthony's visit," occupancy is up, revenue has increased, and management's ability to respond to online criticism has improved. However, there is no mention of the housekeepers. The viewer does not learn whether or not Melchiorri's orders about the fifteen-room limit have been followed. Once Melchiorri's narrative enforces the mandate of becoming a good economic citizen, the housekeeper, and her role in maintaining the design integrity of the hotel, becomes insignificant. She remains invisible, and while the future of the hotel has been ensured, her future has been omitted.

"That Room Was a Disaster"

One of the most emotional episodes of *Hotel Impossible*'s first season occurs at the bucolic Vermont Inn. The Vermont Inn sits on five acres in Mendon, Vermont. Samantha McLemore and Jeremy Smith recently purchased the property, and since they live in Maryland, they have hired Samantha's brother-in-law, Tim, to run the inn. Jeremy explains his concerns to Melchiorri early in the episode: "The inn has been losing money since day one."[21] During his initial room visit, Melchiorri finds a number of issues with the way the inn has been operating. He finds the decor unappealing and there are specific housekeeping issues that he highlights during his inspection. For instance, water has been left in the iron. And, as Melchiorri explains, this water, which has probably been sitting for days, can lead to stains when guests use the iron to steam their clothes. Even more upsetting is the plunger that Melchiorri spots next to the toilet. He looks at the camera and grimaces as he describes "the disgust, the filth, the germs" that are being given free rein in this bathroom.

Like all reality television, *Hotel Impossible* attempts to bring its subjects to a point of crisis to reassure the viewer that a moment of catharsis has been achieved and now the subject can learn from his mistakes, change his ways, and reform. Melchiorri seeks this reaction, this extreme emotional response, during his postinspection conversation with the Vermont Inn's owners. Immediately, Samantha and Jeremy make it clear that there is tension between them and Samantha's sister, Jen, and brother-in-law, Tim. Melchiorri emphatically describes the fiscal crisis that the inn is going through because of its low occupancy rate, and Samantha begins to cry. "This is exactly what I didn't want to do," she meekly explains through a gush of tears. "Me and my sister are just fighting a lot more," she continues. The familial drama becomes the core of this episode's narrative, and here Samantha's affective response initiates Melchiorri's call to action. He is ready to help the Vermont Inn through its difficulties, and he focuses on design issues to ameliorate the situation.

After bringing in the show's designer, Blanche Garcia, who appears repeatedly during the series to perform renovations, Melchiorri describes a very strange encounter he had with the hotel's shortcomings in terms of housekeeping and service design. Editing brings us back in time, and we learn that while walking down a hall at the inn, Melchiorri noticed an unmarked door. He was curious, so he opened the unlocked door and realized that he had found a space that he wished he had never walked into. "This is basically a housekeeper's supply station disguised as a junk room," Melchiorri explains. He remarks that a guest could just as easily wander into this space and see the lack of organization and, even worse, witness the filth that has accumulated in the hotel's service areas.[22] To highlight his disdain, Melchiorri points to a rollaway bed in the space and rhetorically asks his audience: "Do you wanna sleep in this rollaway bed that's next to all this dusty, filthy stuff?" The camera reveals the extent of the mess in this cramped room, and then Melchiorri becomes even more upset when he notices that open rolls of toilet paper have been stored here, as well. "I don't want my toilet paper exposed; I wipe my butt with this." To make certain that the viewer understands how upset he is with this disorganized space, he succinctly relates after leaving, "That room was a disaster."

We, the viewers, may be horrified and entertained with this discovery, but Melchiorri needs more; in order to drive the narrative, he requires an affective response to this "disaster" from the inn's management. Following the usual story line found in every episode of *Hotel Impossible*, Melchiorri goes from the design issue to the staff. Once again, individual deficiencies are to blame, and to understand the supply station debacle, he calls a meeting with Tim and the inn's owners. They are all brought to the offensive space, and Melchiorri points out the obvious problems. Then, after shaming the owners and Tim, he therapeutically asks Tim, "How does that feel?" Tim sheepishly responds that it feels "tough," and he breaks down. His head hangs low and he cries while uttering, "When they see this [the disorganized room], they see me." This is the emotional break that Melchiorri, and, no doubt, his producers, had been hoping for. Melchiorri is now ready to begin the larger transformation, and he explains to the owners, "The pressure on innkeeper Tim is overwhelming, and it's taking a toll on the entire family." In a separate meeting held with Tim and his wife, Jen, we learn that Tim works late hours and the familial drama has become too much to handle. Jen discloses that the real battle is between her and her sister, Samantha. Melchiorri assures the couple that Tim is going to get a reasonable schedule so that he can be home with his family every night by 6:30. The responses of the show's subjects offer a glimmer of hope, as the episode quickly turns to the hotel's design makeover.

And what a makeover it is. Design guru Garcia has worked her magic on the hotel's bridal suite and created a "shabby-chic" fantasy. She has also redone housekeeping's service space, which Melchiorri reassures the owners is now "a work of efficiency." The housekeepers have an organized room, and Melchiorri has also purchased a new housekeeping cart on wheels that makes it much easier to get products from room to room. He declares that the service area is "efficient for your housekeeper, efficient for your guest." Jeremy adds, "This room provides the systems and the structures Tim needs to be efficient. It's now a functional space, as opposed to a safety hazard."

"Before" and "after" imagery enhances the show's emotional tenor in relation to design. Directly after Jeremy's praise of the "systems and the structures," there is a quick cut to the "before" image of what was once the disastrous service room. The camera pans upward and reminds us of the disarray and overall chaos. To accentuate the eventual change, "BEFORE" is written in all capitals in white over a wide, black rectangle that has been superimposed over the lower left side of the frame. Then, the editors use a montage technique to bring up the "AFTER" shot, where neatly folded towels line shelves and the back window opens to what appears to be an idyllic Vermont landscape. The housekeeping tools have also been organized, both in the new cart that Melchiorri provides and on the tidy shelves. As Brenda Weber has explored, "before" and "after" imagery is "the promise of cause and effect" that drives makeover television.[23] Moreover, "The camera's evidence offers not only shaming information but also affective reclamation: After-subjects feel joy because they now perceive the Before-danger that was previously invisible to them."[24] Following the standard arc of reality TV, *Hotel Impossible* traces this "before" to "after" transformation throughout each episode: endless repetition and reminders reinforce our visual understanding of the significant change that has occurred. These obsessive reassurances about positive outcomes heighten our own emotional reaction, reflected in the responses on screen, and this enables us to "feel" connected with the show's representation of renovation. Yet this connection between "before" and "after" all takes place without an understanding of who will actually be using this service space. We hear about the inn's "housekeeper," but she has no say in this renovation. She clearly has a lot at stake in terms of being able to use this newly devised "efficient" space, but where is she? The voice of the actual housekeeper who must contend with these design choices is missing.

Even more moving than the service design makeover is Samantha's emotional response to the inn's renovated bridal suite. Garcia and Melchiorri have been working on this redesign throughout the episode, and Samantha praises Garcia as "amazing" and notes that "all the details are perfect." Jeremy chimes in, "This has reestablished our vision of the potential that this space has." After the reveal, Melchiorri asks Blanche to come out, and here is when the emotional state reaches its peak. Since the room is a bridal suite, Blanche shows everyone that she has included a "baby hope chest" where newlyweds can place the names of what they hope will be their future children. Samantha's tears continue down her face as she tells Blanche that her mother, who passed away two years before, loved "shabby chic" and would have adored Garcia's design. She adds that her mother would want her and her sister Jen to stop fighting. In short, the redesign of the inn has facilitated this emotional resolve; now the Vermont Inn and its proprietors are ready for a new start, which has been symbolically signified through the hope chest's not-so-subtle references to birth and new beginnings.

The Vermont Inn's renaissance never involves housekeepers. Again, housekeeping's response to the realities of using this newly devised service room and cleaning the shabby chic bridal suite is noticeably absent. In a typical act of labor's erasure, we see design's celebrated surfaces without having to witness how it will be construed or maintained after the Travel Channel's cameras leave Vermont. The future of the inn has been secured through Melchiorri's makeover prowess, yet the lives of individual workers have been disenfranchised from this miraculous process.

*

Let's return to Jason the housekeeper's black light and the idea that through proper techniques of surveillance, problems in the hotel industry can be solved. As Mark Andrejevic has observed, surveillance is a critical component to reality television. It allows for entertainment, and it promotes a form of training for viewers, since the all-knowing camera eye can capture behaviors that are frequently made to seem, through the power of editing, inappropriate. Through surveillance the viewer witnesses and learns through a type of televisual pedagogy.[25] Week after week on *Hotel Impossible*, Melchiorri takes his viewers through teachable moments: first he exposes problems because of his seeming omnipotence, and then he helps to resolve these complications within the temporal confines of each episode. All of this takes place on the screen so that viewers can see, listen, and learn from these lessons about business savvy, economic prudence, and design sense. Hence, Jason's black light metaphorically raises the stakes on the show's emphasis on surveillance. The cameras and microphones may capture myriad issues, but sometimes extrasensitive equipment is necessary to identify what may be hidden. Jason's exposure of excretion, which would otherwise be invisible, offers the viewer a better sense of just how careful workers and managers have to be in the world of hotels. What would happen without Jason's device? Would the semen, urine, and blood simply go undetected, hidden from guests yet dangerously ubiquitous?

By carrying around a device that bares the most secretive of secretions, Jason's technique gets our attention; it is a reminder that at its core reality television is all about exposure and shame. Every episode of *Hotel Impossible* takes the viewer through a predictable cycle where problems get uncovered, followed by embarrassment and emotional upheaval. Ultimately, it is through the affective crises of each week's guests that resolution occurs, as we witness the ways in which Melchiorri transforms these problem hotels into success stories. It is the maintenance of design and the creation of service design systems that foster many of these makeovers, offering us an understanding of popular culture's compelling representation of hotel labor. And while there are occasional moments where the voices of individual workers are heard, such as the Southern Oaks Inn episode where we meet Jason, the housekeepers in *Hotel Impossible* usually remain silent. They follow Melchiorri's edicts and make certain that everything looks perfect, but they accomplish these tasks in silence.

YOU'RE DOING RESEARCH WHERE?

I fell hard for Kauai. I had heard about the "Garden Island" for a long time, especially about its mythic green landscape, spectacular beaches, and the "road to Hanalei," the famous single-lane highway that offers scenic views of pristine sand and verdant foliage.[1] I went to Hawaii to research an environmentally sensitive program implemented by Starwood Hotels and Resorts that offered guests the chance to opt out of housekeeping in exchange for meal vouchers or Starwood Preferred Guest points. The time I spent interviewing housekeepers on Kauai made the thorny implications of Starwood's Make a Green Choice program and its connections to design clear. Between these interviews on Kauai, at prosaic locations that could have been found anywhere in the United States, including a Starbucks and a McDonald's, I drove around the island, visiting sites like the awe-inspiring Waimea Canyon and the bucolic "End of the Road." I drove almost five hundred miles in a very short forty-eight-hour period, all while circumnavigating the perimeter of the 562-square-mile island.

The Filipina housekeepers I interviewed on Kauai were very much aware of the beauty that defined Hawaii; after all, they worked at hotels filled with tourists who did, via car and tour bus, exactly what I did, traveling the island and taking in the remarkable views. But to these women Kauai meant work, while to the tourists I found at Tunnels Beach and at Wailua Falls (the location of the famous double falls from the ABC television show *Fantasy Island*) Kauai meant an Edenic paradise far removed from the daily grind.

The sublime coastline of Kauai, coupled with its mythic interior, which is inaccessible and receives over four hundred inches of rain a year, made me think about how a large hotel management company like Starwood could mitigate the environmental impact of tourism by asking guests and management to rethink their notions of service and upkeep. As will soon become apparent, the weight of these green decisions on the house-keepers I spoke with was enormous, as Starwood's initiative not only sold the idea that the individual consumer could "make a difference" but also enhanced their corporate bottom line, since housekeepers suddenly had less work and faced the consequences of lower pay and fewer benefits. This human side to green choices must be thought through, and it seems that Starwood could have devised a plan that paid attention to sustainable choices and the labor discord that followed the implementation of this policy.

Designers, along with those of us who theorize and historically contextualize design, must consider how overusing the planet's resources has extended our environmental crisis, but, as my discussion of Starwood reveals, we often ignore the human dimension that is integral to these issues. As a result of our ongoing conversations about sustainability, the relationship between design and the environment is a serious topic at design schools. Having taught at the Parsons School of Design since 2004, I have heard the word "sustainability" raised, praised, and debated repeatedly. Sustainability, at least in the context of design education, has instigated a critical reevaluation of ethics and what it means to create things, environments, and contexts. Design education now demands that rather than simply designing things for the world to use, the designer must assess how her creative output will interact with larger environmental forces, such as the very real—and still shockingly contested—ramifications of climate change. What follows is, in some ways, a retort to design education's sometimes-superficial fetishization of environmental concerns, as we ask our students to question matters related to the environment without demanding that they understand some of the consequences that have attended these supposedly sustainable practices.

The next chapter asks if there is a space where labor and sustainable design can work together. The example of Starwood Hotels makes it evident that this connection is tenuous, as many hotels utilize the banner of sustainability as mere greenwashing, or a way to tend to fiscal prudence instead of devising programs that will both alleviate the crisis of climate change and foster a work environment that is beneficial to employees. Current practices in the hotel industry, especially when it comes to housekeepers, seem reliant on creating a further divide that separates guests, management, and employees. This is particularly salient in locations like Hawaii, where guests have astounding experiences surrounded by the beauty of a place they want to "defend" through fantasies about environmental protectionism, while the human cost of programs, like Starwood's Make a Green Choice, are easy to ignore. As my own visit to Kauai made clear, the spectacles of sightseeing are far removed from the actual experiences of the housekeepers who have to clean visitors' rooms, where an information card about a hotel's sustainability program may provide a hint of solace for the guest even though the housekeeper responsible for displaying that card may face hardships as a result of its unsustainable message.

5
GO GREEN
Design, Hotels, and the
Sustainability Paradox

In his now-famous article on the sociology of "things," titled "Mixing Humans and Nonhumans Together: The Sociology of a Door-Closer," Bruno Latour briefly, and somewhat humorously, turns to the world of hotels as an anomaly when it comes to disciplining bodies to perform labor.[1] Latour, writing as the pseudonymous Jim Johnson, notes that getting people to do menial tasks is not easy. Indeed, "two hundred years of capitalism has not completely solved" how to get people "to reliably fulfill a boring and underpaid duty."[2] To problematize this labor dynamic, Latour mentions the complications of race and how the history of inequitable economic accessibility continues to taint our perceptions of labor and fair wages. In other words, people and physical work make life knotty. But hotels, according to Latour, seem to have solved this dilemma; they have disentangled the skein. At the end of his discussion about getting a "groom" to act as a doorman, he claims: "Disciplining a groom is an enormous and costly task that only Hilton Hotels can tackle, and that for other reasons that have nothing to do with keeping the door properly closed."[3] This is the only mention that Latour makes of hotels in his article, but this raises questions: What are hotels doing that others have not mastered? Why is work, and getting people to accomplish work, so difficult?

Latour broaches some possible answers when he claims that non-human agents—those designed objects—affect human interactions. Latour asks that we take the inanimate world of things seriously. Using the example of the door—that most common of designed objects that gives meaning to our lives through spatial definition and control—Latour claims that we now "have this relatively new choice: either to discipline the people or to substitute for the unreliable humans a delegated non-human character whose only function is to open and close the door."[4]

The doorman cannot be disciplined without a series of complex social interactions and society has tried to become adept at understanding the problematic nature of physical work. Hiring, firing, surveying, and judging plague the world of labor, but what we often take for granted is that while we turn to the inhuman for solutions to these labor-oriented conundrums, we often disavow the power of the inanimate. We may replace the door groom with the hinged door-closer, but this machine (this designed thing) offers a new set of complications that we, the possible users, often overlook under the guise of the banal interactions that we have with the world of the insensate. This is the rub, this is Latour's point of contention: "Studying social relations without the nonhumans is impossible."[5]

So how do Hilton and other hotels circumvent this dynamic and "tackle" the social complexities of disciplining the "live" door groom with such aplomb? We can take Latour's argument to its logical extension and find an answer to this question in the writing of Langdon Winner, whom Latour mentions in his essay. For Winner, the world of technology offers "ways of building order in our world." Societies make deliberate choices in creating, implementing, and using these technologies, and these choices lead to scenarios in which "different people are situated differently and possess unequal degrees of power as well as unequal levels of awareness."[6] In short, design is an inherently political process that might mask itself in a container of democratization but that, in fact, helps solidify distinctions and hierarchies that "divide" society. It is our responsibility, Winner claims, to pay "careful attention" to these systems, things, and relationships we advance in our designed world. Like Latour, Winner wants us to understand that we may fetishize the innocent nature of technology, but this ideological stance—this dream of the apolitical—is false. This facade of design's apolitical nature, what Gui Bonsiepe might also claim as boutiquization, needs to be questioned.[7] Getting objects to accomplish tasks is often easy, but we need to be more critical of design's relationship to us.[8] Returning to Latour's hotel doorman, we can unpack some of these concerns.

Let's assume that the doorman just got word that the hotel he works for has started a green initiative. A few specifics about the program have been released in the form of a well-crafted public relations statement. Moving forward, guests will be able to signal to housekeeping that towels and sheets do not have to be washed each day; a recycling bin has been placed in each room; and many rooms will be redesigned, replete with energy-saving lighting systems and new decor, including an overabundance of glass and "tasteful" wood, all of which signal the hotel's commitment to "going green." The doorman and the hotel's guests are enthusiastic as the hotel's marketing department hangs signs about the new program in the lobby, right next to the reception desk. Even though the doorman may also realize that he and his fellow employees have not been asked their thoughts about the design of this highly anticipated program, he realizes that his hotel is doing what thousands of hotels worldwide have engaged in during the past decade. Guests now expect some mention of sustainable practices in the tourism industry.

Although they may not be immediately apparent, the doorman's hotel has also introduced several new, nonhuman design elements into the metaphoric and literal fabric of its property. These "green" decisions are design decisions that affect the work of the employees who maintain and service this property. Moreover, returning to Winner's contention, these decisions cause new power relationships and systems of inequity to come to the fore. The doorman, the guests, the housekeeping staff, and even the hotel's management probably do not comprehend the enormity of the changes put in place, but all design decisions matter—especially those by which intentions and realities become obfuscated by putatively innocent agendas.

Because of design's centrality and often-overlooked significance in relation to hotels, this chapter questions specific choices the hotel industry has made about sustainable practices. As I have done throughout this book, I look at this decision making about design from two different, yet interrelated, perspectives. First, I am interested in the actual material design choices that are integral to these green spaces. Second, I am interested in how the adoption of ecologically minded design influences, hinders, and sometimes enhances the design of workflow systems, or service design. To get at this topic, I first examine a program that the Aspen Skiing Company embraced at its famous luxury hotel, the Little Nell, in Aspen, Colorado. Then I turn to hotel sites in Hawaii, where the ecofriendly practices at Starwood Hotels and Resorts led to a very particular outcry from workers who had to cope with these changes—changes that had led to lost wages, decreased benefits, and much more taxing work. These voices from the field of hotel labor open up another set of issues that Latour's and Winner's theoretical conjectures intimate. These workers on the front lines of the tourism industry contextualize my larger argument that, when executed without input from the workforce, specific design choices can negatively affect labor. By exploring design's connection to people and social relationships, and the ways in which design can hinder work and reduce wages, this chapter proffers a number of ethical conundrums about the greening of the hotel business.

Devising Green Initiatives

Auden Schendler, the vice president of sustainability for Aspen Skiing Company, is very open about the conflicts that arise between green initiatives and hotel labor. Aspen owns three hotels, but Schendler is particularly fond of discussing the Little Nell, a world-renowned property situated next to the base of the gondola at Aspen Mountain. The Little Nell has ninety rooms and is arguably the most luxurious hotel in Aspen—a town where luxury lines the city's streets with high-end boutiques and gourmet restaurants. In 2000, Kris Loan, who was the Nell's engineer, developed several proposals that would help the hotel save energy and money. A more efficient boiler was installed, the temperature of the snowmelt system that makes certain guest room patios remain clean was lowered, and the roof's electric heater (a miraculous device that keeps snowfall off the roof) was turned off during the summer. Each of these changes seemed like a wise decision, based on logical thinking that would not prevent the Nell's staff from delivering the utmost in customer service. But there was a backlash, as many hotel workers found these decisions untenable.[9]

The conflict that Schendler discusses brings us back to Latour's notion that human actors do not always perfectly mesh with nonhuman agents, especially when humans make decisions that radically change how we interact with nonhuman things. In this case, members of the maintenance staff at the hotel were not keen about having their authority usurped by these new mandates. Other staff members at the Nell were also reluctant to embrace these modifications. Then, in a moment of sheer ecological madness, the manager of the Nell went to visit a hotel in Sun Valley, Idaho, where he saw steam rising from the swimming pool. He wanted to create the same effect at the Nell, which required raising the pool's temperature to 103°F, "creating 'Aspen's biggest hot tub' and negating much of the natural gas savings realized" by other initiatives.[10] People, both consciously and unconsciously, rebelled against Aspen Skiing Company's sustainable decisions, which they thought would detract from the luxury experiences the hotel was delivering, albeit through enormous expenditures on energy, both in terms of cost and environmental impact.

Today, the Little Nell continues its attempts to deliver ecologically sound luxury to its guests. Its website lists a number of "green initiatives," such as "energy efficient lighting throughout," "use of environmentally friendly cleaning products," "florescent lighting" in the garage, and "a comprehensive hotel-wide recycling program."[11] In addition, guests can opt into the hotel's Eco-Luxe program (fig. 18). For an additional two-dollar nightly fee donated to the Aspen Valley Land Trust, an organization that helps preserve undeveloped land, the environmentally minded

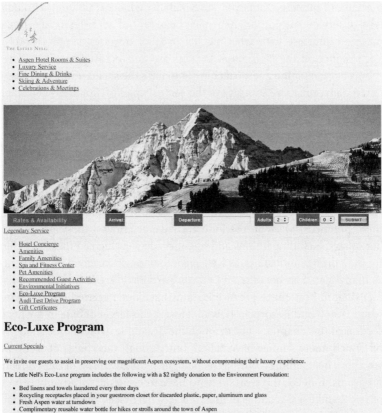

FIGURE 18 "Eco-Luxe Program," http://www.thelittlenell.com/Luxury-Service/
EcoLuxe. Courtesy of Aspen Skiing Company.

guests receive the following: the use of the hotel's fleet of bikes, a guarantee that water will be placed in pitchers during turndown service, the
placement of recycling bins in their rooms, and the option to skip daily
bed linen and towel cleaning. As the website details, "Bed linens and
towels are laundered every three days," which deviates from the standard
daily change that occurs at most luxury hotels.[12]

Schendler describes how the hotel's wealthy clientele do not always
respond enthusiastically to these sustainable practices.[13] Although many
guests embrace these ideas, some, understandably, do not want their
vacations interrupted by the guilt that can attend sustainable thinking.
Part of the hotel's challenge is to make these programs visible while not
burdening those who pay premium prices to stay at a five-star property.
Schendler has worked hard at Aspen and the Little Nell to stress the im-

portance of spending money on sustainability while maintaining a unique level of service. In addition, Aspen has been careful not to let its Eco-Luxe program interfere with what has led to labor disputes at other hotels. For instance, at the Nell, housekeepers are not required to clean more rooms because some guests decide not to have the sheets and linens laundered daily; the expectations are the same, explains Gioanna Villabrille, the hotel's director of housekeeping, "whether the guest has Eco-Luxe or not."[14]

These decisions about waste, energy, products, and building are, of course, design decisions. These programs create challenges in terms of designing hotel properties that successfully implement such codes of green conduct. Sustainable practices also force attention on new types of service design that allow workflow, and its concomitant, labor, to expedite these practices. Many in the industry have celebrated these programs, but others, including unions and scientists, have criticized these policies for their disingenuousness, as well as for their negative effect on workers, as many have lost benefits and pay as a result of green initiatives.[15] By focusing on how these green programs have been carried out by Starwood Hotels and Resorts in Hawaii, I assess this larger debate in the next section of this chapter—not through the discourse of economic models, on which many studies have relied, but through the voices of workers who have been ignored during the planning and execution of these green programs. Indeed, the workers who have to contend with many of the physical and fiscal realities of green design have been overlooked for far too long.

Going Green in Paradise

In 2009, Starwood Hotels and Resorts, an enormous hospitality management company, instituted a program called Make a Green Choice on several Hawaiian Islands, including Oahu, Kauai, and Maui. Starwood's reach in the industry is vast. It manages many brands, including Sheraton, Westin, and W Hotels. The Make a Green Choice program, which Starwood offers at select properties, allows guests to opt out of housekeeping services for one to three days, in return for which the guest receives either a five-dollar meal voucher or five hundred Starwood Preferred Guest Starpoints for each day of participation (fig. 19).[16] According to the company's website, the program helps save electricity, water, natural gas, and chemicals. Starwood proclaims the virtues of these savings by declaring, "See what a difference a night can make!" This "difference," which is clearly marked as a progreen choice on the company's website through color (light green) and visual tropes (fauna)—signs that cus-

MAKE A
green choice

The less water, energy and other resources we use, the more there is to go around. Reward yourself with a $5 voucher at participating food and beverage outlets or 500 Starwood Preferred Guest Starpoints® awarded at check out for each night you decline housekeeping services (except day of departure).

Conservation matters. Make A Green Choice.

Terms & Conditions

difference a night can make!

Save Water	Save Electricity	Save Natural Gas	Save Chemicals
37.2 Gallons*	0.19 KWH*	25,000 btu*	7 oz*
37.2 gallons is 596 cups, enough for 1 person to drink almost 2 cups per day for a year.	That's enough to run an Energy Star-rated laptop for 10 hours.	Enough energy to heat a 400 square foot room at 70°F for 4 hours - when it's 10°F outside.	Fewer chemicals equals less toxicity in the environment. And that's good for everyone.

*All amounts estimated based on average guestroom size and materials usage. Program availability may vary by hotel.

FIGURE 19 "Make a Green Choice," http://www.starwoodpromos.com /westingreenchoice/?EM=VTY_WI_GREENCHOICE_PROMOTION. Courtesy of Starwood Hotels and Resorts.

tomers look for when making "green" decisions—may have been good for Starwood and its guests but, as my fieldwork in Hawaii revealed, not for the housekeepers. These decisions about "savings" had dramatic service design implications that affected the lives of housekeepers in significant ways. Noting such effects forces us to think about Latour's mandate to consider how decisions about the nonhuman world alter the lives of workers through pay cuts, the dissolution of benefits, and difficult reconfigurations of service related to Starwood's green initiative.

According to the general manager at the Sheraton Seattle, Matthieu Van Der Peet, many of Starwood's "guests are environmentally conscious in their day-to-day lives." The program "is a great way to give our guests a choice to continue their green practices while at the Sheraton."[17] This idea of helping guests feel at home, and giving them what they want, is also how Starwood described the program to its employees. Many of the housekeepers I spoke with in Hawaii explained that their managers promoted the program by claiming that guests wanted these changes; it was deemed good for business to "treat the guests to be comfortable [like the way they feel] at home."[18] Some Starwood guests in Hawaii helped promote the program with their web-based reviews of the hotels' green efforts. One guest on the popular website TripAdvisor.com wrote that the

Sheraton on Kauai has "pioneered a commendable Go-Green program where they offer restaurant credit in exchange for not having maid service on any given day. We've found this program to be attractive financially, but also think it's a great idea environmentally—just imagine the energy and resource savings of not having linens replaced every day."[19] Traveling to a place like Kauai and seeing a large hotel corporation make an effort to lower its environmental impact was heartening to many guests, who also were given the incentive of free food and award points.

These "green" guests may have been surprised to learn that opting into the program dramatically affected the lives of hotel workers, who had no say in the program's design. Interviews with eleven housekeepers in Hawaii, eight who work in Honolulu, and three who work on Kauai made clear the human costs of going green. Although the program mitigated the environmental effects of chemicals, detergents, and electricity, it had unintended consequences, such as the unsanitary condition of the rooms, the problematic workflow for the housekeepers, and the loss of work resulting from the lack of rooms to clean. This gendered work is often done with enormous pride, but the difficulties these women encountered in Hawaii became too demanding.[20] As Lydia Agustin, who works at the Moana Surfrider, a Starwood property in Honolulu, explained, "Housekeepers [are] the backbone of the hotel industry." She noted, "We are the one making the guest coming back to the hotel. . . . We take care of them."[21] For her, the go-green program, as she and the other housekeepers referred to it during our interviews, hindered the delivery of "caring." If they could not clean the room, and the room became in their estimation unsanitary, their positive perceptions of their work quickly became negative. Moreover, if they and their colleagues were losing pay, their assessment of the value of their jobs would only worsen.

The go-green program degraded the integrity of the room's physical design, which made cleaning more difficult for housekeepers. One woman with whom I spoke had worked as a housekeeper at the Sheraton Waikiki for over a decade, and she talked about the sunscreen and oils that would get into bathtubs. Because the hotel is on one of the most famous beaches in the world, guests would go to the beach, use tanning oil or sunscreen, and then wash the oils off their bodies when they returned to their rooms. Each day the room could not be serviced meant more of a buildup of lotions in the tub.[22] Several housekeepers also talked about the presence of mold. Given the beach location of these hotels, mold is already a problem; several days without service meant more dirt and more of a chance for mold to infiltrate tiled and cloth surfaces. Lilibeth Herrell of the Sheraton Waikiki explained, "It's so filthy, get mold everything." The lack of cleaning led to smells, "especially if they [the guests] have kids."[23] In terms of children, one of the more surprising things about the program was the guests' diaper disposal practices. When housekeeping entered the rooms only every third day, the trash would accumulate into a mess of filth. Carolina Cacal, of the Sheraton on Kauai, described guests' tendency to leave used diapers either on the room's balcony or outside the room door in the hallway.[24] The additional odors and mess complicated the housekeepers' cleaning responsibilities.

The go-green program also affected and interrupted the design of the workflow systems, or service design, on which housekeeping depends for efficiency. Room cleaning could no longer be scheduled in advance because of the opt-in/opt-out decision of the guest. In hotels, the room-cleaning schedule—or "board," as it is often called—functions as a work plan detailing the rooms that a housekeeper needs to clean. The board also identifies which rooms are checkouts and which rooms are midstay. Housekeepers tend to work on the same section of rooms each day, with little variation; to minimize movement of the loaded service carts, these rooms are typically next to each other. But under Starwood's green initiative, the slate of fifteen rooms that the housekeepers had to service could now be more randomly located throughout the property. The housekeepers no longer serviced fifteen rooms on the same floor (in Honolulu) or in the same building (on Kauai). Carolina Cacal explained, "I have to pick up rooms from the other buildings, from floor to floor, and it's very hard for me; it's too stressful."[25] The Sheraton Kauai's eight separate buildings are spread out across the property (fig. 20). Maneuvering her cart and supplies became more difficult for Cacal because the rooms that she needed to clean were in various locations. The highly orchestrated workflow of housekeeping became disorganized, which made Cacal's task more complicated. Even in the high-rise structure in Honolulu, many of the housekeepers described a scenario in which they had to move their carts from floor to floor. "Let's say [in] my station, I have fifteen rooms, and let's say five rooms refuse service because of the so-called 'go-green,' so I gotta bump another station to make my fifteen rooms, which is hard," noted Rosemary Esperanza.[26]

In other unexpected ways the go-green program wreaked havoc on the hotel's carefully orchestrated service design strategy. The housekeepers could not enter the room of a guest who opted in, but if that same guest asked for other housekeeping services, these requests could not be refused. Housekeepers did not get a room credit for cleaning a room that was participating in go-green, but they might still be called by a guest in the hallway to deliver new towels, or to take out the trash, which added to the housekeeper's workload.[27]

This excess work, coupled with the loss of hours from the reduced

FIGURE 20 Aerial view, Sheraton Kauai Resort, Kauai, Hawaii.

cleaning needs, made life for housekeepers in Hawaii very difficult, as Starwood's management was not hearing their design-related grievances. Latour's warning about nonhuman agents changing human lives became very relevant in the situations of Caridad Rodrigues and Rizalyn Balisacan, two housekeepers at the Sheraton on Kauai. They explained how ecotourism had reduced their vacation time and sick days, both of which accrue after working a set number of days in a given year. In other words, they remained "on call" (waiting to be called into work) for so many days as a result of go-green that they did not accumulate paid time off. Moreover, while on call, they did not earn their hourly wage. In addition to losing wages and benefits, they received no additional credit for servicing rooms that had not been cleaned in three days. Rodrigues had to ask the state of Hawaii for medical insurance, "but they said no, I cannot qualify because my husband, he get the pension. Then they ask everything, it's like you going to welfare; they ask [everything] in the papers."[28] Her sense of humiliation at having to go outside her workplace for this assistance was palpable. Balisacan noted that because her income had declined, she could not send funds to her family in the Philippines, which created hardships for those who depended on her remittance.[29]

Many of the housekeepers working in Hawaiian hotels are Filipina, and in fact all of the women I interviewed in Hawaii were born in the

Philippines.[30] One housekeeper explained that the history of Filipinos in Hawaii is important to consider when looking at labor on the islands. Lilia Olsen, from the Hyatt in Honolulu, talked about the history of plantation life in Hawaii. She noted that generations of Filipinos have struggled for fair working conditions and that "old timers . . . pass it on to us to be strong." Explaining the generational issues, she stated, "We have to think about the future . . . for grandkids. . . . That's why we are fighting." Labor issues came to the fore with the sugar cane plantations: "The old senior citizen, and all the people that retired . . . they started that [battle], and we have to continue that."[31] Filipinos began to immigrate to Hawaii in the early twentieth century to work on sugar plantations. The Hawaiian Sugar Planter's Association (HSPA) was not very kind to Filipino workers during the first decade of the century, in which the wave of immigrants numbered 18,144.[32] However, by 1920 Filipinos were starting to organize aggressively, and large strikes occurred to protest unfair wages and deplorable working conditions. Several of these actions became violent, as the Hawaiian police used rifles to try to control the protesters.[33] This tension, which led to deaths, did eventually foster a better working environment and the development of unions, but the mistreatment of Filipino workers in Hawaii created a legacy of labor disharmony that Olsen sought to explain.

This legacy, perhaps in part, led to the vocal outcry that eventually ended Starwood's go-green program in Hawaii. Housekeepers and their union representatives from UNITE HERE had voiced their overwhelming concern with the program from its inception, but during contract negotiations in early 2011, Starwood Hotels canceled Make a Green Choice in Hawaii. Through potential strikes and campaigns that brought the program to the public's attention, UNITE HERE was able to negotiate its discontinuation.[34] It is important to note that these union-based actions did not initially transpire at the invitation of management, but a collective uprising against these policies led to design-related changes. Although the program still exists in other locations, the housekeepers in Hawaii successfully countered established perspectives about Make a Green Choice. Consequences that had included reduced work hours, additional time and effort to maintain the integrity of the room's design, and upheaval in the delicate balance of workflow became too burdensome. As a result of the housekeepers' unified voice, Starwood's Hawaiian properties stopped asking guests to forgo housekeeping.

The 2011 contract provided other innovative benefits to housekeepers beyond the dissolution of Make a Green Choice. The housekeepers did receive a modest increase in pay, but perhaps most telling in the wake of the Make a Green Choice debacle were the ways in which management offered service design concessions in the new contract. The language of the agreement makes it obvious that the service design conflicts, which defined the debate about Starwood's sustainability program, had affected these negotiations. In the previous 2006 contract, for instance, there was an acknowledgment of the importance of getting credit for checkout rooms, but the 2011 agreement includes additional credits for these more labor-intensive situations, where sheets and towels must be changed. Thus, before 2011 housekeepers could only receive a maximum of three room credits (out of their total of fifteen) for ten checkouts, but now there is the potential for four room credits if there are "11 or more check-outs." Perhaps most significant to the contract is the clause that, according to a summary of the agreement given to me by Benjamin Sadoski, a research analyst for UNITE HERE, asserts that the "employer may not discipline an employee for cleaning fewer than the standard number of guest rooms, except where the employee has persistently and without reasonable justification failed to meet the standard." Sadoski explained the significance of this clause in an email: "This competes with the need for housekeepers to finish all the rooms they have been assigned. Most often, the sacrifice that housekeepers make is to their lunch breaks, which many housekeepers don't take. That's not good for them—their bodies need a break, and they need food. Housekeepers also might rush to clean each room, which can be unsafe—sometimes they slip and fall, sometimes they incur strain injuries, etc." He further noted that this rush to clean rooms could also have negative implications for guests and management, as housekeepers "might be inclined to cut corners and skip some parts of the checklist that are likely not to be noticed."[35] The inclusion of this important caveat in 2011 meant that several service design issues I talked about with housekeepers in Hawaii, such as working with untenable workflow situations, had been addressed by the 2011 contract that offered some relief.

The ratification of this new contract makes it evident that these housekeepers had become design activists by raising important questions about the conventional wisdom that equates environmental decisions with ethical standards. Starwood had not heeded the wisdom of Bruno Latour about paying attention to the human costs of design decisions. So the housekeepers, led by UNITE HERE, demanded that Starwood attend to the human consequences of its decisions.[36] Many guests clearly embraced the program, with its meal vouchers and rewards points, and general managers probably were happy with the cost savings associated with lower operational expenses, but the dissatisfaction and hardships that the housekeepers faced brought Starwood's myopic vision into focus. None of the housekeepers I spoke with intimated a sense of pride in the program's ecological effects. Instead, the message that accompanied their organized action stressed the human-centered aspects of daily work that Starwood ignored during its implementation of a presumed ethical set of practices. The Starwood example should be extrapolated into other arenas where the unquestioned flag of "green" praxis needs to be interrogated.

∗

Many guests who stay at hotels with programs that show environmental sensitivity revel in the tourism industry's commitment to sustainability. That Starwood offers sustainable options for conference planners that use its hotels is telling.[37] Meeting planners who book enormous blocks of rooms look for programs like Starwood's so they can tell their attendees what they are doing to lessen their carbon footprint, all while still putting on what many perceive to be an "old-fashioned" professional meeting. However, what the industry elides in this process of greening hotels is the labor of individual workers: the consequences to the workforce remain hidden in the promotion of these sustainable practices.

This paradox—that politically progressive guests are unknowingly condoning practices they would find abhorrent by supporting these green programs—needs to be addressed.[38] As one housekeeper in Honolulu explained, "We are suffering, the workers are suffering, and the guests are going to suffer."[39] Her distress about Starwood's move in this direction, and the details she (along with all the other housekeepers I interviewed) provided about the program's effect on the room's design integrity, made the paradox of sustainability palpable. Despite the focus here on the human problems that arise in relation to corporations' efforts to promote ecological thinking, the challenge is that climate change—the dire consequences of global warming—are very real. So what can be done? How do we negotiate between the need to change our thinking about ecology and the realities of work? How can workers share more of their own difficulties with some of these seemingly well-intentioned plans?

A solution to this dilemma may be found in the context of further union organizing, which would foster a culture where workers had more of a voice in the hotel industry. As geographer Steven Tufts has explained, "There are opportunities for hotel unions such as UNITE HERE to intervene in the green certification process. Specifically, the union itself could rate its employers and issue a union 'rating' similar to the well known diamond and star systems used by travel providers." Along these lines, UNITE HERE helped create the Informed Meetings Exchange (INMEX) system, which is a web-based resource that allows conference planners to see the ways in which various hotel properties treat their workers.[40] Tufts wants a similar system in place that would help guests understand just how genuine a corporation is being when it comes to green practices.[41] By taking the lead, workers and labor organizers could change the conversation and help hotel owners and managers understand the critical nature of these decisions. Such programs may have limitations, but they would undoubtedly foster a dialogue that could change the larger discussion about programs, such as Starwood's attempt with Make a Green Choice. This type of initiative would make Latour's mandate about being aware of design's consequences come to life.

The hotel industry needs to implement changes that account for design's relationship to workers. Many of the guests at these hotels who laud the virtues of sustainable practices might not think about how employees suffer as a result of additional work requirements and the potential of layoffs. As Latour tells us, the hotel industry has tamed the doorman and made his plight invisible, but at what cost? These housekeepers in Hawaii, whose collective ire led to changes and a heightened sense of awareness, need to be heard by other hotel owners and managers. The industry should pursue sustainable initiatives, but the human toll—the effects that these choices have on individual workers—demands further consideration.

Vignette Six
CHICAGO AND THICK DESCRIPTION

In June of 2011, I went to Chicago because a contact I had made with the hotel workers' union, UNITE HERE, had put me in touch with a local labor organizer named Noah Dobin-Bernstein. Dobin-Bernstein was eager for me to meet a group of housekeepers who had been working for the Hyatt Regency Chicago and who had been greatly affected by, as I detail in the following chapter, the hotel's recent renovation. I expected to find out what had transpired at the hotel and the ways in which design became intertwined with the realities of labor. What I did not expect to learn, and what emerged very quickly, were the ways in which the politically charged nature of the relationship between workers and their union, and workers and the hotel's management, would surface. I found myself in the midst of some very awkward situations that I have debated including in the pages of this book. With Clifford Geertz's ideas about "thick description" in mind, as well as James Clifford's warning about the cultural biases and relativistic limitations that attend thick description, I want to use this space to try to unpack some of the complications that I witnessed at the Hyatt Regency Chicago in 2011.[1] Moreover, since the next chapter attempts to interpret the words, actions, and gestures that I learned while going into the field and assessing a labor dispute, I want to be certain that this analysis offers interpretative depth that digs deeper than the "thin description" that Geertz asks us to avoid.[2]

I knew that Hyatt had been repeatedly taken to task because of the management company's ambivalence toward labor, but Hyatt's extreme discomfort around this topic took me by surprise. Initially, the hotel had no hesitancy about having Dobin-Bernstein take me into the back of the house of the Chicago Regency. When we arrived at the employee entrance to the hotel, security did not even blink as Dobin-Bernstein explained that

I was there doing research. Human resources was not called; no manager was asked if I was allowed in, as the officer at the security desk gave me a visitor's badge and off I went with full access to the vast employees-only area at the hotel. While at the Hyatt, I was confident that nobody from Hyatt's management was watching me. Dobin-Bernstein and I went up and down back staircases and used service elevators looking for house-keepers to interview. I kept looking at Dobin-Bernstein as though something was going to happen, but as we spoke with housekeepers and wandered the guest floors, Hyatt seemed complacent and accepting—or, perhaps just blissfully ignorant—about my presence.

That complacency changed when Dobin-Bernstein brought me into a meeting between the human resources department and housekeeping. He explained that the meeting had been called to discuss specific work-load concerns. Before the meeting officially began, a manager from Hyatt asked Dobin-Bernstein and me to leave. I had a feeling that suddenly Hyatt had a sense that I was up to something. In fact, attempts to get further information and even interview Hyatt management about the hotel's ongoing labor dispute led nowhere.

As surprised as I was by Dobin-Bernstein's access to the hotel's service areas, I had not anticipated his sway over the unionized employees we encountered. Granted, he is an organizer, so his role is to build trust and have employees come together as a unified voice, but it became apparent that his authoritative word was significant among the hotel's staff. I am quite confident that if he had not been with me that day I would not have conducted any interviews, because by introducing me to the house-keepers he put them at ease. In an environment where there is heightened tension between management and line workers, an outsider can be seen as an unwanted interloper whose only purpose is to break confidences and deter progress. Dobin-Bernstein made it clear that I was there to conduct research and not to act as an agent on Hyatt's behalf.

I was interested in Hyatt's and UNITE HERE's perspectives, but I was particularly excited about the prospect of speaking with housekeepers to learn about the individuals who have to maintain the hotel's design features. And even though these interviews happened within the confines of the hotel, the women that I spoke with were remarkably open about the joys and pains associated with their work. The amount of pride they took in their work was obvious. This is a theme that became readily apparent during all of my conversations with housekeepers that I conducted for this book, but that pride came at a cost, and many of these housekeepers had trouble reconciling what they understood as the taxing nature of their own physical labor with management's apparent ignorance. The idea of respect, and even, as you will soon read, teaching respect to one's children by being a role model, is a critical issue and these housekeepers wanted Hyatt to acknowledge their labor.

My trip to Chicago in 2011 was the first time I had a chance to sit down and speak with housekeepers. I had been mindful of some of the issues I would encounter, but my time at the Hyatt made me very cognizant of the personal side to this story that I had not considered. The stories that unfolded as I interviewed these housekeepers helped me understand hotel labor as a multifaceted issue laden with emotional and physical repercussions, since it became apparent that these women's lives had been changed by the difficult nature of their work. Connected to this, of course, were the ways in which the actual specifics of hotel labor became much more tangible to me by speaking with these women. If Marx helps us understand that labor becomes abstracted under capitalism, my discussion with these women in Chicago made that labor far more, as Marx would explain, concrete.[3]

Both historically, as discussed in my chapter on *The Practical Housekeeper*, and today, as seen in my earlier assessment of hotel management textbooks, the goal of the hotel industry is to take the elements of housekeeping—including time, physical capabilities, and attention to details—and make these components fit together in a harmonious system where work flows in a seamless fashion. This is at the core of the industry's uncompromising vision of labor and service design. One of the most telling guest surveys I have ever received from a hotel is the Hotel Bel-Air's poststay survey that includes this statement, which it asks guests to rate on a scale of 1 to 5 (5 being "strongly agree" and 1 being "strongly disagree"): "The hotel staff all worked together seamlessly."[4] This sentence, buried in a long list of other interrogatives, summarizes the way in which we reflexively consider labor at hotels. We want a clean, well-appointed space that will facilitate our travels, yet we do not want to think about how that space gets maintained and serviced. Moreover, the idea of learning about the physical and emotional toll that cleaning these spaces entails is not high on the typical hotel guest's list of desires. We do not want to see the seams of service.

My final chapter, on Hyatt, further exposes the invisibility that obscures housekeeping. Learning about how complicated it is to lift a mattress, roll a towel, or deal with the stresses of other poor design choices are not what most people have in mind when you tell them you are writing a book about hotels and design. However, by revealing some of these realities, and coming up with a potential way of rethinking the design process found at hotels, we can begin to imagine new possibilities where abstracted labor becomes more tangible, relatable, and concrete. And, most critically, where workers can begin to have a voice in the design process at hotels.

6

"WE TRULY LISTENED TO OUR GUESTS"

Rethinking the Redesign of the Hyatt Regency Chicago

Maria Hernandez has been a housekeeper at the Hyatt Regency Chicago for thirty-five years.[1] When she discusses the hotel's recent renovation, she becomes particularly upset about the changes to the guest room bathrooms. She notes that there is more glass in these updated spaces, and this abundance of glass takes more time to clean. She also spends time describing the second roll of toilet paper that must be placed in the renovated rooms. At first, these may seem like banal design choices, or simple extras that would not interfere in any way with the normal upkeep of a hotel room. But to Hernandez, these additional amenities are a problem because they take up more of her time. Adding to an already difficult work schedule, the extra minutes it takes to clean the new glass surfaces and monitor and install a second roll of toilet paper accumulate over the course of a sixteen-room shift.[2]

This focus on the bathroom and its appearance is prevalent in the travel industry. One place where the bathroom receives ample attention is on the travel website TripAdvisor.com, where, as I explain in other sections of this book, guests feel free to share all kinds of details about hotels. For instance, the reviews of the bed and breakfast property Kimeret Place in Mapua, New Zealand, are, for the most part, very positive. Guests describe the B & B's idyllic location and the hospitality at the small guesthouse. With only five rooms, everything seems to be about attention to detail.[3] One review, in particular, by a TripAdvisor member named emc1, who is from Monterey, California, is markedly glowing. Although she does not identify her actual name, emc1 is a 50–64-year-old woman who has been a member of the site since 2008. She has written eleven reviews, and three of her reviews have been given helpful votes by other TripAdvisor users. This is not a distinguished number, given the dedication that some

FIGURE 21 Toilet paper roll. Photograph by Abby Brazina.

users have to the site, but it shows her active participation in this virtual community of travelers. In a typically short and formulaic review, emc1 describes the beauty of Kimeret Place's location as well as its exceptional service, beautiful guest rooms, and delicious food. She also spends some time on the B & B's staff's attention to details. These "small touches," to use emc1's helpful phrase, relate directly to design as they focus on the presentation of extraordinary design details, the superb upkeep of the property's interiors, and the way in which service design delivers unexpected extras. This mention of "small touches" is the one part of emc1's review that stands out, since she includes a design detail that may seem somewhat absurd to some travelers, but, in fact, many guests adore. She writes, "I loved the small touches" that the owner of the Kimeret made, "such as her expertise with toilet paper origami (yes), where she fashions little roses, fans etc. . . . on the toilet paper roll, or leaves sheaves of lavender in the bathroom."[4]

In hotels throughout the world, there is now an almost universal expectation that the toilet paper will be folded by housekeeping (fig. 21). This fold, which has in some places, like the Kimeret, become much more elaborate, is a mark of cleanliness. It is a sign that housekeeping has been there; the room attendant has done her job, and that added touch of labor—that extra bit of work—signifies that the room is sanitary. There is, after all, a long history in hotels of marking the toilet with signage that reveals the absence of germs. Think about the white paper that still wraps the toilet seat at some motels. Here the "touch" is "smaller," but the subtle act is equally reassuring: it makes the guest confident that a housekeeper has entered the premise and given that most intimate of shared spaces a clean bill of health.

The toilet paper fold is, to use the language of service design, a "touch-point" between the guest and labor.[5] The bathroom is, as Elizabeth Shove has demonstrated, an important design element that helps us organize our lives around notions of normativity and hygiene.[6] While these norms of cleanliness are socially constructed, they define our everyday lives. When we check into hotels, we expect that the bathroom, that sacred space where fantasies and nightmares about sanitary surfaces become most critical, should be "clean" and should utilize design in a way that fosters a sense of organization around this ideal of being antiseptic. One of the odd paradoxes of the folded toilet paper is that it signifies that a thorough and careful cleaning has occurred, but, in reality, it means that another individual has repeatedly touched and manipulated that product that will soon touch our bodies, revealing a type of handling of a surface that many guests—if they spent a moment thinking about this—might find unacceptable. The hotel bathroom, where design meets—or does not meet—expectations becomes heavily freighted with meaning. It is not surprising that the bathroom is one of the hotel room's designed features that guests most critique. This emphasis on the bathroom has led to many renovations of hotel properties as a result of bathrooms that seem outdated, drab, and in need of attention.

In this chapter, I explore the ways in which renovation choices in hotel guest rooms affect the work of housekeepers who maintain these spaces. I also question why hotel owners and managers do not seek the advice of housekeepers before these renovations begin. To get at these questions about the link between renovations and labor, I interviewed a number of housekeepers at the Hyatt Regency Chicago, where a renovation that ended in 2011 led to conflict between the hotel's management and line workers, or those who hold nonmanagement positions at hotels. To get a sense of the larger context that incited this conflict, I also interviewed the designer who led the redesign of the hotel's guest rooms, and I spent time talking with officials from UNITE HERE, the union that represents Hyatt's workers. While management from Hyatt was unwilling to discuss my questions, the hotel's public relations arm has released statements that clarify their position on this conflict, and I have looked at this material to discern the multiple perspectives that are integral to this complicated story. In what follows, I consider the Hyatt renovation and some of the ways in which seemingly straightforward design decisions led to unforeseen repercussions. I conclude this chapter with some thoughts about the ways in which a co-design process could have fostered different outcomes in Chicago.

The YouTube Wars

Like so many public relations campaigns in the twenty-first century, the fight between the Hyatt Regency Chicago and its employees' union, UNITE HERE, can be viewed on YouTube. In a response to what it positions as UNITE HERE's "scare tactics," Hyatt begins their 2010 video titled *Just the Facts* with text that suggests they are about to deliver "An Important Message to our Valued Employees." The slick production, replete with pleasant piano music, claims that Hyatt has repeatedly come to the bargaining table with offers of more money and generous benefit packages, but the union has refused this kindness and fostered a hostile work environment that has provoked potential guests to boycott the hotel. The African American actor notes that this controversy is not about issues happening in Chicago; instead it is about "someone else, somewhere else": namely, workers in other parts of the United States, such as Indianapolis, where Hyatt and its line workers have entered into very disagreeable labor disputes. The fireplace that the actor sits in front of toward the end of the video, and the overall cozy atmosphere of the video's set, domesticates the message, making its delivery appear friendlier in tone, but the constant refrain about "respect," pride, and mutuality provides a pedantic tenor. By concluding the video with faceless images of work (specifically, bed making and vacuuming), along with the actor's voiceover, which offers a sentiment of thanks to Hyatt's employees, the almost four-minute video appears to embrace and praise labor. This message of inclusivity and acknowledgment appears so critical that there is also a Chinese version of the same video, to ensure that all hotel staff get the message that, as the video states, "enough is enough": it is time to end the conflict, get back to work, and make each other proud.[7]

UNITE HERE's 2011 satirical response to Hyatt's video deploys the visual and the aural to offer what they title "The Real Truth" in a more than six-minute video. The union uses Hyatt's stock footage throughout their retort, but instead of the dapper spokesman who pleads "enough is enough" in the well-appointed interior found in the Hyatt version, the union video includes a farcical representation of a "fat cat" capitalist. This stereotyped character is also African American, but his clothes are less refined and he smokes a cigar and sips brandy, reminding us of Thomas Nast–like imagery from the late nineteenth century. Everything in the UNITE HERE video makes the viewer aware of the artifice of Hyatt's public relations machine (fig. 22): UNITE HERE changes the beautiful

FIGURE 22 Still from "Hyatt: The Real Truth," Youtube.com, March 29, 2011, accessed January 12, 2012, http://www.youtube.com/watch?v=wFi4k3qRD_Y. Courtesy of UNITE HERE.

FIGURE 23 Still from "Hyatt: The Real Truth," Youtube.com, March 29, 2011, accessed January 12, 2012, http://www.youtube.com/watch?v=wFi4k3qRD_Y. Courtesy of UNITE HERE.

flowers that appoint the Hyatt interior to plastic flowers; the fireplace is now a television that plays a video of a fire burning; and the maps and diagrams found in the Hyatt video become a display for humorous and exaggerated sounds that poke fun at the hotel management company's attempts to debunk what it claims are the union's talents at mythmaking. At one point, the pedantic spokesman exclaims, "Despite what your Union says, you don't need mops to clean floors. You can have as much water as you would like from one of our brand new, state of the art, water coolers." Like the Hyatt video, UNITE HERE concludes with the same images of housekeeping vacuuming and making beds, but in this instance an African American woman comes in to serve the spokesman, yet the spokesman's demands get thwarted—the performance of work stops—after he asks the hotel worker if she expects a tip (fig. 23). Suddenly, the woman playing the part of the line worker puts up her hand (as if to signal "talk to the hand," this will go no further) and declares, "Hyatt, stop playing games, give us a fair contract."[8] Through this sudden narrative twist, which includes a worker's affective response to being taken advantage of, UNITE HERE disavows Hyatt's claims about its employees' petty behavior.

This battle on YouTube was a result of the lapsed contract between Hyatt management and its Chicago hotel workers represented by UNITE HERE. In fact, it is important to note that the Regency was only one of four hotels affected by these failed negotiations.[9] The previous contract went into force on September 1, 2006, and expired on August 31, 2009. From 2009 until the ratification of a new contract in 2013, those represented by the union, including the housekeeping staff and many of those in food and beverage, worked without a contract. This meant a protracted series of conflicts centered on wages, conditions, and benefits. One aspect of the 2006 contract that is of particular interest for this book is "Supplement VI," which focuses on housekeeping. The language details how specific benefits will be available to the housekeepers and also mentions how Hyatt will provide the guest room attendants with certain items for protection, such as work gloves. But it is the daily room quota, set at sixteen, that is very significant. This number can be reduced if there are over ten "checkouts," as checkouts, with their mandatory linen changes and more regimented cleaning requirements, demand much more work.[10] This "board" (again, a term housekeepers use to refer to the number of rooms that they must complete in a day) was set in accordance with the design of the Hyatt Regency Chicago's rooms in 2006. As a result of the renovation of these rooms, which began in 2010, the appearance and design of these spaces radically changed, which resulted in housekeepers requesting less rooms on their daily board. Yes, finances and benefits were critical to the postrenovation round of labor talks and disputes that went on for four years in Chicago, but line workers also protested the physical changes to the interior that made their jobs more demanding. The maintenance of the interior's aesthetics, and coping with problematic service design realities in the face of these renovations, became a serious issue, one that was particularly difficult for the housekeepers, who had been given no say in the design choices that circumscribed the hotel's multi-million-dollar facelift.

The Renovation and the Renovators

Starting with the West Tower of the hotel, and then moving to the East Tower, the Hyatt Regency Chicago completed the renovation of its 2,019 rooms in 2011. The hotel's website details many of the design elements included in this massive undertaking. In a web page that offers "fun facts" about the West Tower renovation, the list of changes includes: 1,480 pillows, 2,694 accent pillows, and 2,918 mirrors. The hotel, once again, turned to YouTube to give further details about the changes that took place. The hotel's head of engineering, who speaks throughout this video, notes, "The improved product is extremely well received by our guests. It was definitely the right thing to do."[11] Hyatt stresses the importance of the guest in other public relations material related to the renovation. The hotel's general manager, Patrick Donelly, explains on another Hyatt web page that offers an image of the new rooms, "We truly listened to our guests, and in turn, several aspects of this renovation were incorporated as a direct result of guest feedback. We are excited to provide our guests an even better experience through innovative, top-of-the line guest room accommodations featuring the latest in design and technology."[12] The ongoing message purported by Hyatt is that by listening closely to customers the hotel management company was able to deliver a better product. Indeed, guests' reviews of the hotel prior to the renovation make it evident that the appearance of the rooms was stale. As one guest noted on TripAdvisor in 2007, "The décor and the furniture was tired" and the property needed to be updated.[13]

While the guests' desires were clearly the driving force behind these design changes, the voices of hotel workers—especially housekeepers—were not included in the design process, as housekeeping became, instead, something that designers wanted to discipline within the context of the hotel. The firm Indidesign, based in California, led the $90 million renovation. A conversation with Beatrice Girelli, the firm's principal and owner, helps shed light on both their design brief from Hyatt and some of the challenges that went into the enormous project. Girelli is very open about the tension that exists between corporations, like Hyatt, and a more ambitious design vision. Often this has to do with finances, and these limitations can affect creativity, since Girelli's firm does what it can to push the possibilities of design into territory that will, in her words, "wow the guest." Indidesign is committed to what Girelli describes as the "longevity" of the materials and objects that fill the room. If the furniture and equipment does not last, the space loses its economic viability and the renovation gets labeled a failure, so her team thinks extensively about durability. Girelli is also very frank about housekeeping and concerns that her firm has with the women who clean the spaces she has designed. She notes, "We design [things] that fit only in one place," which makes certain that the room is "housekeeping proof." She emphasizes that there are many hotels where "housekeeping is the designer," as they move objects, they do not follow the manuals that design firms give to hotels, and they disregard the importance of appearance. To avoid this, Girelli and

FIGURE 24 Guest room before the renovation. Hyatt Regency Chicago, Chicago, IL. Courtesy of Hyatt Hotels.

her team keep a careful record of where each object should be placed and create a "manual for housekeeping" that gives explicit directions about where objects should be kept. In this instance, the housekeepers become another aspect of the hotel that needs to be disciplined through vigilant design.[14]

Indidesign's changes at Chicago's Hyatt Regency focused on the palette, fixtures, and textures found in the guest rooms, while seemingly unaware about what housekeepers would experience while cleaning these spaces. The beds and pillows in the old rooms were multicolored, with vertical lights attached to many of the enormous wood headboards (fig. 24). A grid-like pattern defined the overall appearance of the earlier rooms, while Girelli's new rooms are more monochromatic (fig. 25). The new lighting fixtures are subtle, and the furniture has cleaner lines, without the cluttered look that must have led to the decision to renovate. The bathrooms extend this motif of cleaner lines with new sinks and vanities and the absence of towel racks. The sinks are now set within a wood base, and underneath the sink are three bath towels that, instead of hanging from a rack, are rolled and tucked out of the line of sight, which would be unavoidable with towel racks. Instead of the sink's surface extending over the back of the toilet to create a ledge for bathroom products, Indidesign

FIGURE 25 Guest room after the renovation. Hyatt Regency Chicago, Chicago, IL. Courtesy of Hyatt Hotels.

uses a simple ledge where the Hyatt's bath amenities can be placed. In several of the hotel's images of the renovation, a small bamboo plant, in a glass jar, is on the sink, adding to the overall spa-like aesthetic that defines the renovation.

The Renovation's Aftermath

Not all of the housekeepers at the Hyatt have embraced this renovation, and many note that the changes have led to injuries and other difficulties. Several of the housekeepers explained that the new mattresses in the rooms are heavier and difficult to maneuver, especially in terms of tucking in bottom sheets. Girelli, from Indidesign, noted that Hyatt bought these beds without the consultation of her firm, but the position of the bed, which her firm did devise, is also a point of contestation between housekeeping and the Hyatt's management.[15] As Ann Small-Gonzalez, who is a floor runner in housekeeping, remarked, "The bed is so close to the wall, in order to get that tuck is so uncomfortable, I think that's how a lot of people might be getting hurt."[16] In order to alleviate the complexity of getting the tuck perfect, managers gave the housekeepers a plastic wedge. This small device putatively provides leverage, allowing the housekeeper to lift the heavy mattress and insert the bottom sheet. Two long-time housekeepers at the Hyatt, Angela Martinez and Tina Marmolejo, contended that this invention has not helped. Martinez further claimed that placing the mattress on a wooden box, rather than the box spring that was in the old rooms, also makes the bed-making process far more difficult, since the box spring was more flexible than the wooden platform. The new bed also has more pillows than the previous bed. There are now six pillows, according to Marmolejo and Martinez, and these "fluffier" pillows are longer and require more reaching and extending of the housekeeper's arm to place the pillow in its case. Both women complained that this has led to shoulder and back pain.[17] Other guest room attendants that I interviewed at hotels in other parts of the United States complained about the growing numbers of pillows placed on beds.[18] These extra creature comforts for guests have only led to increased back, shoulder, and joint pain for those who must maintain these additional design features. As Niklas Krause, Teresa Scherzer, and Reiner Rugulies have noted in their study of Las Vegas housekeepers, and as I have detailed in other sections of *Housekeeping by Design*, "Hotel workers have higher rates of occupational injury and illness compared to workers in the service sector at large."[19]

Other seemingly benign design choices in Chicago meant further complications for the hotel workers at the Hyatt Regency. One guest room attendant noted that the new carpeting makes it much harder to maintain the appearance of cleanliness. She explained that the darker color shows all the dirt, which necessitates more vacuuming. The new, updated bathrooms have also led to more work. Some of the bathrooms have glass partitions that separate the tub from the rest of the bathroom, and many rooms that have shower curtains no longer use a plastic liner, so housekeepers have to scrub the white surface, which shows even miniscule amounts of dirt. Also, since the towel racks have been removed, housekeepers must roll towels and place them under the counter, below the sink. The towels are hidden from view, achieving the type of clean-line aesthetic found throughout the renovated rooms, but using a napkin as a model, one housekeeper revealed how exacting the rolling process is and how much longer it takes than folding a towel and placing it on a rack.[20]

These design decisions, which did not heed the voice of workers, created a tense work atmosphere at the Hyatt Regency Chicago that, in part, led to workers taking action. On May 26, 2010, about four hundred employees walked out of the hotel for a brief period of time to protest issues related to the workload increase caused by the renovation. Hyatt and UNITE HERE's inability to resolve a contract dispute exacerbated this issue, and a controversy about the hotel's management's refusal to allow a union representative into the hotel, during a particularly heated moment, only made the situation worse. As reported in the local press, Hyatt's management blamed the situation on the workers, and the workers blamed the tension on hotel management. During the action, John Schafer, the vice president and managing director of the Regency, told NBC Chicago, "Today's union action . . . is regrettable, especially in light of current economic conditions. We believe the most productive place to address important workplace matters is at the negotiating table." He noted that "by working together, we can reach an agreement that provides our guests with the level of service they have come to expect from Hyatt, and continues to provide team members with competitive wages, good benefits, and quality health care."[21] Shafer's comments focus on pay and benefits, but his remarks do not mention the problems related to design that Hyatt's line workers described to me in such detail. Hyatt repeatedly embraces the idea that only guests can benefit and respond to the design choices made at the hotel. As the Hyatt workers I interviewed explained, they became fed up with the situation. One of the housekeepers I spoke with emotionally revealed, "They [management] didn't think we were serious." However, "we got everybody out of there (the majority)" during the walkout.[22]

The walkout only lasted a few brief hours, but the stage was set for what continued to be a protracted contract negotiation that had, for several employees, an enormous emotional impact. Maria Sanchez, a pastry chef at the hotel, discussed the walkout in terms of her family and pride. If she did not speak out against management, how, she asked, "can I tell her [my daughter] to stand up for yourself, to be brave, to know your place, and make sure that everyone gives you respect. . . . How can I look her in the eye, if I put my head down when someone tries to step on me?"[23] Continuing this theme of pride in work, an employee who had been at the hotel for over a decade commented, "The guests come here because of us, not because of corporate, they come here because of the service that we provide . . . the service . . . that those housekeepers provide, not because, you know, Mark Hoplamazian, the CEO guy, is waiting at the door to check their bags."[24] Like the YouTube videos that UNITE HERE produced to challenge the videos put out by Hyatt, this woman's observation — and her specific reference to the CEO of Hyatt Hotels, Mark Hoplamazian, as unable to deliver the actual service that the guest enjoys — exemplifies the sense of pride that hotel workers share, especially in the face of struggles for improving difficult work environments.[25] Moreover, she related that management was unwilling to embrace the idea that labor delivers service (design) to the hotel's guests.

The emotional responses that I heard in Chicago were somewhat mediated by the hotel worker's union, UNITE HERE. Like many other hotel workers who have contracts throughout the United States, Hyatt employees can have a union representative at the hotel. The contract language includes this clause: "Authorized representatives of the Union shall be permitted to visit the Employer's establishment for purposes of communication with employees and supervisors regarding union business and collecting Union dues, assessments and initiation fees."[26] As discussed earlier, a UNITE HERE organizer named Noah Dobin-Bernstein accompanied me everywhere. Dobin-Bernstein seemed very keen to have specific workers talk to me so that I could grasp what he understood as the full story about the problematic renovation.[27] Moreover, his run of the hotel, which included most of the back of the house, was surprising, and it was obvious that after he signed in at the security desk he could move freely throughout the property without any interference from Hyatt management.[28]

There were, as I explained in the vignette before this chapter, limits to Dobin-Bernstein's access, and at two in the afternoon, on the day that I was at the hotel, he brought me into a meeting between housekeepers and the Regency's human resources department. He explained that the meeting had been set to continue a larger dialogue about housekeeping and workload. However, when the HR representatives saw that Dobin-Bernstein was in the room, they refused to hold the meeting. Dobin-Bernstein became adamant and exclaimed that the housekeepers should not hold this meeting about workload issues without a union presence. He became further animated when he saw that there were no Chinese workers at the meeting, only Latina and African American housekeepers. After about five minutes of back and forth, Dobin-Bernstein and I left the meeting, and it became evident that HR was going to conduct the meeting with the housekeepers, regardless of whether or not Dobin-Bernstein was in the room. Although this could certainly be the topic for another study, I could not help but be intrigued by the extent of UNITE HERE's influence at the Hyatt Regency Chicago. That presence—fostered by Dobin-Bernstein's influence—must affect employees' perceptions of the complicated politics between management and labor at the hotel.[29]

In watching this untenable exchange among the workers, the union, and Hyatt management it became apparent that something had to change, and it is my contention that design could take the lead in implementing this change. The tension, according to the hotel's management, was linked to some of the employees' ignorance about their work situation since they only adhered to what the union demanded. On the other hand, many workers wanted more of a voice, which could lead to better pay, improved work conditions, and more benefits. I would contend that what both sides should, in part, focus on achieving is a democratic sense of design that would give workers more influence over a process that is now far too removed from the everyday realities of labor. After a week-long strike in September of 2011, tensions between both sides only escalated.[30] Issues related to design did not get reported by the press, but from what I could determine through my conversations with workers, this was a major concern that only exacerbated the conflict. Then, finally, in August of 2013, Hyatt and its employees reached an agreement at the four Chicago hotels, including the Chicago Regency, and signed a contract that would be in force until 2018. As a result of the new contract, housekeepers would get a $1.80 raise per hour, taking their pay to $16.40 per hour, and workers now have the right to protest the way in which Hyatt treats its employees in cities outside Chicago.[31] Nevertheless, while many of the pressing concerns appear to have been resolved, there is still the matter of design. There are still the difficulties associated with contending with guest rooms that have not been designed to facilitate the hard work of housekeeping.

A Call for Co-Design

Design should be a more democratic process and attend to the physical realities of labor. As Gui Bonsiepe has argued, design has now become too entrenched in the spectacle of a media event. Instead of focusing on intelligent solutions, design has "drawn nearer to the ephemeral, fashionable and quickly obsolete." This has led "to the 'boutiquization' of the universe of products for everyday life."[32] While he does not mention hotels specifically, Bonsiepe's argument is certainly applicable, as hotel chains like Hyatt redesign their rooms not with design solutions in mind, but with the idea of keeping up appearances that will be fashionable. Bonsiepe wants the design community to move away from this unsustainable model and move toward a "sense of participation, so that dominated citizens transform themselves into subjects opening a space for self-determination."[33] This ability to instill self-determination is at the heart of Bonsiepe's larger wish for an emancipative type of design that will encourage less subjugation in the face of a design establishment enamored of the seductive power of manipulating users with and through design.

One way of embracing the participatory notion of design is to foster co-design. Elizabeth Sanders and Pieter Jan Stappers describe co-design as a subversion of what designers usually accept as best practices. In co-design, as briefly mentioned earlier in my book, "the person who will eventually be served through the design process is given the position of 'expert of his/her experience,' and plays a large role in knowledge development, idea generation and concept development."[34] Sanders and Stappers still claim that the role of the professional designer is important, but in their model, the designer cannot do his or her job without input from the individuals who will have to utilize the product or system being produced. In the context of hotels, it could be myopically conceivable that those being "served" are only guests, and this is, in fact, what Hyatt appears to believe, but design has other constituents in the context of hotels. And labor, I would argue, is a key, but often ignored, actor in these spaces. Sanders and Stappers claim that with more of an inclusive process—that would permit the voice and presence of those who are directly affected by the design being considered—"what is being designed will change."[35]

Imagine, then, a scenario at the Hyatt Regency Chicago where housekeepers, management, and potential guests work together to come up with design solutions. This form of co-design could include conversations about the current rooms that raise questions about what design choices work and what design choices could be improved upon. Perhaps, for instance, a housekeeper could explain to Beatrice Girelli how the weight of the mattress in relation to its placement on a nonflexible bed frame makes it very difficult to change the sheets and how this burdensome procedure leads to injuries. In reaction to this, the housekeepers and the designers could come up with novel solutions for different types of mattresses and frames that would enable rooms to look presentable to guests without causing the hardships described by many of the housekeepers I interviewed.

This model of co-design would, ultimately, lead to what Lucy Suchman describes as a "located" design practice. Taking a cue from Donna Haraway's feminist conception of "situated knowledge," Suchman defines "locating design" as critical to lifting the veil of social ignorance that plagues the field, since in its current form designers are frequently unaware "of their own positions within the social relations that comprise technical systems."[36] She tasks us with identifying design's "participation in the various mediations that define the production and use of new technologies, and taking some responsibility for them. It requires analyzing the process by which boundaries within and between technology production and use are constructed and maintained, and understanding our contributions to their reproduction or transformation." This active engagement with a situated form of design also "means mapping not only our local networks, but locating those as well within more extended networks, including an increasingly globalized division of labor."[37] If we take Suchman's call to action into account, this would mean, in the context of the Hyatt Regency Chicago, that line workers, management, guests, and designers would all be charged with understanding how decisions affect a chain of stakeholders who historically have been uninformed about design's ramifications.

In her conclusion, Suchman points to some possible "transformations" that would happen in the wake of "locating design." Her first transformation loudly resonates with this book. She claims that this new arrangement could lead to "recognizing the various forms of visible and invisible work that make up the production/use of technical systems, locating ourselves within that extended web of connections, and taking responsibility for our participation."[38] This "responsibility" is, at the moment, elided in the hotel industry, where conversations about the consequences of design among makers, users, and investors do not occur. This becomes very apparent if we think back to General Manager Donelly's remarks about "truly listen[ing] to our guests." Hyatt's focus on the guest's pleasure may appear to make sense from the standpoint of a corporate model beholden to profits. After all, it is the guest who purchases, or rents, the room at the hotel. Yet the contentious nature of the industry could be mitigated by embracing and listening to the multiple stakeholders and agents who must contend with the aesthetic and service design choices made at hotels.

∗

One company that appears to be engaged with a form of co-design that is trying to remedy some of the issues related to hotel work is WorkSafe Technology. Started by design entrepreneur Dan Koval, WorkSafe is finding a growing market at hotels, and Koval, along with his design team, has worked closely with housekeepers to come up with a tool that makes it easier to make beds. Think back to those "wedges" that management gave to housekeepers at the Chicago Regency. According to the women I interviewed, these wedges did nothing to alleviate the difficulty of getting leverage to lift heavy mattresses that had been awkwardly located in the redesigned rooms. Koval and his lead designer, Tom Jarvis, have been devising a paddle-like tool that actually does the work that the wedge could never do. It gives housekeepers the chance to make beds efficiently and safely. From the video demonstrations that I watched while talking with Koval, it became obvious that he and WorkSafe are changing the way in which beds are made.[39] And, remember, the bed is one of the most controversial design elements in the hotel room, since its weight causes countless injuries to housekeepers, who try to use their shoulders, arms, and body weight to lift mattresses that only seem to be getting heavier.

While the jury is still out on how successful Koval's efforts will be, the difference in his approach to housekeeping has to do with co-design. Koval and Jarvis have taken their product through multiple iterations, and with each prototype they have asked housekeepers to test their product. Koval gave me details about this process that made it evident that he was working with housekeepers to make the best possible tool: "We found that [housekeepers] did not like completely changing the way they make the beds. So we had two groups of really very interested users: the people who were already in a lot of pain, and the people who were brand new to housekeeping. And both of them embraced it quickly." He further noted, "The [housekeepers] who didn't embrace it were this middle ground where they have their way of making the bed, they're under a lot of time pressure, and a radically different way to do it, that takes them away from the bed," is going to make them hesitant. Koval understands the importance of being physically proximate to the bed. He continued:

> So usually you kneel very close to the side of the bed, and you're using your hands and you're getting all this tactile feedback from the process of making the bed, right? Is this right, is it looking good, you can smooth quickly, you can do so many things so quickly, and while this tool we give them ergonomically is very good because their back's not bent so much, they're not doing lots of frequent bends, they're not jamming their hands under the mattress, it is moving them away [from the actual bed].[40]

Granted, Koval's sample group is not as large as he and his designers would like, but the fact that they are bringing their tool into hotels and running focus groups where feedback is taken seriously is telling. Note how Koval is even willing to admit that not every housekeeper has been delighted with what he calls the "Tuck-it."[41] And yet he continues to devise new iterations of his product, looking for that ideal interface that will make the life of the guest room attendant a bit easier. Koval appears to be on the cutting edge of a new group of entrepreneurs in the hotel industry that is thinking about changing the nature of the business.

Koval's perspective is unusual in that it represents the possibility of offering guest room attendants a voice. At the moment, that is a rarity in a business where the corporate stakeholders only tend to listen to guests. One of the more vocal housekeepers I spoke with in Chicago summarized labor's position eloquently: management personnel "don't listen to their people, they don't take that in consideration, that people are actually getting hurt from doing what they are doing in these rooms, and that the changes they made are affecting peoples' life."[42] In order to get management to "listen," changes have to occur that will enable a dialogue to take place. Ways of conceptualizing design as an inclusive process where various constituents—including workers—can take part in decision making about specific design elements is never easy. Too often the design process becomes disenfranchised from the lives that will be affected by these decisions. Thinking about design as a democratic practice where myriad voices inform options ultimately makes designing more complex, but this also has the potential to make the process equitable to both bodies and minds.

CONCLUSION
A Cinderella Story

Hollywood's interest in fairy tales far surpasses its interest in tackling workers' rights. The film *Maid in Manhattan* (2002), directed by Wayne Wang, offers the typical Hollywood redux of the Cinderella story through a credulous narrative about a New York City housekeeper. The movie's premise is predictable: a Latina hotel maid, named Marisa Ventura (Jennifer Lopez), gets mistaken for another hotel guest by a senatorial candidate, named Christopher Marshall (Ralph Fiennes), and impassioned hijinks ensue at the fictional Beresford Hotel.[1] However, love is not enough for this big-screen tale. Ventura is also able to reform Marshall's political views about labor, minorities, and the working poor. While this narrative about transformation, romance, and interracial harmony has become cliché in the film industry, it is unusual for a big-budget movie to represent housekeeping at a luxury hotel.

In this upstairs-downstairs narrative, Wang shows us the back of the house of the fictional Beresford.[2] After an opening set of shots filled with pathos about Ventura's predicament as a single mom in New York, we watch the director of housekeeping, Paula Burns (Frances Conroy), check off a list of pithy remarks to her staff of housekeepers. Uniformed women follow Burns down the hall as she recites, "A Beresford maid is expedient. A Beresford maid is thorough. A Beresford maid serves with a smile. And, above all, a Beresford maid strives to be invisible." To make the point even more obvious, the camera moves from Burns to a shot of two signs written in dramatically large cursive loops. One reads, "Strive to be Invisible." And the other declares, "Strive to Serve." This rather humorous play on the typical overabundance of inspirational signage and aphorisms found in the back of the house of hotels is punctuated by a housekeeper's subtle response to Burns, stated in a witty aside, "Maybe we can disappear one day all together."

As with all of the examples I have discussed in this book, housekeeping is a highly designed service activity in *Maid in Manhattan*, where the invisibility of labor is paramount. Yet here, in a typical Hollywood effort that shuns subtlety, the design of housekeeping and its relationship to service and subservience get accentuated. Christopher and Marisa's first meeting, which occurs in a bathroom where Marisa is on her knees, helps to establish this point. Christopher has arrived at the hotel, and he and his staff are in their suite. He quickly moves to the bathroom in a rush to urinate and get on with his busy day of campaigning. As he stands over the toilet about to open his fly, he suddenly realizes that Marisa is cleaning the floor. She looks up at him and apologizes with, "Oh my god, I'm sorry, sir," and then hurriedly gets up to leave. She smirks at this putatively bad timing, but to reveal his kind nature, Christopher thanks Marisa on her way out of the suite's beautifully appointed bath. The idea that we, together with Marisa, almost see Chris's genitalia makes the joke of this strange happenstance, and the duo's eventual bliss, that much funnier and poignant, but through this rather sophomoric plot twist we also get a clear indication about Marisa's literal subservience to this powerful man, whose phallus is almost—but not quite—in hand.

This type of service design snafu—specifically, the idea of a guest room attendant in the bathroom cleaning the floor while the guest is about to use the toilet—is improbable. Hotel management, especially at luxury hotels, goes out of its way to make certain that housekeepers are not in a room while the guest is present. As described in my discussion of hotel management textbooks, the industry consistently demands that a housekeeper enter the guest room by pausing at the door for several seconds after ringing the bell or knocking. I also detailed how the Four Seasons Hotels and Resorts, in training DVDs, depict the guest room attendant's long pause before entering. The instructional DVD then directs the housekeeper to put only her head into the room after opening the door, and to call out one final time to make certain that nobody is there.[3] Guest privacy and housekeeper safety have become even more significant since the Dominique Strauss-Kahn (DSK) scandal that occurred at New York's Sofitel Hotel in 2011, when, as I mentioned at the start of this book, a housekeeper named Nafissatou Diallo claimed that Strauss-Kahn had sexually assaulted her in his guest room.[4]

Maid in Manhattan predates the infamous DSK case, but in an industry that so carefully orchestrates service design, the idea that Marisa could catch Chris with his pants almost down is still suspect. Moreover, the camera's attention on Marisa's knowing or sexy smirk, as she quickly exits the bathroom, is not how this vignette would have actually concluded in a contemporary hotel. Marisa never reports this event to management, and while Chris's declaration of "thank you" may add to our understanding of his character's beneficence, this type of encounter would have led to much more intensive scrutiny about how Marisa could have been behind the closed door of a bathroom at the same time as this VIP guest.

And what would Marx have said about this almost hand-on-the-phallus mishap? The film's intention is to provide the viewer with an initial interaction between the future husband and wife who come from different class and racial backgrounds. While the straitlaced Marshall becomes startled by Ventura's presence, her smirk—a sign of knowing and flirtation—foreshadows her character's tenacious transcendence of her own socioeconomic and racial circumstance. But this narrative where the prince gets entangled with the help is highly implausible, both in terms of the carefully orchestrated logistics of hotel service design and in relation to societal norms. This unlikely meeting in the bathroom does, however, help to promulgate one of the key myths of capitalism, namely, that a housekeeper can leave her class-laden challenges behind and get off her bended knee to climb the hierarchy of class effortlessly. Yet beyond the humor and not-so-subtle cues about character development, is it surprising that *Maid in Manhattan* places these two characters in these choreographed positions: Marisa on bended knee with cleaning rags in her hand and Chris standing about to place his "equipment" in his own hand? This physical enactment of male privilege and dominance foreshadows the gendered essence of this Cinderella story.

Even though *Maid in Manhattan* elides and satirizes much of the reality of hotel work, it does offer an explicit look at issues related to the design of worker surveillance in our neoliberal era. During the film's opening credits, we watch as Marisa travels to work via subway. The sequence of shots makes it clear that her commute is difficult, crowded, and rushed, and we also see her fellow commuters holding tabloid newspapers that foreshadow the arrival of Chris Marshall, the politician, in New York. Once Marisa enters the hotel through the staff entrance, she proceeds downstairs, deep into the back of the house, where she punches in on the time clock and has a brief conversation with the security officer who watches over a bank of closed-circuit televisions. Marisa jokes with him, and they have a humorous exchange as we witness a naked man who has been locked outside his suite by his disgruntled wife. During this jocular moment, which is reminiscent of some of the stories of odd hotel guest behavior we read about in Rufus Jarman's biography of E. M. Statler, we also see just how far reaching these security cameras are within the hotel.[5] Marisa tells the security officer, "I call you God because you see everything and you still smile."

As I have discussed, security, surveillance, and the carefully designed overall intrusiveness of the managerial presence is something that guest room attendants must contend with. Indeed, capitalism is reliant on, in the words of Henri Lefebvre, "the visual space of transparency" where "nothing in it escapes the surveillance of power."[6] Think of Mary Bresnan's description of watching over her charges in the *Practical Hotel Housekeeper* or the way in which management judges the bed making in the contests I describe in my consideration of management textbooks. The specter of panopticism is everywhere in hotels. It is most obvious in the closed-circuit video booth in *Maid in Manhattan*, but it is also explicit in the back-of-the-house signage and in the managers' dialogue, especially during those scenes when Marisa gets called into offices. These are the very surveillance cameras that will catch Marisa as she escapes the drudgery of her housekeeping life and transgresses against the paradigm of subservience by pretending to be a guest, or a Cinderella who is able to catch the wealthy and politically powerful Chris Marshall. Yet Marisa's character is so fantastical in this film that she is able to get "caught" but still have her Hollywood ending. The panoptic system finds, records, and helps prosecute her subversion, but she still rides off into the sunset with her man, the wealthy guest who appears oblivious to the class and racial distinctions that the film spends so much time defining and then erasing.

Lest we think that the panoptic order of things allows Marisa a pass, it is the system of celebrity surveillance that provides a neat and tidy conclusion to her ascent above the housekeeping cart. The film ends with an old-fashioned newspaper-spinning effect, a nod to earlier cinema, which leads to myriad headlines. A fictional *People* magazine displays "A Romance Maid in Manhattan" as a headline and then below, on the cover, we read, "Will they Make It?" *Newsweek* has the bold and rather academic headline "Politics and the Working Class," which is printed above the somewhat paradoxical "Senator Marshall Second Generation Senator to Hold Seat." Then we see the cover of *Hotel Management*, where Marisa is now wearing a professional blazer, the sartorial sign of hotel management mentioned at other points in the film. The headline here is "The Maid also Rises," and below we see Ventura's fellow ex-maids wearing blazers with the tagline "The New Breed of Manager." There is also *New York* magazine, which shows a rather glamorous photograph of Fiennes and Lopez together with the tagline "The Ex-Maid and the New Senator." These news stories about Ventura and Marshall solidify our understanding of the couple's romantic bliss and their ability to tackle what is often understood as an insurmountable line between privileged hotel guests and workers, and between race and class difference.[7] But what is at stake here is the entertainment industry's contention that one can become an "ex" member of the working class and, in Horatio Alger–like fashion, "rise" in a way that questions the hotel industry's embrace of a rigid hierarchy. With Ventura and Marshall's sudden love, the issues that divided those wearing blazers from those wearing maid's uniforms dissolve and we now have a "new breed of manager" who will, we assume, use past work experiences to make things better for those who have not been so fortunate. Hollywood, as expected, provides a narrative trajectory that rejects our cultural expectations for its own sentimental finale.

And what about the realities of work and physical labor? Remember it is the director of housekeeping, Paula Burns, who wants her housekeepers to remain invisible. They should do their job, but the guest should always remain unaware of this hard labor. Thus, it is somewhat odd that even though the camera purportedly provides access to Marisa's daily routine—as we watch her commute, punch her time clock, and navigate the hotel with her heavy housekeeping cart—we rarely get the chance to see her perform the actual work of maintaining the design integrity of the Beresford. We do see her on her knees when she first meets Marshall and we do watch her make the bed in another suite, but the narrative moves Ventura through a romantic journey that elides physical work. Her efforts seem more focused on gossip among the housekeepers and her pretending to be someone of a higher social status and less on the demanding labor associated with housekeeping.

It is Marisa's donning of an outfit by designers Dolce & Gabbana, the film's own twist on Cinderella's shoe, that best exemplifies *Maid in Manhattan's* elision of work. Caroline Lane, played by Natasha Richardson, has checked into the Beresford because she is, we learn early in the film, no longer satisfied with the Four Seasons Hotel. Lane is an executive at Sotheby's. Her job, her disappointment with the Four Seasons, and her British accent make it evident that she should immediately be understood as a difficult guest—a VIP who will be impossible to satisfy. While Ventura puts in extra effort to make Lane's room perfect, she is enticed by something in Lane's room that becomes irresistible, a Dolce & Gabbana ensemble that costs, as the price tag announces, $5,000. It is while Marisa is making Lane's bed (fig. 26)—one of the few moments of actual work we witness in *Maid in Manhattan*—that her coworker discovers the stunning designer outfit in Lane's closet. Ventura is hesitant as her colleague implores her to "feel how the other half feels" by trying on Lane's clothes. The music becomes somewhat lighter, and its pace quickens, alerting us that something magical is about to transpire. The camera then cuts to Ventura's young son, named Ty, who just happens to be at the hotel and, deciding he wants to go for a walk, meets senator-to-be Marshall in the elevator. The two immediately hit it off, and after their meeting Ty takes

FIGURE 26 Still from *Maid in Manhattan* © 2002 Revolution Studios Distribution Company, LLC. All Rights Reserved. Courtesy of Sony Pictures Entertainment.

Marshall back to meet his mother. Meanwhile, Ventura has already put on the white and perfectly tailored Dolce & Gabbana coat, turtleneck, and pants. She has, although her hair and jewelry remain modestly the same, been transformed by the film's own version of the glass slipper. The surface of this sartorial reference to luxury and privilege becomes the perfect antidote to Lopez's character's physical labor and her hotel uniform, which nullifies individuality. Now that she has changed out of her drab work clothes, and into the pure, white luxury of a guest's pricey outfit, she and Marshall can fall in love. Suddenly, Ventura's onerous daily allotment of rooms, an issue I have returned to repeatedly in *Housekeeping by Design*, is no longer a concern. She is free to escape to Central Park, flirt with her handsome suitor, and pretend to be somebody else, a somebody of higher social status, power, and prestige.

By pretending to be a hotel guest, and wearing the markers of socioeconomic success, Ventura offers us a twist on Thorstein Veblen's theory of conspicuous consumption. Hotels are, as explored throughout *House-keeping by Design*, important sites for the display of status and what Veblen described as "pecuniary strength."[8] By imitating a Beresford guest, Ventura becomes more acceptable to Marshall, as it shows that they travel and consume in the same circles. The hotel, in a way, vets Ventura's standing for Marshall, as its luxurious confines turn out to be a shared space of conspicuous consumption, a location that offers economic legitimacy. Although the film wrestles with the class-based complexity of Ventura's playacting, her Dolce & Gabbana garb and her supposed room at the Beresford suggest her secure place in the upper echelons of society. Somewhat ironically, these recognized trappings of the rich—which she flawlessly wears without the taint of labor—become the charade that she must eventually let go of, as the film claims that we can all transcend our status-weighted position. Veblen's rigid depiction of class gets left behind in *Maid in Manhattan's* willingness to forgo the realities of hotel work.

The film's ignorance about the design of hotel work is particularly absurd if we return to the Four Seasons training DVDs that describe the housekeeper's duties. On one particular DVD, titled *Sequence of Service for Cleaning a Guest Room Safely*, there are seven chapters that take the housekeeper through a carefully orchestrated set of movements to clean a guest room. A disembodied voice asks the guest room attendant to perform everything from a maintenance check to an assessment about potential lost items. Then there are also chapters about how to make the bed properly, how to best clean the bathroom, and how to dust and tidy up the room.[9] This highly designed activity, where each detail must be performed in a particular sequence and with enormous attention to detail and consistency, is time consuming and onerous. I highlighted some of the hardships related to these rigidly designed activities in my chapters on the Hyatt Regency Chicago and Starwood Hotels in Hawaii. An honest film depiction of the industry-wide surveillance, pedagogy, and uniformity about how to clean and maintain a guest room would not have attracted the over 150 million dollars in worldwide box office returns that *Maid in Manhattan* grossed.[10] Thus, it is the movie's utterly incongruous distortion of these circumstances—its representation of Marisa Ventura in Dolce & Gabbana flirting in Central Park—that is particularly problematic.

The movie's perversion of labor allows for its Hollywood ending to unfold in a way that mentions race without having to grapple with racism. Without Marisa's ability to subvert expectations and leave her highly scheduled work behind, she would not have been able to turn in her maid uniform and move up to wearing the managerial blazer we learn about in the headlines at the film's conclusion. As my book has detailed, house-keeping at hotels is work that is most often performed by women of color. *Maid in Manhattan* casts Lopez to make this point. And, in fact, the opening scenes that highlight her Uptown (or, perhaps outer-borough) life further raise questions related to race. This is Hollywood, so to make the case obvious, the film opens by using Paul Simon's 1972 single "Me and Julio Down by the Schoolyard" to highlight images of Ventura's Latino inner-city neighborhood, where the colorful graffiti, trash, and sneakers hanging from telephone wire leave little doubt about the class of people who call this home. Ventura's eventual rescue by the wealthy Caucasian politician (Chris Marshall) makes it obvious that these stereotypical scenes of working poverty and single parenthood have happily come to an end. Ironically, it is through her position as a housekeeper that Ventura meets her white knight who takes her out of the "hood" and offers her a better life, far removed from what we saw at the film's beginning. Ventura's journey up the class ladder takes less than one hour and forty-five minutes. Jenny may be from the block, but she no longer lives there.

Housekeeping by Design has, it is my hope, revealed the mythic representations of housekeeping that are pervasive in popular culture. I have included *Hotel Impossible* and *Maid in Manhattan* because just as I began each chapter with my own memories of hotels that have occasionally been entangled with my own misperceptions about work, popular culture furthers our collective ignorance about the actualities of how hotels operate while at the same time reifying the fantasy that labor happens magically in these complicated spaces. Labor disputes and affective turmoil quickly get resolved in these narratives, and some of the long-standing contestation about housekeeping, as I identified in my case studies that focused on hotels in Chicago, Honolulu, and Kauai, disappear in a matter of a few well-edited minutes. By describing the history of hotels in relation to hotel management theory and labor challenges, *Housekeeping by Design* has interrogated issues of design to expose the complex and demanding nature of hotel work. Design's presence at hotels is a vexed problem, something that is almost too difficult to resolve in the choreographed realm of the hotel, where service design and choices made about the materiality of spaces often confound and problematize labor. This is precisely why these examples from popular culture offer such a quick fix. Presented with this Hollywood fantasy of happy endings, we, the audience of potential guests, will continue to believe that hotels are not contested spaces.

Maid in Manhattan reinforces the notion that hotels can remain places where, as Bruno Latour explains, work can be "tackled" and "disciplined" in a manner that makes the process appear seamless, as if hotels and their managerial efficacy can wish away the voices of individual workers.[11] In the film, the narrative arc, furthered by the ideal of "service with a smile," permits the movie's Pollyannaish conclusion, where the hotel can continue to be a site where we can escape into a world of fantasy. And the make-believe notion of Marissa gaining a voice in the highly designed managerial process, which comes to fruition as a result of her marriage to Marshall, is a critical component of the film's foray into the illusory. Prior to this Hollywood ending, Marissa is under the watchful eye of security and her superiors. She has no say in the various design elements that define the Beresford. Finally, after she magically ascends into the sphere of management, her ideas do become viable, as she is able to become part of a "new breed of manager" whose understanding and empathy will transcend the Beresford's oppressive past.

*

What can be done by the hotel industry to better the hardships associated with housekeeping and design, to move us away from our collective ignorance of these important design issues? There have been a few encouraging first steps, such as Marriott's decision to place tip envelopes in guest rooms for housekeepers. This initiative, started in 2014 in cooperation with Maria Shriver's group A Woman's Nation, "enable[s] hotel guests to express their gratitude by leaving tips and notes of thanks for hotel room attendants in designated envelopes provided in hotel rooms."[12] This action, although certainly forward thinking, places the burden on the guest, offering management a free pass.[13] Instead of these types of guest-focused schemes, I would urge the industry to heed Elizabeth Sanders and Pieter Jan Stappers's call for co-design. As I explained in my investigation of the Hyatt Regency Chicago, these two scholars ask that "the person who will eventually be served through the design process [be] given the position of 'expert of his/her experience,'" which will allow her to perform "a large role in knowledge development, idea generation and concept development."[14] The professional designer is still there to mediate, create, and, in the words of Herbert Simon, promote design as that practice that works at "devis[ing] courses of action aimed at changing existing situations into preferred ones."[15] Yet this work needs to incorporate the ideas and experiences of all end users; otherwise the process takes place in a vacuum, ignoring the critical voices of those whose day-to-day work must contend with the designer's choices. If we invite housekeeping to the design table and allow guest room attendants to contribute to the design process, I am confident that many of the labor disputes and the overall contestation I describe in *Housekeeping by Design* would be resolved. There will always be ways in which management attempts to exploit labor, especially in our current neoliberal epoch, but listening to the voices of disenfranchised workers would dramatically improve their working and living conditions.

Let us briefly return to an email survey about my experience at the Hotel Bel-Air that I mentioned earlier in my book to explore some of the ways in which the industry furthers the fantasy of seamless service while obviating the benefits that could come from engaging with co-design. The expected litany of questions covering everything from the check-in process to room service's punctuality was part of this rather extensive post-stay, online questionnaire. However, as you may remember, in the middle of the survey I was asked to rate a statement that made me pause: "The hotel staff all worked together seamlessly."[16] This notion of offering the guest a seamless experience, where everyone and every service happens without the presence of any disruption, is at the core of what many hotels want so desperately to offer their guests. Moreover, our memories and fantasies about hotels further this fiction of a seamless narrative by allowing for the fantastical to take hold. Hotel guests are always seeking an ideal escape, and the industry wants to provide the perfect conditions where that escape can be experienced unhindered, uninterrupted, and unencumbered by the realities of labor.

It is design's role in fostering this illusory realm that each chapter of this book has sought to unpack. Design delineates every aspect of the hotel experience, for guests, for management, and for line workers. *Housekeeping by Design* has explored how those who create these particular spaces are ignorant about how design functions and dysfunctions within the context of these strange locations where people come to sleep, eat, celebrate, and fantasize for short stays, being blissfully unaware about the ways in which their expectations about design—both in its material and service manifestations—affect labor. Once we engage with design as a process that involves multiple constituents and actors, we can begin to encourage more equitable work environments.

ACKNOWLEDGMENTS

This project began with my passion for hotels, but this book could never have been written without the generosity of my interviewees. I am particularly grateful to the housekeepers I had the opportunity to interview and learn from in Chicago, in Honolulu, and on Kauai. Many of these women are named in my book, and *Housekeeping by Design* benefited enormously from their enthusiasm, support, and wisdom.

I am also very appreciative of several union organizers from UNITE HERE. These union representatives trusted me and were willing to put me in touch with hotel housekeepers.

There were several organizations and universities that gave me the chance to speak about hotels, and having a group of scholars comment on and critique this project was invaluable. In particular, Boston University, the College Art Association, the University of Delaware, the Fashion Institute of Technology, the Winterthur Museum, and, especially, Hertfordshire University's Theorizing Visual Art and Design group all provided venues where I could share ideas. Grace Lees-Maffei offered me a visiting research position at Hertfordshire that changed this project. She provided an audience of smart students and faculty over two weeklong periods, and her insight and clever thoughts about design made this book stronger.

Ideas from two of the chapters in this book appeared in journals. I am grateful for Victor Margolin's enthusiasm for my article about Starwood's sustainability program, which appeared in *Design Issues*. Early in my research, Elizabeth Guffey and several peer reviewers made excellent suggestions for an earlier version of the chapter about hotel management textbooks, which appeared in *Design and Culture*.

One of the remarkable opportunities that came out of this project was being given the chance to spend time at the Rockefeller Foundation's Bellagio Center in Bellagio, Italy. The staff at the center coddled me, fed me, and provided everything I could possibly want during my residency. This is where I completed the first draft of the book, and I cannot think of a better place for inspiration, especially while surrounded by brilliant scholars and spectacular vistas.

My home institution, Parsons School of Design (a division of the New School), has been incredibly supportive. I had two sabbaticals over the past seven years that gave me the time and space to conduct research and write. The New School also funded research trips, research assistance, and money for image permissions, reproductions, and an index. I am especially grateful for my dean, Sarah Lawrence, and my executive dean, Joel Towers, for being so generous. Other colleagues at Parsons provided feedback and helped me understand aspects of design that I had not previously considered. Laura Auricchio, Margot Bouman, Emma Bowen, Lucy Chudson, Hazel Clark, Clive Dilnot, Orit Halpern, Janet Kraynak, Sarah Lichtman, Ethan Robey, Emily Shapiro, and Jilly Traganou were terrific resources. My research assistants at the New School during this project, including Emily Shapiro, Claire Waugh, and Ansley Whipple, all made life easier.

An additional thanks goes to several other New School colleagues. Shana Agid and Vicky Hattam read several chapters of this book, and their ideas and criticism were essential. Shana also helped me understand and grasp the nuances of service design. Having Rachel Sherman (the author of the indispensable *Class Acts: Service and Inequality in Luxury Hotels*) as a faculty member at the New School meant that I could bombard her with countless questions about institutional review board intricacies, sociological literature, and the minutiae of hotels.

There are a number of other scholars and experts who have helped me with *Housekeeping by Design*. Daniel Levinson Wilk gave me a forum at the Fashion Institute of Technology where I could discuss my historical chapter on Mary Bresnan, and he met with me early in this project, directing me to some terrific sources. In fact, without Dan I would never have tackled E. M. Statler or understood how important the Statler "service code" was to my story. Diana Linden read drafts of chapters, and her kindness and suggestions were very valuable. Patricia Hills has continued to be a mentor and friend. Others provided enthusiasm via editing suggestions, emails, union contacts, or Facebook cheer, including Steven Adams, Molly Berger, Jonathan Cohen, John Davis, Thomas Denenberg, Noah Dobin-Bernstein, Saraleah Fordyce, Ramiro Gomez, Rob Garris, Michael Golec, Carma Gorman, Sean Haley, John Howard, Charlie James, Stuart Kendall, Leland Monk, Will Moore, Keith Morgan, Steven Nelson,

Rebecca Noel, Benjamin Sadoski, Cameron Tonkinwise, Michelle Travis, Shirley Wajda, and Bess Williamson.

I have continued to have the pleasure to work with the University of Chicago Press. Doug Mitchell is the best kind of editor there is. He supported aspects of this project that I was initially afraid to experiment with and his open-mindedness is a wonderful gift. Tim McGovern guided *Housekeeping by Design* along, and his understanding of copyright and permissions quelled my anxieties, as he helped me devise some alternative plans for the images I use in this book. Kyle Wagner has been a very welcome addition to the Chicago crew, and Erik Carlson's careful eye helped polish my prose. Chicago also sent my first draft to two very thoughtful readers, whose insights made this book more cohesive and comprehensive.

My friends outside academia have made a tremendous difference. A special thanks to Ian Abadilla, Paul Aferiat, Andrew Arrick, Ivan Averchenko, Todd Bishop, Frank Borsa, John Cuomo, Maria Goretti, Michael Hofemann, Paul Johnson, Michael Jones, John Mahler, Erica Martin, Bob O'Leary, Eric Orner, Dan Poth, Craig Spano, Amy Sagan Srebnick, Peter Stamberg, Kevin Steen, Tas Steiner, Christopher Sullivan, Jeff Wallace, Greg Weithman, and R. J. Williams. This book also benefited from my friend Josh Srebnick's insight, as he was willing to read anything and everything at a moment's notice. Josh's thoughtful cheering makes everything better.

My family continues to be a tremendous fund of support. My parents, Michael and Shelley, are always at the ready to celebrate the publication of an article or the completion of a chapter. My brother Jonathan is an extraordinary academic. Moreover, his kindness and reassurance sustain me. Additionally, it was terrific to have the encouragement of other family members, including Abby Brazina, Terri McCullough, and Howard Wolfson. I also want to mention my grandmother, Nanny Helene Barnett. Although she died a couple of years before the publication of this book, she set an example for us all as a traveler extraordinaire and as a fabulous neighbor.

Finally, I would be at a loss without James Castillo. James is there for me everyday; he is my toughest critic, but he is also my biggest fan. He read various drafts and sections of this book and offered countless suggestions. Most of all, James demanded that I write as clearly as possible, to avoid distancing myself from my readers through jargon and confusing prose. He is also, and this is no small feat, willing to indulge my hotel passions, and for this I am forever grateful.

Bellagio, Italy

NOTES

Introduction

1. Dell Upton, "Architectural History or Landscape History?," *Journal of Architectural Education* 44 (1991): 195–99. Much of Upton's argument also takes to task the idea of only looking at "high"-style examples of architecture. For a book-length example of Upton's scholarship, see his *Holy Things and Profane: Anglican Parish Churches in Colonial Virginia* (Cambridge, MA: MIT Press, 1986).

2. Neil Maycroft, "The Objectness of Everyday Life: Disburdenment or Engagement?," *Geoforum* 35 (2004): 714.

3. For Jameson's analysis, see his *Postmodernism; or, The Cultural Logic of Late Capitalism* (Durham: Duke University Press, [1991] 2003), 38–45.

4. Karl Marx, *Capital: A Critique of Political Economy*, vol. 1, ed. Frederich Engels, trans. Samuel Moore and Edward Aveling (Chicago: Charles H. Kerr & Co., 1915).

5. Harry Braverman, *Labor and Monopoly Capital: The Degradation of Work in the Twentieth Century* (New York: Monthly Review Press, 1998).

6. A helpful model of scholarship that describes this less rigid understanding of work and power dynamics can be found in Susan Porter Benson's *Counter Cultures: Saleswomen, Managers, and Customers in American Department Stores, 1890–1940* (Urbana: University of Illinois Press, 1986).

7. For a useful overview of service design, see Marc Stickdorn, Jakob Schneider, et al., *This Is Service Design Thinking: Basics—Tools—Cases* (Hoboken, NJ: John Wiley & Sons, 2011). Stickdorn describes the five interrelated elements of service design as user centered ("services should be experienced through the customer's eyes"), co-creative ("all stakeholders should be included in the service design process"), sequencing ("the service should be visualised as a sequence of interrelated actions"), evidencing ("intangible services should be visualised in terms of physical artefacts"), and holistic ("the entire environment of a service should be considered"). For more specifics about these overarching definitions, see Stickdorn, "What Is Service Design?," in Stickdorn, Schneider, et al., 34–45. Lucy Kimbell also provides a valuable discussion of the field of service design, and its differences from what we typically think of as design practice, in her essay "The Turn to Service

Design," in *Design and Creativity: Policy, Management and Practice*, ed. Guy Julier and Liz Moor (Oxford: Berg, 2009), 157-73. I am using the phrase "touchpoint" as a reference to *Touchpoint, the Journal of Service Design*. A touchpoint is a manifestation of service design that a customer experiences while in a designed environment. A classic example of a hotel-related touchpoint is the chocolate that housekeeping places on the guest's pillow as a marker of turndown service at luxury hotels. The journal *Touchpoint* contains some of the most recent thinking about this expanding academic field. For more on the journal, see its website, accessed June 13, 2014, http://www.service-design-network.org/read/touchpoint/.

8. In other words, they do not adhere to Stickdorn's focus on "all stakeholders."

9. For more on this, see my "Go Green: Hotels, Design, and the Sustainability Paradox," *Design Issues* 30 (2014): 5-15; and chapter 5.

10. Jim Johnson (Bruno Latour), "Mixing Humans and Nonhumans Together: The Sociology of a Door-Closer," *Social Problems* 35 (1988): 298-310.

11. Herbert A. Simon, *The Sciences of the Artificial* (Cambridge, MA: MIT Press, 1996), 111.

12. The history of hotels and hospitality is extensive. A. K. Sandoval-Strausz's *Hotel: An American History* (New Haven: Yale University Press, 2007) offers a comprehensive history of the hotel in American culture, from its inception in the early republic to its transformation into a larger business. Another insightful example of hotel history is Phil Brown's *Catskill Culture: A Mountain Rat's Memories of the Great Jewish Resort Area* (Philadelphia: Temple University Press, 2003), which discusses one specific geographic region of hotels and its relevance to American Jewish history. Additionally, historian Daniel Levinson Wilk urges us to assess hotels as places that encourage socioeconomic freedom, especially when we look at the service industry in relation to previous centuries' commitments to slavery and inequitable work environments. Levinson Wilk argues "that the modern service sector was not only better to its workers than its masters and mistresses were to servants, but that it played a significant role in the decline of servitude in the United States." See Levinson Wilk, "Tales from the Elevator and Other Stories of Modern Service in New York City," *Enterprise and Society*, 7 (2006): 695-704 (quote on 696). Further, Molly W. Berger has used a historic perspective to explore how technology affected the hotel industry in her *Hotel Dreams: Luxury, Technology, and Urban Ambition in America, 1829-1929* (Baltimore: Johns Hopkins University Press, 2011), and Annabel Jane Wharton examines how Hilton hotels became a design metaphor for Cold War politics in her book *Building the Cold War: Hilton International Hotels and Modern Architecture* (Chicago: University of Chicago Press, 2001).

13. Mary Bresnan, *The Practical Hotel Housekeeper* (Chicago: Hotel Monthly, 1900).

14. The study of work and emotions is extensive, especially in the sociological literature. One of the books that initiated this larger body of research is Arlie Russell Hochschild's *The Managed Heart: Commercialization of Human Feeling* (Berkeley: University of California Press, 1983). The idea that labor has an affective component comes up repeatedly in my book. Lauren Berlant offers one of the best definitions of affect I have found. She explains "affect [as] naming at once the somatic manifes-

tation of psychic activity and the subject's relation to bodily action." For this definition, see Lauren Berlant and Lee Edelman, *Sex, or the Unbearable* (Durham: Duke
University Press, 2014), 95.

15. Donald A. Schön, "Designing: Rules, Types and Worlds," *Design Studies* 9
(1988): 181–90.

16. Attendants' racial or ethnic background tends to vary in different regions due
to demographics and labor patterns in relation to a hotel's locale.

17. According to what the Bureau of Labor Statistics describes as "employed
persons by detailed occupation, sex, race, and Hispanic or Latino ethnicity," out
of 1,514,000 "maids and housekeeping cleaners" in 2014 who worked in "buildings
and grounds cleaning and maintenance occupation" in the United States, 88.6 percent were women, 16.8 percent were black, 5.5 percent were Asian, and 43.8 percent
were Hispanic or Latino. For this information, see Department of Labor, Bureau of
Labor Statistics, *Employed Persons by Detailed Occupation, Sex, Race, and Hispanic
or Latino Ethnicity*, 2014, February 12, 2015, accessed July 9, 2015, http://www.bls
.gov/cps/cpsaat11.htm. For more on the racial and gender divide within the hotel
workforce, see Rachel Sherman, *Class Acts: Service and Inequality in Luxury Hotels*
(Berkeley: University of California Press, 2007), especially her appendix on the
breakdown of race and gender by jobs, 291–93. Also, see Yvonne Guerrier and Amel
Adib, "The Interlocking of Gender with Nationality, Race, Ethnicity and Class: The
Narratives of Women in Hotel Work," *Gender, Work & Organization* 10 (2003): 413–
32. And, for an example of the racial and gender breakdown of hotels in Hawaii, the
subject of my fifth chapter, see Patricia A. Adler and Peter Adler, *Paradise Laborers:
Hotel Work in the Global Economy* (Ithaca: Cornell University Press, 2004).

18. For a helpful discussion of the media spectacle that surrounded this event,
see Hannah Brenner, "Beyond Seduction: Lessons Learned about Rape, Politics,
and Power from Dominique Strauss-Kahn and Moshe Katsav," *Michigan Journal
of Gender and Law* 20 (2013): 225–90. Also, Caroline Field Levander and Matthew
Pratt Guterl provide an insightful reading of the Strauss-Kahn scandal in their *Hotel
Life: The Story of a Place Where Anything Can Happen* (Chapel Hill: University of
North Carolina Press, 2015), especially in their second chapter.

19. Sarah Chaplin, *Japanese Love Hotels: A Cultural History* (London: Routledge,
2007); Barbara Penner, *Newlyweds on Tour: Honeymooning in Nineteenth-Century
America.* (Lebanon, NH: University of New England Press, 2009); Jilly Traganou,
The Tōkaidō Road: Travelling and Representation in Edo and Meiji Japan (London:
Routledge, 2004); and Miodrag Mitrašinović, *Total Landscape, Theme Parks, Public
Space* (Aldershot: Ashgate, 2006). Several articles in the journal *Annals of Tourism
Research* deal with design. See, for instance, Les M. Lumsdon, "Factors Affecting
the Design of Tourism Bus Services," *Annals of Tourism Research* 33 (2006): 748–66;
and Sigal Haber and Arie Reichel, "Physical Design Correlates of Small Ventures'
Profitability," *Annals of Tourism Research* 32 (2005): 269–72.

20. Sherman. For another sociological study about hotels that provides details
about labor's place in the hierarchical structure of hotel management, see Adler
and Adler.

21. Orvar Löfgren, *On Holiday: A History of Vacationing* (Berkeley: University of

California Press, 1999), 7. Also, see Dean MacCannell, *The Tourist: A New Theory of the Leisure Class* (Berkeley: University of California Press, 1999). For another approach to leisure, see Mika Pantzar and Elizabeth Shove, *Manufacturing Leisure: Innovations in Happiness, Well-Being and Fun* (Helsinki: National Consumer Research Centre, 2005), which is available online, accessed June 25, 2015, http://www.researchgate.net/profile/Mika_Pantzar/publication/242523535_Manufacturing_leisure/links/0c96052a076b46d878000000.pdf.

22. Karl Spracklen, *Whiteness and Leisure* (New York: Palgrave Macmillan, 2013), 5.

23. Wayne Koestenbaum, *Hotel Theory* (Brooklyn: Soft Skull Press, 2007). The three key texts I will be looking at by Marx, Lefebvre, and Veblen are Marx; Henri Lefebvre, *The Production of Space*, trans. Donald Nicholson-Smith (Oxford: Blackwell, [1974] 2000); and Thorstein Veblen, *The Theory of the Leisure Class* (New York: Dover Publications, [1899] 1994).

24. Frederick Winslow Taylor, *The Principles of Scientific Management* (New York: Harper Brothers, 1911).

25. See Ruth Schwartz Cowan, *More Work for Mother: The Ironies of Household Technology from the Open Hearth to the Microwave* (New York: Basic Books, 1983); and Grace Lees-Maffei, *Design at Home: Domestic Advice Books in Britain and the USA since 1945* (Abingdon, United Kingdom: Routledge, 2014).

26. I also discuss this in my article "A Textbook Case: Design, Housekeeping, and Labor," *Design and Culture: The Journal of the Design Studies Forum* 3 (2011): 25-49.

27. For more on co-design, see Elizabeth B. N. Sanders and Pieter Jan Stappers, "Co-creation and the New Landscapes of Design," *CoDesign: International Journal of CoCreation in Design and the Arts* 4 (2008): 5-18; and my discussion of co-design in chapter 6.

28. Dan Zuberi, *Differences That Matter: Social Policy and the Working Poor in the United States and Canada* (Ithaca: Cornell University Press, 2006), 50.

29. Department of Labor, Bureau of Labor Statistics, *Occupational Employment and Wages: Maids and Housekeeping Cleaners*, 2012, May 2013, Report 27-2012, accessed July 19, 2014, http://www.bls.gov/oes/current/oes372012.htm. For the national figures for all professions, see Department of Labor, Bureau of Labor Statistics, *National Occupational Employment and Wage Estimates United States*, 2012, May 2013, accessed July 22, 2014, http://www.bls.gov/oes/current/oes_nat.htm#00-0000.

30. Niklas Krause, Teresa Scherzer, and Reiner Rugulies, "Physical Workload, Work Intensification, and Prevalence of Pain in Low Wage Workers: Results from a Participatory Research Project with Hotel Room Cleaners in Las Vegas," *American Journal of Industrial Medicine* 48 (2005): 326-37. For more on this topic, see Luis L. M. Aguiar and Andrew Herod, eds., *The Dirty Work of Neoliberalism: Cleaners in the Global Economy* (Malden, MA: Blackwell Publishing, 2006).

31. Susan Buchanan et al., "Occupational Injury Disparities in the US Hotel Industry," *American Journal of Industrial Medicine* 53 (2010): 120.

32. Berger, 2.

33. I received IRB approval at the beginning of this project and renewed my application for each of the following years I conducted research.

34. For some helpful examples of discussions about anonymity and interviewing, see Anne Grinyer, "The Anonymity of Research Participants: Assumptions, Ethics and Practicalities," *Social Research Update* 36 (2002); Katja Guenther, "The Politics of Names: Rethinking the Methodological and Ethical Significance of Naming People, Organizations, and Places," *Qualitative Research* 9 (2009): 411–21; Benjamin Baez, "Confidentiality in Qualitative Research: Reflections on Secrets, Power and Agency," *Qualitative Research* 2 (2002): 35–58; and Karen Kaiser, "Protecting Respondent Confidentiality in Qualitative Research," *Qualitative Health Research* 19 (2009): 1632–41.

35. See, for instance, Dan Zuberi, "Organizing for Better Working Conditions and Wages: The Unite Here! *Hotel Workers Rising* Campaign," *Just Labour: A Canadian Journal of Work and Society* 10 (2007): 60–73.

36. The interviews I conducted in Chicago took place in the staff cafeteria of the Hyatt Regency Chicago, and the interviews on Kauai took place at public locations, such as a Starbucks, removed from the union and the hotels. Several other interviews, especially those with designers and management, occurred via telephone.

37. For a discussion about paying subjects in research, see Emma Head, "The Ethics and Implications of Paying Participants in Qualitative Research," *International Journal of Social Research Methodology* 12 (2009): 335–44; and Elizabeth B. D. Ripley, "A Review of Paying Research Participants: It's Time to Move beyond the Ethical Debate," *Journal of Empirical Research on Human Research Ethics: An International Journal* 1 (2006): 9–19.

Vignette 1

1. Irish Hotel Faked Reviews," TripAdvisorWatch: Hotel Reviews in Focus, accessed March 24, 2014, http://tripadvisorwatch.wordpress.com/2010/10/30/irish-hotel-faked-reviews/.

2. "Irish Hotel Told Staff to Fake TripAdvisor Reviews," *Belfast Telegraph*, accessed March 24, 2014, http://www.belfasttelegraph.co.uk/news/local-national/republic-of-ireland/irish-hotel-told-staff-to-fake-tripadvisor-reviews-28567768.html.

3. "Review of Hyatt Regency Chicago," TripAdvisor, accessed February 5, 2014, http://www.tripadvisor.com/ShowUserReviews-g35805-d87617-r171891462-Hyatt_Regency_Chicago-Chicago_Illinois.html#CHECK_RATES_CONT.

4. "Review of Hyatt Regency Chicago," TripAdvisor, accessed February 5, 2014, http://www.tripadvisor.com/ShowUserReviews-g35805-d87617-r171544975-Hyatt_Regency_Chicago-Chicago_Illinois.html#REVIEWS.

5. See, for instance, the reviews of the Jack London Inn in Oakland, California: "Jack London Inn," TripAdvisor, accessed March 24, 2014, http://www.tripadvisor.com/Hotel_Review-g32810-d84777-Reviews-Jack_London_Inn-Oakland_California.html.

6. "Review of Hyatt Regency Chicago," TripAdvisor, accessed March 24, 2014, http://www.tripadvisor.co.uk/ShowUserReviews-g35805-d87617-r118002719 -Hyatt_Regency_Chicago-Chicago_Illinois.html.

Chapter 1

1. Margie Garay, interview by David Brody, New York, NY, February 9, 2009.

2. For more on this issue, see Rachel Sherman, *Class Acts: Service and Inequality in Luxury Hotels* (Berkeley: University of California Press, 2007), 40–41.

3. Wayne Koestenbaum, *Hotel Theory* (Brooklyn: Soft Skull Press, 2007), 7.

4. The phrase was used by the director of PR at a luxury hotel: anonymous, interview by David Brody, January 8, 2009.

5. Sherman discusses this extensively in her book.

6. Karl Marx, *Capital: A Critique of Political Economy*, vol. 1, trans. Samuel Moore and Edward Aveling (Chicago: Charles H. Kerr & Co., 1915), 82.

7. Ibid., 82.

8. Ibid., 91.

9. Samantha Alfafara, interview by David Brody via telephone, January 28, 2009. In the interview with this frequent guest of luxury hotels, the importance of amenities became very obvious. She spoke at length about the significance of brand names and having specific products available at hotels.

10. "Gold Standards," The Ritz-Carlton, accessed February 15, 2009, http://cor porate.ritzcarlton.com/en/About/GoldStandards.htm.

11. Information on the Four Seasons and its use of housekeeping carts was ob-tained from both site visits and my interview with Margie Garay. Additionally, sev-eral companies that design and manufacture housekeeping carts now sell carts that replicate the veneer of a particular hotel's hallway. This, of course, is another example where design hides the presence of labor. For an illustration of this, see Forbes Industries, "Guest Room Attendant Carts," accessed March 24, 2014, http:// www.forbesindustries.com/media/MasterCatalog/(17)%20Guest%20Room %20Attendant%20Carts.pdf.

12. Marx; and Harry Braverman, *Labor and Monopoly Capital: The Degradation of Work in the Twentieth Century* (New York: Monthly Review Press, 1998).

13. Sherman, 11. For an overview and critique of this scholarly phenomenon, see Michael Burawoy, "Toward a Marxist Theory of the Labor Process: Braverman and Beyond," *Politics and Society* 8 (1978): 247–312.

14. Daniel Levinson Wilk, "Tales from the Elevator and Other Stories of Mod-ern Service in New York City," *Enterprise and Society* 7 (2006): 696. For more on hotel workers and labor organizations, see Michelle Madsen Camacho, "Dissent-ing Workers and Social Control: A Case Study of the Hotel Industry in Huatulco, Oaxaca," *Human Organization* 55 (1996): 33–40; and Miriam J. Wells, "Unionization and Immigrant Incorporation in San Francisco Hotels," *Social Problems* 47 (2000): 241–65.

15. Erving Goffman, *The Presentation of Self in Everyday Life* (New York: Double-day, 1959), 151–52.

16. *Four Seasons: Introductory Training Program*, Four Seasons Hotels and Resorts, DVD. As Goffman notes, "Perhaps the classic type of non-person in our society is the servant," 151.

17. Anonymous, interview by David Brody via telephone, February 5, 2009.

18. Goffman claims that a subordinate nonperson can also reverse the expectation and treat a superordinate "as if he were not present," 153.

19. Yvonne Guerrier and Amel S. Adib, "'No, We Don't Provide That Service:' The Harassment of Hotel Employees by Customers," *Work, Employment & Society* 14 (2000): 689–705; and Yvonne Guerrier and Amel S. Adib, "The Interlocking of Gender with Nationality, Race, Ethnicity and Class: The Narratives of Women in Hotel Work," *Gender, Work & Organization* 10 (2003): 413–32. For more on this issue, see Rosemary Lucas, *Employment Relations in the Hospitality and Tourism Industries* (London: Routledge, 2004); and Yvonne Guerrier's longer book, *Organizational Behavior in Hotels and Restaurants: An International Perspective* (New York: John Wiley & Sons, 1999).

20. Patricia A. Adler and Peter Adler, *Paradise Laborers: Hotel Work in the Global Economy* (Ithaca: Cornell University Press, 2004); and see Sherman, especially her helpful chart about the division of labor at hotels on page 51.

21. Susan Porter Benson describes the complex and often humanizing interactions between customers and service workers in her *Counter Cultures: Saleswomen, Managers, and Customers in American Department Stores, 1890–1940* (Urbana: University of Illinois Press, 1986).

22. Thomas J. A. Jones, *Professional Management of Housekeeping Operations* (Hoboken, NJ: John Wiley & Sons, 2005), 11.

23. Thorstein Veblen, *The Theory of the Leisure Class* (New York: Dover Publications, [1899] 1994), 15.

24. Ibid., 54.

25. Bettina Matthias, *The Hotel as Setting in Early 20th-Century German and Austrian Literature* (Rochester, NY: Camden House, 2006), 32.

26. For a helpful biography of Veblen, see John Patrick Diggins, *Thorstein Veblen: Theorist of the Leisure Class* (Princeton: Princeton University Press, 1999). My use of the term "fancy" comes from Molly W. Berger's book *Hotel Dreams: Luxury, Technology, and Urban Ambition in America, 1829–1929* (Baltimore: Johns Hopkins University Press, 2011).

27. Veblen, 41.

28. Ibid.

29. Ibid., 39.

30. Henri Lefebvre, *The Production of Space*, trans. Donald Nicholson-Smith (Oxford: Blackwell, [1974] 2000), 59.

31. Ibid. For a helpful study that looks at design, labor, and Lefebvre's theoretical premise, see Miodrag Mitrašinović, *Total Landscape, Theme Parks, Public Space* (Aldershot: Ashgate, 2006).

32. Lefebvre, *The Production of Space*, 353.

33. Ibid., 58–59.

34. Ibid., 384.

35. Ibid.

36. Ibid., 353.

37. In a recently discovered manuscript, published in 2014, Lefebvre does describe the possibility for spaces that will allow us to engage with enjoyment. In this book, titled *Toward an Architecture of Enjoyment*, he seems to celebrate the idea of alternative spaces, especially "the countryside or a landscape" where there will exist "a genuine space, one of moments, encounters, friendships, festivals, rest, quiet, joy, exaltation, love, sensuality, as well as understanding, enigma, the unknown, and the known, struggle, play." See Henri Lefebvre, *Toward an Architecture of Enjoyment*, ed. Lukasz Stanek, trans. Robert Bononno (Minneapolis: University of Minnesota Press, 2014), 152.

38. Bruno Latour (as Jim Johnson), "Mixing Humans and Nonhumans Together: The Sociology of a Door-Closer," *Social Problems* 35 (1988): 298–310.

39. For an overview of the field, see Victor Margolin, *The Politics of the Artificial: Essays on Design and Design Studies* (Chicago: University of Chicago Press, 2002).

40. Elizabeth B. N. Sanders and Pieter Jan Stappers, "Co-creation and the New Landscapes of Design," *CoDesign: International Journal of CoCreation in Design and the Arts* 4 (2008): 12.

41. Co-design should be understood in relation to earlier models of "participatory design." Participatory design often focused on technology, and its principles about democratic design came out of political and civil rights movements from the 1960s and '70s. For more on participatory design, see Jesper Simonsen and Toni Robertson, eds., *Routledge International Handbook of Participatory Design* (New York: Routledge, 2013).

42. Margolin.

Vignette 2

1. Merrill Folsom, G*reat American Mansions and Their Stories* (New York: Hastings House Publishers, 1979).

2. See David Lowenthal, *The Past Is a Foreign Country* (Cambridge: Cambridge University Press, 1999).

3. The New York City Landmarks Preservation Commission sponsored a report that details the Plaza's architectural history. See Mary Beth Betts et al., *Plaza Hotel Interior Designation Report*, New York City Landmarks Preservation Commission, 2005, accessed June 1, 2013, http://www.nyc.gov/html/lpc/downloads/pdf/reports /plazahotel.pdf.

4. Donald Trump, "Why I Bought the Plaza," *New York*, September 12, 1988, 27.

5. See, for example, Cityrealty, accessed June 2, 2015, http://www.cityrealty.com /nyc/midtown-west/the-plaza-768-fifth-avenue/30362.

6. The four titles by Thompson and Knight are *Eloise* (New York: Simon & Schuster, 1955), *Eloise in Paris* (New York: Simon & Schuster, 1957), *Eloise at Christmas Time* (New York: Random House, 1958), and *Eloise in Moscow* (New York: Simon & Schuster, 1959).

7. Rachel Sherman, *Class Acts: Service and Inequality in Luxury Hotels* (Berkeley: University of California Press, 2007), 24.

8. Ibid., 26.

Chapter 2

1. For this advertisement, see *Hotel Monthly* 5 (April 1897): 3.

2. Mary Bresnan, *The Practical Hotel Housekeeper* (Chicago: Hotel Monthly, 1900). The initial pages of the book also mention that Bresnan wrote several of her early columns with another housekeeper named Mary Cavanaugh. However, the two women were not able to continue their work together, and the book's copyright is only under Bresnan's name.

3. For more on the luxury hotel during the nineteenth century and early twentieth century, see Molly W. Berger, *Hotel Dreams: Luxury, Technology, and Urban Ambition in America, 1829–1929* (Baltimore: Johns Hopkins University Press, 2011). For an excellent historical survey of hotels in the United States, see A. K. Sandoval-Strausz, *Hotel: An American History* (New Haven: Yale University Press, 2007).

4. See my introduction for more about definitions of design. Also, see Herbert A. Simon, *The Sciences of the Artificial* (Cambridge, MA: MIT Press, 1996), 111.

5. Daniel Levinson Wilk, "Tales from the Elevator and Other Stories of Modern Service in New York City," *Enterprise & Society* 7 (2006): 700. This article relates directly to the important work that Levinson Wilk did in his dissertation, "Cliff Dwellers: Modern Service in New York City, 1800–1945" (Ph.D. dissertation, Duke University, 2005). Susan Porter Benson also describes this relationship among workers, customers, and managers in her book *Counter Cultures: Saleswomen, Managers, and Customers in American Department Stores, 1890–1940* (Urbana: University of Illinois Press, 1986). Rachel Sherman expands on ideas about emotional labor in a contemporary context in her book *Class Acts: Service and Inequality in Luxury Hotels* (Berkeley: University of California Press, 2007).

6. E. M. Statler, "Statler Service Codes," *Hotel Monthly* 23 (May 1915): 32.

7. While I tried repeatedly to find out more about Bresnan's biography, these searches were unsuccessful. I do assume that a successful housekeeper wrote *The Practical Hotel Housekeeper*, but it is unclear whether or not the book was written under a pseudonym.

8. Bresnan, 3–4.

9. Ibid., 9–11.

10. "How a Woman Acts in a Hotel: Things Which Try the Patience of the Knights of the Counter," *Chicago Daily Tribune*, November 2, 1891.

11. For more on women as guests in eighteenth- and nineteenth-century American hotels, see Sandoval-Strausz. Carolyn E. Brucken also examines women in nineteenth-century hotels in her "Consuming Luxury: Hotels and the Rise of Middle-Class Public Space, 1825–1860" (Ph.D. dissertation, George Washington University, 1997).

12. Bresnan, 6–7.

13. Ibid., 7.

14. Ibid., 24.

15. Ibid., 25-26.

16. In chapter 6 of *Housekeeping by Design* I describe how a renovation relates to the experience of housekeepers at Chicago's Hyatt Regency, and in chapter 5 I assess the concerns of a number of housekeepers in Hawaii, whose required quota became very problematic in the aftermath of a sustainability program adopted by Starwood Hotels and Resorts.

17. Bresnan, 56-57.

18. For a discussion of these issues in relation to the cultural sphere, see Martha Banta, *Taylored Lives: Narrative Productions in the Age of Taylor, Veblen, and Ford* (Chicago: University of Chicago Press, 1993).

19. "Preston's Hotel Time Chart," *Hotel Monthly* 5 (October 1897): 27.

20. Bresnan includes two other charts titled "List of Linen Sent to Laundry" and "List of Linen Returned from Laundry."

21. See the beginning of the book for these foldout pages and see Bresnan, 1, for this quote.

22. Ibid., 3.

23. Ibid., 39-41.

24. For definitions of service design and a current understanding of this developing field, see Marc Stickdorn, Jakob Schneider, et al., *This Is Service Design Thinking: Basics—Tools—Cases* (Hoboken, NJ: John Wiley & Sons, 2011); and my introduction.

25. Edward F. Clark, "Plan of the Help's Quarters," *Hotel Monthly* 8 (July 1900): 15. Other period magazines mention Clark as an important figure in the hotel world; see, for instance, the article on his Hotel Chieftain in *Hotel Monthly* 35 (March 1927): 55.

26. Clark, 15.

27. Bresnan, 53-54.

28. Ibid., 52-53.

29. Clark, 15.

30. Bresnan, 94.

31. Ibid., 95.

32. Ibid., 101-2.

33. Ibid., 99-100.

34. Ibid., 103.

35. Ibid., 103-4.

36. Ibid., 102.

37. Ibid., 98.

38. Ibid., 163-64.

39. For these helpful statistics, see Wilk, "Cliff Dwellers," 181.

40. Merle Crowell, "A Great Salesman of Service," *American Magazine* 83 (1917): 20.

41. Wilk, "Cliff Dwellers," 177-78. And for more on Statler's background, see Berger, 201-2.

42. See Crowell, 21, for more about Statler and this catchphrase.

43. E. M. Statler, "How We Practice Business Good Manners," *System* 31 (1917): 370.

44. Ibid., 370–71.

45. Ibid., 377.

46. For more on this phrase and the larger context of Wagner's idea, see Lisa Pfueller Davidson, "'A Service Machine': Hotel Guests and the Development of an Early-Twentieth-Century Building Type," *Perspectives in Vernacular Architecture* 10 (2005): 113–29.

47. Berger, especially pages 199–214.

48. "Fourth Hotel Statler Is Located in St. Louis," *Hotel Monthly* 26 (1918): 42.

49. Ibid., 52-53 and Berger discuss the telautograph as a technological device that provided new forms of luxury in modern hotels. See Berger, 196. Another device that helped with communication within many of these hotels was the annunciator, which moved sound through tubes. For more on the annunciator, see Berger, 105, 156, and 158.

50. Berger, 197.

51. For two very helpful descriptions of these bathrooms, see Wilk, "Cliff Dwellers," 181; and Berger, 211–12.

52. "Hotel Pennsylvania New York," *Architecture and Building* 51 (1919): 21. An advertisement for the Servidor Company can be found in *Hotel Monthly* 29 (1921): 59. And Berger (254) also mentions the Servidor at the Hotel Pennsylvania.

53. Rufus Jarman, *A Bed for the Night: The Story of E. M. Statler and His Remarkable Hotels* (New York: Harper & Brothers, 1950), 256–57. Of course, Statler did not seem to understand the complex nature of tipping. Rachel Sherman offers insight into the "money games" that circumscribe tipping in the third chapter of her *Class Acts* (n. 5 above).

54. For more on the invention of the Servidor, see Wilk, "Cliff Dwellers," 328–329. And for this article on the Matchette system, see "The First Master of Hotel Accounting," *Hotel Monthly* 29 (July 1921): 44–46.

55. Jarman, 8.

56. Ibid., 163.

57. Frederick Winslow Taylor, *The Principles of Scientific Management* (New York: Harper Brothers, 1911).

58. Berger, 208; and see Annabel Jane Wharton on Statler's Fordist ideas, as well. Annabel Jane Wharton, *Building the Cold War: Hilton International Hotels and Modern Architecture* (Chicago: University of Chicago Press, 2001), 171.

59. Wharton, 161.

60. For more on the Statler Foundation and Cornell, see Morris Bishop, *A History of Cornell* (Ithaca: Cornell University Press, 1962).

61. "Hilton Completes Statler Purchase," *New York Times*, October 28, 1954.

62. Herbert K. Witzky, "The Changing Role of the Manager," *Cornell Hotel and Restaurant Administration Quarterly* 10 (1969): 17.

63. The 1947 date is from Wharton, 2.

64. Ibid., 18.

65. For more on the rise of union power in the twentieth century, see Wilk, "Cliff Dwellers."

66. Gerald Mygatt, "The Chambermaid in Your Hotel," *Ladies' Home Journal* 32 (1915): 14.

67. Ibid.

68. Here, of course, I am thinking of Foucault's famous discussion of panoptic discipline in his *Discipline and Punish: The Birth of the Prison*, trans. Alan Sheridan (New York: Vintage Books, [1977] 1995).

69. Anna Steese Richardson, "Hotel Work for Women," *Woman's Home Companion* 37 (1910): 28.

70. Thorstein Veblen, *The Theory of the Leisure Class* (New York: Dover Publications, [1899] 1994), 43.

71. See Elizabeth Clark-Lewis, *Living In, Living Out: African American Domestics in Washington, D.C., 1910–1940* (Washington D.C.: Smithsonian Books, 2010).

72. Statler did continue to use workers' quarters. See, for instance, a description of his Statler-Detroit in "Statler-Detroit, the Complete Hotel," *Hotel Monthly* 23 (1915): 44–76.

73. Witzky, 20.

Vignette 3

1. Arlie Russell Hochschild discusses the role of employee's emotions in relation to customer satisfaction and perceptions in her book *The Managed Heart: Commercialization of Human Feeling* (Berkeley: University of California Press, 1983).

2. Rachel Sherman offers a close analysis of emotional labor in the hotel industry in her *Class Acts: Service and Inequality in Luxury Hotels* (Berkeley: University of California Press, 2007).

3. I would be remiss if I did not mention a number of challenges that the Hotel Bel-Air has recently encountered. In 2009, the hotel's owners, the Dorchester Group, closed the property for an extensive renovation. At the same time, the hotel decided to sever its union ties and refused to guarantee jobs for its previously unionized staff. UNITE HERE Local 11 (of Los Angeles) has been vocal about this decision, and the union has staged a number of protests since the 2009–11 renovation. Even more recently, the owner of the Dorchester Group, the Brunei Investment Agency (the investment arm of the royal government of Brunei), has come under fire as a result of Brunei's embrace of Sharia law. Part of this rigid penal code includes the possibility of execution, through stoning, for same-sex relationships and adultery. Beginning in the spring of 2014, the entire Dorchester Group, including the Bel-Air, faced a boycott from the entertainment and fashion industries that has been devised to protest Brunei's laws. As of this writing, the boycott continues. For more on the union issues, see Hugo Martin and Patrick J. McDonnell, "Hotel Bel-Air Closes for Renovations, Laying Off 250 Union Workers," *Los Angeles Times*, October 1, 2009, accessed July 15, 2014, http://articles.latimes.com/2009/oct/01/business/fi-belair1. For more on the recent boycott, see Martha Groves, "Islamic Laws in

Brunei Spark Protests at L.A.-Area Luxury Hotels," *Los Angeles Times*, May 5, 2014, accessed July 15, 2014, http://www.latimes.com/local/la-me-0506-beverly-hills -brunei-20140506-story.html.

Chapter 3

1. A version of this chapter was published previously as "A Textbook Case: Design, Housekeeping, and Labor," *Design and Culture: The Journal of the Design Studies Forum* 3 (2011): 25-49.

2. Alta M. La Belle and Jane Perkins Barton, *Administrative Housekeeping* (New York: G. P. Putnam's Sons, 1951).

3. Grace H. Brigham, *Housekeeping for Hotels, Motels, Hospitals, Clubs, Schools* (New York: Ahrens Publishing, 1955); Georgina Tucker and Madelin Schneider, *The Professional Housekeeper* (New York: Van Nostrand Reinhold, 1982); Thomas J. A. Jones, *Professional Management of Housekeeping Operations* (Hoboken, NJ: John Wiley & Sons, 2005). For a historiographical look at these textbooks, see Denney G. Rutherford, ed., *Hotel Management and Operations* (New York: Wiley & Sons, 2002), 143-45. Conducting an online Google search makes it obvious that various editions of the book that I analyze in depth, Thomas Jones's *Professional Management of Housekeeping Operations*, are used in a number of university courses. Here is a brief sample from a few online syllabi: "Food & Beverage Service Foundation," West Bengal University of Technology, West Bengal, India, 2008, accessed April 1, 2009, http://74.125.93.104/search?q=cache:Lp79Pppc4rUJ:www.wbut.ac .in/syllabus/Hotel_Mgnt_Syllabus_Revised_2008.pdf+jones+professional+man agement+of+housekeeping+operations+syllabus&cd=2&hl=en&ct=clnk&gl= us&client=firefox-a; "Housekeeping Supervision," Austin Community College in Austin, Texas, 2009, accessed April 1, 2009, www2.austincc.edu/hospmgmt/ehkp 1301; Dr. Scott Dahlberg, "Rooms Division Management—Housekeeping," Wor-Wic Community College in Salisbury, MD, 2008, accessed April 1, 2009, http:// 74.125.93.104/search?q=cache:ke3giUzHzWUJ:www.worwic.edu/Media/Docu ments/Syllabi/Samples/HMR%2520203%2520Sample.pdf; Akita Brooks, "Professional Housekeeping," Walnut Hill College, Philadelphia, PA, 2009, accessed April 1, 2009, http://74.125.93.104/search?q=cache:JwVuRxJg09YJ:www.walnut hillcollege.com/Instructors/Brooks/documents/Syllabus_Housekeeping_Term3 _09.pdf+jones+professional+management+of+housekeeping+operations+sylla bus&cd=22&hl=en&ct=clnk&gl=us&client=firefox-a; Suzanne Holmes, "Hotel and Catering Studies IV," University of Portsmouth in Portsmouth, UK, 2006-7, accessed April 1, 2009, http://techfaculty.port.ac.uk/tud/dbp/UnivPort/level_2 /ACCMAN.htm; and "Front Desk and Housekeeping Operations," Canadian Tourism College, 2009, accessed April 1, 2009, http://www.tourismcollege.com/show Page.php?id=21. Note that many of these links are no longer available, since this initial research was conducted in 2009 and 2010.

4. Mary Bresnan, *The Practical Hotel Housekeeper* (Chicago: Hotel Monthly, 1900).

5. Richard J. Boland Jr. and Fred Collopy, eds., *Managing as Designing* (Palo Alto: Stanford University Press, 2004), 3-7.

6. Elizabeth Shove, *Comfort, Cleanliness, and Convenience: The Social Organization of Normality* (Oxford: Berg Publishers, 2003).

7. Ruth Schwartz Cowan, *More Work for Mother: The Ironies of Household Technology from the Open Hearth to the Microwave* (New York: Basic Books, 1983).

8. David R. Olson, "On the Language and Authority of Textbooks," *Journal of Communication* 30 (1980): 186-96.

9. Claire Kramsch, *Context and Culture in Language Teaching* (Oxford: Oxford University Press, 1993), 181.

10. Ibid., 201.

11. "Professional Management of Housekeeping Operations, 5th Edition," Wiley Online Library, wiley.com, accessed April 30, 2009, http://www.wiley.com/Wiley CDA/WileyTitle/productCd-EHEP000843.html.

12. Kramsch, 24.

13. Clifford Geertz, *The Interpretation of Cultures* (New York: Basic Books, 1977), 27.

14. Ibid., 19.

15. David Morrow, "Housekeeping (HRA 125)," Walnut Hill College, Philadelphia, Pennsylvania, accessed May 1, 2009, http://74.125.47.132/search?q=cache:D0 Ce-iLBZMgJ:www.walnuthillcollege.com/Instructors/documents/Syllabus _Housekeeping_2006_dem.doc+jones+professional+management+of+house keeping+operations&cd=75&hl=en&ct=clnk&gl=us&client=firefox-a.

16. I focus on the 2005 edition, which is very similar to the 2008 edition. There have been five editions of this book. There are, of course, other textbooks that focus on housekeeping, but while I was doing this research, Jones's book stood out as a preferred text.

17. Dahlberg.

18. Jones, 3.

19. Madelin Schneider, Georgina Tucker, and Mary Scoviak, *The Professional Housekeeper* (New York: John Wiley & Sons, 1999), 35. Note that this is a later edition of this book's 1982 edition, which I cite above.

20. Frederick Winslow Taylor, *The Principles of Scientific Management* (New York: Harper Brothers, 1911).

21. Jones, 5-7.

22. Ibid., 4.

23. Ibid.

24. Ibid., 11.

25. There is a history to this stereotype of the housekeeper; see A. K. Sandoval-Strausz and Daniel Levinson Wilk's essay "Princes and Maids of the City Hotel: The Cultural Politics of Commercial Hospitality in America," *Journal of Decorative and Propaganda Arts* 25 (2005): 161-85.

26. As I have discussed elsewhere in this book, Rachel Sherman, in her *Class Acts: Service and Inequality in Luxury Hotels* (Berkeley: University of California

Press, 2007), offers her readers a comprehensive understanding of hierarchy and work at hotels.

27. Schneider, Tucker, and Scoviak, 74-77.

28. Jones (n. 3 above), 37.

29. Ibid., 42.

30. Ibid., 346.

31. Ibid., 212.

32. *Sequence of Service for Cleaning a Guest Room Safely*, Four Seasons: Introductory Training Program, Four Seasons: Hotels and Resorts, DVD.

33. Margie Garay, interview by David Brody, New York, NY, November 4, 2009.

34. Samantha Alfafara, interview by David Brody via telephone, January 2009.

35. Jones, 211.

36. Margie Garay, interview by David Brody, New York, NY, February 9, 2009.

37. Contract between Walt Disney World Co. and Services Trades Council Union (STCU), UNITE HERE Local 737 (2004), contract period 05/02/04-04/28/07, accessed from the Cornell University, ILR, BLS Contract Collection, accessed January 20, 2016, http://digitalcommons.ilr.cornell.edu/blscontracts/561/.

38. Jones, 214-18.

39. Tucker and Schneider (n. 3 above), 99.

40. See Jones, 212-26, for the images of GRAs in guest rooms and 204 for management photos. Again, for more on race, class, and gender in relation to the hotel industry, see Yvonne Guerrier and Amel S. Adib, "The Interlocking of Gender with Nationality, Race, Ethnicity and Class: The Narratives of Women in Hotel Work," *Gender, Work and Organization* 10 (2003): 413-32. Also, see my introduction and first chapter.

41. Jones, 220 and 223.

42. Karl Marx, *Capital: A Critique of Political Economy*, vol. 1, trans. Samuel Moore and Edward Aveling (Chicago: Charles H. Kerr & Co., 1915); and Harry Braverman, *Labor and Monopoly Capital: The Degradation of Work in the Twentieth Century* (New York: Monthly Review Press, 1998).

43. Jones, 60.

44. Tucker and Schneider, 85.

45. Jones, 121.

46. OSHA, accessed February 26, 2009, http://www.osha.gov.

47. Chris Murray, "Ergonomics and Backpack Vacs," in Jones.

48. Jones, 126.

49. Ibid., 132.

50. While this iteration made by Windsor Industries has since been replaced by the 81-pound Lighting 2000, the Merit 2000 was released in 2002 as "a faster, better, and easier to use product. It allows customers to realize outstanding returns on their investments." Windsor Industries, interview by David Brody via a phone call with their customer service call center, April 13, 2009. This was an unscheduled and informal interview, which happened as a result of wanting to get more specifics about the product.

51. Thomas Net, "Floor Burnisher Provides Dust-Free Operation," thomasnet.com, March 6, 2002, accessed February 27, 2009, http://news.thomasnet.com/full story/7318.

52. Sherman (n. 26 above) also discusses the notion of games in relation to the dynamic of hotel work, especially her pages 110–153.

53. Jones, 18.

54. Ibid., 19.

55. "Bed Making Competition," YouTube video, 2:47, posted by "Splendid Video," 2008, accessed April 1, 2009, http://www.youtube.com/watch?v=YrWv_y7xyoA. This video is no longer available online.

56. All Michael Jackson, "Working Day and Night," accessed April 10, 2009, http://www.allmichaeljackson.com/lyrics/workingdayandnight.html.com/song-lyrics.html.

57. A similar narrative can be found in the YouTube video "San Antonio Hotel and Lodging Association—Making Beds," posted by gabriel2411, posted on September 17, 2008, accessed March 2, 2009, http://www.youtube.com/watch?v=0phdx G5jW14&feature=related. In the San Antonio video we see housekeepers congratulating each other with smiles at the end of the video, but we do not see prizes being given out, as the video ends when the inspection concludes. However, the San Antonio Hotel and Lodging Association's website does announce that prizes are given during the bed-making contest (accessed March 2, 2009, http://www.san antonio-lodging.org/index.php?pr=Bed_Making_Contest_application).

58. Victor Margolin, "Casualties of the Bedding Wars," *Design Altruism Project*, September 25, 2006, accessed March 2, 2009, http://www.design-altruism-project.org/?p=31. For other information on design, ergonomics, and housekeeping, see Niklas Krause, Teresa Scherzer, and Reiner Rugulies, "Physical Workload, Work Intensification, and Prevalence of Pain in Low Wage Workers: Results from a Participatory Research Project with Hotel Room Cleaners in Las Vegas," *American Journal of Industrial Medicine* 48 (2005): 326–37.

59. Sherman, 110–53.

60. Garay, November 4, 2009.

61. UNITE HERE, *Creating Luxury, Enduring Pain: How Hotel Work Is Hurting Housekeepers*, April 2006, accessed April 8, 2009, http://www.hotelworkersrising.org/pdf/Injury_Paper.pdf.

Vignette 4

1. *Plaza Suite*, iTunes, directed by Arthur Hiller (Los Angeles: Paramount Pictures, 1971). All references to the film can be found in this version on iTunes. I will not cite references to the film after the initial note.

Chapter 4

1. *Hotel Impossible*, iTunes, episode 8: "Southern Oaks Inn," Travel Channel, first aired June 4, 2012. All other references to this episode can be found in this ver-

sion on iTunes. Note that when I discuss separate episodes, I will cite each episode. However, I will not cite references to the episode after the initial note.

2. Brenda R. Weber's *Makeover TV: Selfhood, Citizenship, and Celebrity* (Durham: Duke University Press, 2009) discusses how reality television works on corporeal and psychic transformation.

3. Anita Biressi and Heather Nunn discuss the idea that reality television is an excellent resource for understanding the cultural zeitgeist because of its popularity. See their *Reality TV: Realism and Revelation* (London: Wallflower Press, 2005).

4. For more on reality television and surveillance, see Mark Andrejevic, "The Kinder, Gentler Gaze of Big Brother: Reality TV in the Era of Digital Capitalism," *New Media and Society* 4 (2002): 251–70. Also, see Andrejevic's book-length study *Reality TV: The Work of Being Watched* (Lanham, MD: Rowman & Littlefield Publishers, 2004).

5. *Hotel Impossible*, season 1, April–August, 2012, Travel Channel. In the middle of its first season, the show had close to one million viewers. For these ratings, see Amanda Kondolojy, "Wednesday Cable Ratings," TV by the Numbers, May 10, 2012, accessed May 15, 2014, http://tvbythenumbers.zap2it.com/2012/05/10/wednesday -cable-ratings-nba-basketball-nhl-duck-dynasty-south-park-daily-show-restaurant -impossible-more/133240/.

6. Laurie Ouellette and James Hay, *Better Living through Reality TV* (Malden, MA: Blackwell Publishing, 2008), 2.

7. Ibid., 99–100.

8. Weber, 4.

9. This introduction was repeated on each of the thirteen episodes that aired during the first season from April 9, 2012, to August 6, 2012.

10. See his Travel Channel bio at the Travel Channel, accessed January 14, 2013, http://www.travelchannel.com/tv-shows/hotel-impossible/articles/meet-anthony -melchiorri.

11. Argeo Hospitality, accessed September 18, 2012, http://www.argeohospitality .com.

12. Caroline Field Levander and Matthew Pratt Guterl offer a similar reading of Gordon Ramsay's television show *Hotel Hell* in their *Hotel Life: The Story of a Place Where Anything Can Happen* (Chapel Hill: University of North Carolina Press, 2015), 179–83.

13. *Hotel Impossible*, iTunes, episode 1: "Gurney's Inn," Travel Channel, first aired April 9, 2012. All other references to this episode can be found in this version on iTunes.

14. *Hotel Impossible*, iTunes, episode 2: "The Penguin Hotel," Travel Channel, first aired April 16, 2012. All other references to this episode can be found in this version on iTunes.

15. For more on the importance of the "reveal" in reality television, see Susan Murray and Laurie Ouellette, *Reality TV: Remaking Television Culture* (New York: New York University Press, 2009); and John McMurria, "Desperate Citizens and Good Samaritans: Neoliberalism and Makeover Reality TV," *Television and New Media* 9 (2008): 305–32.

16. Melchiorri also works with a designer named Blanche Garcia, whom I mention later in this chapter, to renovate a few of the public spaces at the Penguin. Thus, the "reveal" in this episode focuses on housekeeping and Garcia's design work.

17. See Eric P. Nash and Randall C. Robinson Jr., *MiMo: Miami Modern Revealed* (San Francisco: Chronicle Books, 2004). And see *Hotel Impossible*, iTunes, episode 3: "The Hotel New Yorker," Travel Channel, first aired April 23, 2012. All other references to this episode can be found in this version on iTunes.

18. Karen W. Tice, "The After-Life of Born-Again Beauty Queens," in *Mediating Faiths: Religion and Socio-cultural Change in the Twenty-First Century*, ed. Michael Bailey and Guy Redden (Surrey, England: Ashgate, 2011), 114. Weber also discusses the idea of "salvation" in the context of reality TV. See Weber, 6.

19. This success at the New Yorker gets highlighted in a special episode that revisits some of sites that Melchiorri has transformed. See *Hotel Impossible*, special episode: "After Anthony," Travel Channel, first aired February 4, 2013. The clip about Melchiorri's revisit to the New Yorker can be found online, accessed February 9, 2014, http://www.travelchannel.com/video/revisiting-the-new-yorker.

20. *Hotel Impossible*, iTunes, episode 6: "The Hotel Corpus Christi Bayfront," Travel Channel, first aired May 14, 2012. All other references to this episode can be found in this version on iTunes.

21. *Hotel Impossible*, iTunes, episode 12: "Vermont Inn," Travel Channel, first aired July 23, 2012. All other references to this episode can be found in this version on iTunes.

22. These service spaces are key locations that allow housekeeping departments to stage service design systems within hotels. They offer storage for supplies and linens, but they often also house paperwork and other essentials that are important to housekeeping. Additionally, they can serve as sites where housekeepers can take breaks.

23. Weber (n. 2 above), 2.

24. Ibid., 96.

25. Andrejevic, *Reality TV: The Work of Being Watched*. (n. 4 above).

Vignette 5

1. The Road to Hanalei is also the name of a souvenir boutique on Kauai, but I am referring here to the actual road (Route 56, also called the Kuhio Highway) that circles the island.

Chapter 5

1. A version of this chapter was published previously as "Go Green: Hotels, Design, and the Sustainability Paradox," *Design Issues* 30 (2014): 5–15.

2. Bruno Latour (as Jim Johnson), "Mixing Humans and Nonhumans Together: The Sociology of a Door-Closer," *Social Problems* 35 (1988): 300.

3. Ibid.

4. Ibid., 301.

5. Ibid., 310.

6. Langdon Winner, *The Whale and the Reactor: A Search for Limits in an Age of High Technology* (Chicago: University of Chicago Press, 1986), 28–29.

7. See Gui Bonsiepe, "Design and Democracy," *Design Issues* 22 (Spring 2006): 27–34.

8. As Neil Maycroft has noted, "Contemporary academic fascination with designed objects has tended to emphasise their semiotic and symbolic attributes." Hence, the prevalence and "goodness" of design is lauded without assessing its actual function, beyond what appears to be its obvious use. Moreover, by turning to functionality, we can begin to assess how design, in the words of Cameron Tonkinwise, does or does not function "as the process of humanizing things." See Neil Maycroft, "The Objectness of Everyday Life: Disburdenment or Engagement?," *Geoforum* 35 (2004): 714; and Cameron Tonkinwise, "Thingly Cosmopolitanism: Caring for the Other By Design," accessed April 10, 2011, http://www.iade.pt/de signist/issues/000_10.html.

9. Auden Schendler, "Applying the Principles of Industrial Ecology to the Guest-Service Sector," *Journal of Industrial Ecology* 7, no. 1 (2003): 130. Also, for more about Schendler's take on ecology, see his book *Getting Green Done: Hard Truths from the Frontlines of the Sustainability Revolution* (New York: Public Affairs, 2010).

10. Ibid.

11. The Little Nell, accessed April 2, 2011, thelittlenell.com.

12. Ibid. Although this was the case in 2011, the land trust is no longer mentioned on the hotel's website. The site now notes that the two dollars given by the guest each night, along with the three dollars given by the hotel, will be donated to a group called the Environmental Foundation. For more on the foundation, see the Aspen Snowmass website, accessed May 28, 2014, http://www.aspensnowmass .com/we-are-different/the-environment-foundation.

13. Auden Schendler, interview by David Brody via telephone, January 20, 2011. There have also been a number of difficult situations that have arisen between Aspen's wealthy citizens and immigrant workers as a result of a xenophobic discourse couched as ecological mindedness. For more on this, see David Naguib Pellow and Lisa Sun-Hee Park, *The Slums of Aspen: Immigrants vs. the Environment in America's Eden* (New York: New York University Press, 2011).

14. Gioanna Villabrille, interview by David Brody via telephone, January 27, 2011.

15. For a critique of ecodesign, see Kate T. Fletcher and Phillip A. Goggin, "The Dominant Stances on Ecodesign: A Critique," *Design Issues* 17 (2001): 15–25. For an assessment of these concerns, see Paul R. Kleindorfer, Kalyan Singhal, and Luk N. Van Wassenhove, "Sustainable Operations Management," *Production and Operations Management* 14 (2005): 482–92.

16. Starwood Hotels, accessed June 16, 2015, http://www.starwoodpromos.com /sheratongreenchoice/?EM=VTY_SI_GREENCHOICE_PROMOTION. Note that awards for a free night at Starwood Hotels begin at two thousand points.

17. "Starwood Pays Guests to Go Green," *Terracurve*, 2009, accessed June 20, 2011, http://www.terracurve.com/2009/08/03/starwood-pays-guests-to-go -green/.

18. Anonymous housekeeper, interview by David Brody, Honolulu, July 15, 2011.

19. "Fabulous Kauai Resort," TripAdvisor, accessed April 2, 2011, http://www
.tripadvisor.com/ShowUserReviews-g60625-d111674-r96656893-Sheraton_Kauai
_Resort-Poipu_Kauai_Hawaii.html.

20. For more on the gendered nature of hotel work, see my introduction and
first chapter.

21. Lydia Agustin, interview by David Brody, Honolulu, July 15, 2011.

22. Anonymous housekeeper.

23. Lilibeth Herrell, interview by David Brody, Honolulu, July 15, 2011.

24. Carolina Cacal, interview by David Brody, Lihue, Hawaii, July 17, 2011.

25. Cacal.

26. Rosemary Esperanza, interview by David Brody, Honolulu, July 15, 2011.

27. Cirila Magallanes, interview by David Brody, Honolulu, July 15, 2011.

28. Caridad Rodrigues, interview by David Brody, Poipu, Hawaii, July 17, 2011.

29. Rizalyn Balisacan, interview by David Brody Poipu, Hawaii, July 17, 2011.

30. For more on Filipinos working in Hawaiian hotels, see Patricia A. Adler and
Peter Adler, *Paradise Laborers: Hotel Work in the Global Economy* (Ithaca: Cornell
University Press, 2004).

31. Lilia Olsen, interview by David Brody, Honolulu, July 15, 2011. Although
Olsen works for Hyatt Hotels and Resorts, and not for a Starwood property, she
was involved with the local UNITE HERE chapter (Local 5 Hawaii) and was very
familiar with the issues at Starwood.

32. Edward D. Beechert, *Working in Hawaii: A Labor History* (Honolulu: University of Hawaii Press, 1985), 132. For more on race and the labor movement in Hawaii,
see Moon-Kie Jung, *Reworking Race: The Making of Hawaii's Interracial Labor
Movement* (New York: Columbia University Press, 2006); Ronald Takaki, *Strangers
from a Different Shore: A History of Asian Americans* (New York: Little, Brown and
Company, 1998); and Rick Baldoz, *The Third Asiatic Invasion: Empire and Migration
in Filipino America, 1898–1946* (New York: New York University Press, 2011).

33. Beechert, 199–232.

34. The 2011 collective bargaining agreement on Oahu, Hawaii, includes this language: "Due to the unique characteristics of a resort environment the Employer will
not adopt any program that provides an incentive of value for guests to refuse daily
room cleaning." See *Collective Bargaining Agreement between UNITE HERE Local 5
and Kyo-Ya Hotels & Resorts, LP, dba, the Moana Surfrider Hotel, a Westin Resort &
Spa, the Royal Hawaiian, a Luxury Collection Resort, Sheraton Waikiki Hotel, Sheraton Princess Kaiulani Hotel, & Support Services, July 1, 2010 through June 30, 2013*, rati-
fied on March 18, 2011. Extensive coverage of this issue appeared in the hospitality
press. See, for example, Sean Cole, "Going 'Green' Can Be Cutting Jobs," *Marketplace*, October 15, 2010, accessed October 3, 2012, http://www.marketplace.org
/topics/sustainability/going-green-can-be-cutting-jobs.

35. Benjamin Sadoski gave me this specific contract information in emails dated
April 8 and April 13, 2015. Sadoski explained that UNITE HERE's Hawaii chapter
(Local 5) engages in what he termed "pattern bargaining," where the organization

attempts to achieve parity of benefits and standards across all of the hotels they represent. Therefore, some of the language in this Starwood-specific contract may also have been the result of issues that arose at other non-Starwood hotels in Hawaii.

36. I have made multiple attempts to interview Starwood's management, but these attempts have gone unanswered.

37. Starwood Hotels (n. 16 above).

38. Of course, others have noted various issues related to the "green paradox." See, for instance, Hans-Werner Sinn, *The Green Paradox: A Supply-Side Approach to Global Warming* (Cambridge, MA: MIT Press, 2012).

39. Anonymous housekeeper.

40. For more on INMEX, see their website, accessed June 3, 2014, http://www .inmex.org/.

41. Steven Tufts, "Climate Change and Labour Union Strategy in the Accommodation Sector: Opportunities and Contradictions," Work in a Warming World, working paper 2011-02, accessed February 1, 2016, http://warming.apps01.yorku .ca/wp-content/uploads/WP_2011-02_Tufts_Climate-Change-Labour-in-Accom modation-Sector.pdf. Tufts also mentions Starwood's Make a Green Choice program in his article.

Vignette 6

1. Clifford Geertz, *The Interpretation of Cultures* (New York: Basic Books, 1977), especially his first chapter; and James Clifford, *The Predicament of Culture: Twentieth-Century Ethnography, Literature, and Art* (Cambridge, MA: Harvard University Press, 1988).

2. Geertz's ideas about the distinction between "thin" and "thick" description come from his reading of Gilbert Ryle. Geertz offers Ryle's narrative about three different boys who are "rapidly contracting the eyelids of their right eyes" for three distinct reasons—one has a twitch, one is trying to communicate with a wink, and a third is parodying the poor boy who cannot control his involuntary twitch. Without thick description, these actions would all appear the same, thus disallowing a clear and accurate account of the distinction between these three seemingly similar gestures. For more on this, see Geertz, 6–7.

3. For Marx's discussion about concrete and abstract labor, see his *Capital: A Critique of Political Economy*, vol. 1, trans. Samuel Moore and Edward Aveling (Chicago: Charles H. Kerr & Co., 1915), 64–78.

4. Gallup survey sent guests after staying at Hotel Bel-Air, received via email by David Brody on June 27, 2013.

Chapter 6

1. This is not this woman's actual name. She requested that she remain anonymous during our interview. She also requested that I not record our interview.

2. Anonymous housekeeper, interview by David Brody, Chicago, June 29, 2011.

3. "Kimeret Place: Traveler Reviews," TripAdvisor, accessed January 7, 2012, http://www.tripadvisor.com/ShowUserReviews-g1773688-d602880-r93921791 -Kimeret_Place-Mapua_Nelson_Tasman_Region_South_Island.html.

4. emc1, "In a Class of Its Own," TripAdvisor, December 26, 2010, accessed January 7, 2012, http://www.tripadvisor.com/ShowUserReviews-g1773688-d602880-r9 0742883-Kimeret_Place-Mapua_Nelson_Tasman_Region_South_Island.html.

5. *Touchpoint, the Journal of Service Design* is the name of an important journal in the field. Moreover, Marc Stickdorn writes about this practice in his essay "What Is Service Design?," where he relates: "Service evidencing can thus help reveal inconspicuous backstage services. Sometimes even promoting the once inconspicuous to become standard service signals such as the folded toilet paper representative of housekeeping in hotels. Service evidence needs to be designed according to the service's inherent story and its touchpoint sequence." See Stickdorn, "What Is Service Design?," in *This Is Service Design Thinking: Basics—Tools—Cases*, by Marc Stickdorn, Jakob Schneider, et al. (Hoboken, NJ: John Wiley &Sons, 2011), 43.

6. Elizabeth Shove, *Comfort, Cleanliness and Convenience: The Social Organization of Normality* (Oxford: Berg Publishers, 2004).

7. "Just the Facts: Hyatt Hotels in Chicago & UNITE HERE," Youtube.com, posted by ChicagoHyatt, December 29, 2010, accessed January 12, 2012, http:// www.youtube.com/watch?v=KsCAu3DigBI. And for the Chinese version, see http://www.youtube.com/watch?v=N28my5xrV20.

8. "Hyatt: The Real Truth," Youtube.com, March 29, 2011, accessed January 12, 2012, http://www.youtube.com/watch?v=wFi4k3qRD_Y.

9. "Chicago Hotel Workers Ratify Local Contract with Hyatt Hotels," UNITE HERE, August 8, 2013, accessed March 6, 2014, http://www.unitehere1.org/2013/08 /chicago-hotel-workers-ratify-local-contract-with-hyatt-hotels/. The other three Chicago hotels are the Hyatt Regency McCormick Place, the Park Hyatt, and the Hyatt Regency O'Hare.

10. "Agreement between Chicago Joint Executive Board of the UNITEHERE, Local 1, and UNITEHERE, Local 450 and Hyatt Regency Chicago," September 1, 2006—August 31, 2009.

11. For these facts and the YouTube video, see Hyatt Regency Chicago Blog, accessed January 12, 2012, http://hyattregencychicago.wordpress.com/2011/02/01 /renovation-fun-facts/.

12. See the Chicago Renovation page, accessed January 12, 2012, http://www .hyatt.com/gallery/chircrenovation/.

13. cptjustice, "As Bad as It Gets!," TripAdvisor, July 21, 2007, accessed March 7, 2014, http://www.tripadvisor.com/ShowUserReviews-g35805-d87617-r8 213308-Hyatt_Regency_Chicago-Chicago_Illinois.html#REVIEWS.

14. Beatrice Girelli, interview by David via telephone, July 8, 2011. I asked, but I never was able to review this "manual for housekeeping." The discussion with Girelli directly relates to the idea of human-centered design. Hyatt and her firm appear to be designing these spaces as if the guest room attendants were part of the design, instead of independent agents cleaning these spaces, and this speaks to larger questions about who (as people and actors within the sphere of the hotel) count as

"human." If the guest room attendant is only there as a type of cleaning machine that needs to be trained to avoid interfering with the aesthetics of the room, is the guest the only true human agent in the hotel? And is management merely mediating between these human needs and the housekeeper's delivery of service? As scholars such as Klaus Krippendorff explain, understanding the human-centered notion of design practice is critical. See Krippendorff's *The Semantic Turn: A New Foundation for Design* (Boca Raton, FL: Taylor & Francis Group, 2006).

15. Girelli; Ann Small-Gonzalez, interview by David Brody, Chicago, June 29, 2011. Other housekeepers who described the bed issue include Angela Martinez and Tina Marmolejo, interview with author, June 29, 2011, Chicago; and two anonymous interviewees, interviewed by David Brody simultaneously, Chicago, June 29, 2011. It is important to note that the Martinez and Marmolejo interview was done with live translation. The translator was Noah Dobin-Bernstein, the UNITE HERE organizer who accompanied me to the Hyatt Regency Chicago on June 29, 2011. The inter-vention of a translator who has an obvious stake in the conversation was not ideal, but from my own limited understanding and study of Spanish (along with the hand gestures that Martinez and Marmolejo gave) it does appear that Dobin-Bernstein's translation was accurate.

16. Small-Gonzalez. A floor runner takes amenities, such as an iron or a tooth-brush, to guests upon request. In this instance, Small-Gonzalez is describing rooms with two beds.

17. Martinez and Marmolejo.

18. For instance, Anonymous, interview by David Brody, Honolulu, July 15, 2011.

19. Niklas Krause, Teresa Scherzer, and Reiner Rugulies, "Physical Workload, Work Intensification, and Prevalence of Pain in Low Wage Workers: Results from a Participatory Research Project with Hotel Room Cleaners in Las Vegas," *American Journal of Industrial Medicine* 48 (2005): 327. For more on this issue, also see Victor Margolin, "Casualties of the Bedding Wars," *Design Altruism Project*, September 25, 2006, accessed March 2, 2009, http://www.design-altruism-project.org/?p=31; and Niklas Krause, Reiner Rugulies, and Christina Maslach, "Effort-Reward Imbalance at Work and Health of Las Vegas Hotel Room Cleaners," *American Journal of Indus-trial Medicine* 53 (2010): 372–86.

20. Anonymous, interview by David Brody, Chicago, June 29, 2011.

21. Anthony Ponce, "Hyatt Regency Workers Walk Out, Briefly," 5 NBC Chi-cago, accessed November 5, 2011, http://www.nbcchicago.com/news/local/Hyatt -Regency-Workers-Walk-Out-Briefly-94948924.html.

22. Anonymous, interview by David Brody, Chicago, June 29, 2011.

23. Maria Sanchez, interview by David Brody, Chicago, June 29, 2011.

24. Anonymous, interview by David Brody, Chicago, June 29, 2011.

25. For a helpful discussion of "pride" among workers in a hotel environment, see Rachel Sherman, *Class Acts: Service and Inequality in Luxury Hotels* (Berkeley: University of California Press, 2007).

26. "Agreement between Chicago Joint Executive Board of the UNITEHERE, Local 1, and UNITEHERE, Local 450 and Hyatt Regency Chicago," 30.

27. As I have discussed in my introduction and the vignette before this chap-

ter, experiences in the field cannot be objective. During my visit to Chicago, I was keenly aware of this problematic issue that arises while conducting fieldwork.

28. As discussed in my introduction to this book, UNITE HERE facilitated my visit and organized the interview sessions I held at the hotel.

29. For more on the complexities of worker-organizer relationships, see Teresa Sharpe, "Union Democracy and Successful Campaigns: The Dynamics of Staff Authority and Worker Participation in an Organizing Union," in *Rebuilding Labor: Organizing and Organizers in the New Union Movement*, ed. Ruth Milkman and Kim Voss (Ithaca: Cornell University Press, 2004), 62–87. Also, it became fairly obvious as I interviewed housekeepers at the hotel that there were three distinct ethnic groups of housekeepers—African Americans, Latinas, and Chinese.

30. Francine Knowles, "Hyatt Workers Launch Week-Long Strike," *Chicago Sun Times*, September 8, 2011, accessed March 10, 2014, http://www.suntimes.com/news /metro/7536203-418/hyatt-workers-launch-week-long-strike.html.

31. "Chicago Hotel Workers Ratify Local Contract" (n. 9 above), accessed March 14, 2014.

32. Gui Bonsiepe, "Design and Democracy," *Design Issues* 22 (Spring 2006): 28.

33. Ibid., 29.

34. Elizabeth B. N. Sanders and Pieter Jan Stappers, "Co-creation and the New Landscapes of Design," *CoDesign: International Journal of CoCreation in Design and the Arts* 4 (2008): 12.

35. Ibid., 16.

36. Lucy Suchman, "Located Accountabilities in Technology Production," *Scandinavian Journal of Information Systems* 14 (2002): 95. For an insightful discussion of Suchman and co-design, see Shana Agid, "Worldmaking: Working through Theory/Practice in Design," *Design and Culture: The Journal of the Design Studies Forum* 4 (2012): 27–54.

37. Suchman, 94.

38. Ibid., 101.

39. Dan Koval, interview by David Brody, New York, NY, August 27, 2013; and Tom Jarvis, interview by David Brody via Skype, August 29, 2013. For more on WorkSafe, see their website, accessed March 14, 2014, http://worksafetechnology .com/.

40. Koval.

41. Koval, email to David Brody, March 10, 2014. This is the first time I heard Koval refer to the product using this name.

42. Anonymous, interview by David Brody, Chicago, June 29, 2011.

Conclusion

1. *Maid in Manhattan*, iTunes, directed by Wayne Wang (2002; Culver City, CA: Columbia Pictures). All references to the film can be found in this version on iTunes. I will not cite references to the film after the initial note.

2. The shots of the outside of the hotel are of the Waldorf Astoria in Manhattan.

3. See my third chapter for more on these DVDs.

4. The press and the public debated the veracity of Diallo's claims after the scandal broke, but the hospitality industry responded by looking further into issues related to worker safety. For more on this, see Nathan Greenhalgh, "Safekeeping," *Hotels* 45 (August 2011): 10, about guest room attendants and safety precautions in the aftermath of the DSK case. Also, businesses have begun to sell panic buttons that alert management when housekeepers have been threatened. See, for instance, Enterprise Mobile Duress, accessed April 21, 2014, http://enterprisemobileduress .com/hospitalit/.

5. I am referring here to some of the jocular tales about housekeepers finding guests in compromising positions, which I mention in my second chapter.

6. Henri Lefebvre, *The Production of Space*, trans. Donald Nicholson-Smith (Oxford: Blackwell, [1974] 2000), 147. Lefebvre here is discussing the transparency of modern architecture, but his ideas are certainly applicable to the realm of security surveillance.

7. Others have written about race in the film. See, for instance, Isabel Molina-Guzmán and Angharad N. Valdivia, "Brain, Brow, and Booty: Latina Iconicity in U.S. Popular Culture," *Communication Review* 7 (2004): 205–21.

8. See my first chapter for more on Veblen and hotels.

9. *Sequence of Service for Cleaning a Guest Room Safely*, Four Seasons: Introductory Training Program, Four Seasons: Hotels and Resorts, DVD. While I am dubious of looking to this training DVD as clear evidence of what truly transpires at hotels, it does offer a sense of what management understands as best practice.

10. For this statistic, see Box Office Mojo, accessed April 22, 2014, http://www.box officemojo.com/movies/?id=maidinmanhattan.htm.

11. See my discussion of Latour in my introduction and fifth chapter.

12. See the Marriott press release, "Marriott International Joins The Envelope Please™, A New Initiative Created by Maria Shriver and A Woman's Nation™ in Support of Hotel Room Attendants," Marriott News Center, September 15, 2014, accessed June 8, 2015, http://news.marriott.com/2014/09/marriott-international -joins-the-envelope-pleasetm-a-new-initiative-created-y-maria-shriver-and-a-wo .html.

13. There has been quite a bit of controversy about this program. See, for instance, Bill Chappell, "Marriott's New Envelope for Room Tips Stirs Debate," NPR .org, September 16, 2014, accessed June 8, 2015, http://www.npr.org/sections /thetwo-way/2014/09/16/348961485/marriott-s-new-envelopes-for-room-tips -stirs-debate.

14. Elizabeth B. N. Sanders and Pieter Jan Stappers, "Co-creation and the New Landscapes of Design," *CoDesign: International Journal of CoCreation in Design and the Arts* 4 (2008): 12.

15. See Herbert A. Simon, *The Sciences of the Artificial* (Cambridge, MA: MIT Press, 1996), 111.

16. Gallup survey sent guests after staying at Hotel Bel-Air, received via email by David Brody on June 27, 2013.

INDEX

Page numbers in italic refer to figures.